UNDERSTANDING GRAPHIC ARTS

Kenneth F. Hird

**California State University
Los Angeles**

Published by

IE90　SOUTH-WESTERN
PUBLISHING CO.

CINCINNATI　WEST CHICAGO, ILL.　DALLAS
PELHAM MANOR, N.Y.　PALO ALTO, CALIF.

ISBN: 0-538-33900-4

Library of Congress Catalog Card Number: 82-80077

1 2 3 4 5 6 7 8 D 5 4 3 2

Printed in the United States of America

CONTENTS

PREFACE

Understanding Graphic Arts provides the student with a foundation of knowledge that will contribute to future achievement in a wide range of graphic arts careers. The content of this book establishes an understanding of communication processes that will be valuable to any citizen. In particular, this awareness of communication and production processes will help students to become wiser and more alert consumers. For students who go on into careers in printing and allied industries, this book provides the basic theories and hands-on experiences upon which they can build.

ORGANIZATION

Understanding Graphic Arts is organized in a series of modules that can be presented within any curriculum structure or to meet any school's needs. For example, if a given group of students is to study spirit duplicators and mimeograph processes before taking up offset or letterpress printing, the modules in this book can be covered in the sequence that matches this experience pattern.

Flexibility is inherent in the four-part organization structure of this book.

Part I is general. Content introduces the student to the world of graphic arts. Discussions cover careers in graphic arts, the history and future of graphic arts, and the importance of graphic arts for communication among all people, regardless of working area or special interest.

Part II covers the five major areas of printing use. The content structure of this part of the book is logically organized into teaching modules. The units on offset are placed first because this is the dominant process of printing today. This important printing process is covered in separate units on phototypesetting, offset filmmaking, and offset printing. Similarly, letterpress printing is covered in separate units for typesetting and printing. In this way, the content about typesetting and film preparation can be taught with any process of printing reproduction. These units can be taught in any order.

Part III deals with the materials of graphic arts. Units in this part cover ink and paper, color, and binding and finishing.

Part IV has a single unit dealing with future developments *and opportunities* in graphic arts. This unit looks at the impact of space age technologies on graphic arts methods.

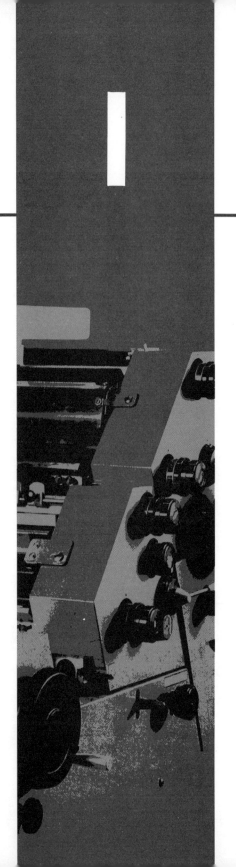

INTRODUCTION

Graphic arts is a series of related skills, materials, and processes. One of the purposes of graphic arts is to organize and deliver information.

The first part of this book uses graphic arts to present information about graphic arts. The idea is to help you begin to build your understanding. In reading the units in this first part, you will gain a basic understanding about graphic arts.

This understanding will be the basis for your work in the remaining units of the book. The same information may become important to your future. Whatever field you choose to work in, graphic arts will certainly play some role in your future. So, the introduction to graphic arts within these first few units will be valuable to you.

TO GRAPHIC ARTS

The units of this first part cover:

1. *Opportunities in Graphic Arts.* This is a review of what graphic arts can mean to your future. Topics include uses of graphic arts in everyday life and in areas of your future work.

2. *Graphic Arts Technology—Past, Present, and Future.* This unit introduces you to the basic methods for producing graphic materials. Topics include the five main printing processes. You will also have an opportunity to learn the reasons these processes were developed, as well as some of their historical highlights.

3. *Communicating with Graphic Arts.* This unit shows how the graphic arts are important to people and how graphic arts products are prepared. Also covered are the techniques followed in preparing printed materials. Areas described include illustration, art, type, and design.

1

OPPORTUNITIES IN GRAPHIC ARTS

THE INTELLIGENT CONSUMER: A UNIVERSAL OPPORTUNITY

No matter which direction your life takes in the future, graphic arts will play a part. Everyone, in every part of society, is a consumer of graphic arts products (Fig. 1-1). You are a graphic arts consumer when you read a newspaper or magazine. You are a graphic arts consumer when you buy food wrapped in printed containers. Graphic arts also affect you when you watch television. Many elements of TV shows are results of graphic arts activities. These include the designs, the scenery, the titles on the screen, and other items.

Figure 1-1. *No matter what the product, graphic arts are involved in its packaging. (National Association of Printing Ink Manufacturers, Inc.)*

An understanding of graphic arts will make you a better consumer. You will be able to appreciate design and quality in newspapers, magazines, and books (Fig. 1-2). You will understand the techniques of advertising and marketing. With this type of understanding, you will become a better consumer. No matter what career you follow, graphic arts will serve you. Graphic arts will be part of your life. Your knowledge of graphic arts will contribute to your success and happiness.

THE GRAPHIC ARTS INDUSTRY:
A LARGE OPPORTUNITY AREA

The graphic arts industry is the sixth largest in the country. There are many parts to this industry, as you will learn. Some 45,000 separate companies make up this industry. These companies vary in size. Many are small companies. These are organizations that employ 10 persons or less. Medium-sized companies employ up to 100 persons. Companies that employ more than 100 persons are considered to be large (Fig. 1-3).

In all, the 45,000 graphic arts companies provide jobs for more than 1,500,000 (a million and a half) people.

Figure 1-2. *Design and quality play important roles in the success of printed products. (South-Western Publishing Co.)*

Figure 1-3. *There are many large companies involved in the various aspects of the graphic arts industry. (W.A. Krueger Company)*

Figure 1-4. *Ideas come from people. People share ideas as an initial step in the graphic arts production process. (W.A. Krueger Company)*

GRAPHIC ARTS OCCUPATIONS

Creative Jobs and Challenges

Graphic arts products deliver information. Information includes ideas. Ideas come from people—not from paper, ink, or printing equipment. People present ideas to other people (Fig. 1-4). Graphic arts techniques are tools for delivering this information.

People who develop ideas are *creative.* This means that they originate sets of words or images (pictures) that have meaning for other people. Creative jobs in graphic arts include:

Writers organize ideas into words. Sometimes writing is the starting point for graphic arts products. The

Figure 1-5. *Illustrators develop artwork that shows ideas in a graphic way.*

stories in newspapers and magazines are examples of how graphic arts products are built from written information. In other situations, writers add words to visual images. Greeting cards and jackets for record albums are examples.

Illustrators are specialized artists. Their job is to develop pictures that present ideas (Fig. 1-5). Cartoons and drawings in newspapers, magazines, and books are examples of their work.

Photographers also illustrate graphic arts products. Their illustration tools are cameras. (Fig. 1-6)

Figure 1-6. *Photographers use cameras as tools for illustration. (Eastman Kodak Company)*

Designers are artists responsible for the appearance of printed items (Fig. 1-7). Designers are sometimes called **layout artists.** They lay out the words and pictures of printed materials. That is, they decide where the words and pictures are placed.

Skilled Workers and Technicians

Skilled workers and technicians are the ones who actually do the printing and create the graphic arts products. Many people in this category require special education at technical schools or colleges. Apprenticeship programs are the source of learning in a

Figure 1-7. *Designers are responsible for the appearance of graphic arts products. (Eastman Kodak Company)*

Figure 1-8. *More and more, typographers work at word processing terminals linked to computers. (Nielsen Lithographing Co.)*

Figure 1-9. *Compositors in cold type facilities paste up type and pictures for photographic reproduction. (South-Western Publishing Co.)*

Figure 1-10. *Strippers prepare film for platemaking. (Eastman Kodak Company)*

Figure 1-11. *Platemakers produce the plates from which printing is done. (Eastman Kodak Company)*

number of occupations. Skilled workers and technicians in the printing and other graphic arts areas include:

Typographers set type for materials to be printed. Some work with actual metal type. Some use machines that form lines or "slugs" of type in metal. Increasing numbers of typographers work at computerized machines that produce images of words on paper (Fig. 1-8).

Compositors put together pages of materials to be printed. Some work with metal type and plates from which pictures are printed. Others paste type and pictures in place for reproduction through processes using photography (Fig. 1-9).

Camera operators convert the pasted up end products produced by compositors to film from which printing plates will be made.

Strippers are specialists in preparing film for platemaking. Their job is to "strip" together film containing images of type and illustrations (Fig. 1-10).

Platemakers produce the plates from which printing is done (Fig. 1-11). They use the positioned film put together by strippers. They deliver plates that are placed on presses.

Press operators run the printing presses. These presses can range from small units that print on one sheet of paper at a time to large complexes of machinery that use rolls of paper (Fig. 1-12).

Binders finish the work of printing. They operate equipment that folds printed material and joins pages together into finished items (Fig. 1-13). Binding is important as the finishing step for magazines and books. In some modern plants, binding is done on portions of the printing equipment.

Figure 1-12. *Press operators run printing presses, performing tasks such as controlling ink flow. (Eastman Kodak Company)*

Check Your Knowledge (True or False)

1. There are only 10 careers in which you can use a knowledge of graphic arts.

2. Designers are sometimes referred to as layout artists.

3. Compositors set type for printed materials.

Figure 1-13. *Bindery workers run equipment that joins printed pages into finished products. (American Printer and AM Varityper)*

Figure 1-14. *Sales is one of many varied business skills vital to the graphic arts industry. (Eastman Kodak Company)*

Figure 1-15. *The graphic arts industry employs people in a wide variety of occupations and professions in addition to those directly related to product production. (Interlake, Inc.)*

Management and Administrative Jobs

Graphic arts companies are businesses. They employ people with the skills necessary for the running of any successful business. These jobs need not be described in detail. However, you should be aware of the general opportunities in the graphic arts field. These opportunities exist for a wide range of occupations and professions (Fig. 1-14). Included are engineers, chemists, business administrators, attorneys, accountants, computer programmers, electronics technicians, electricians, truck drivers, and many others (Fig. 1-15).

GRAPHIC ARTS IN EDUCATION

You have used books and other printed materials throughout your education. You have also looked at displays on bulletin boards in most of your classrooms. You will continue to rely on graphic arts products throughout your education (Fig. 1-16). Preparing the materials you use is an important part of the work of your teachers. Also, there are many companies and people specializing in providing printing materials to schools. Schools at all levels use more than $1 billion worth of printed materials each year.

RELATED INDUSTRIES

Graphic arts is an industry. The industry produces billions of dollars worth of products. Any field this big is part of a broader chain of supply and demand. This is true for every type of business: Automobiles use steel. Bread bakers use flour. Graphic arts companies are also part of a *chain of supply.*

Figure 1-16. *Printed products such as books are a very important part of the education field. (South-Western Publishing Co.)*

A vital industry related to graphic arts is *papermaking.* Billions of trees are cut and processed each year to produce the many tons of paper required for printing.

Ink making is part of the graphic arts industry (Fig. 1-17). To produce ink, chemicals are needed. Companies that develop chemicals from oil provide the raw materials for ink.

Printing plants are consumers of power provided by electric utilities. Printers also depend on trucking companies, railroads, and airlines to deliver the materials they produce.

Figure 1-17. *Ink processing, shown here on a three-roller mill, is a highly scientific and vital part of the graphic arts industry. (National Association of Printing Ink Manufacturers, Inc.)*

In other words, graphic arts companies are an important part of society. They fit into the overall business picture known as the economy, and are therefore known as a service industry.

ROLE OF TECHNOLOGY

For centuries, printing was an industry that saw little change. But as costs of materials and salaries increased, changes became necessary. Without technology, it would have been impossible for people to afford printed products. As a result, newspapers, magazines, and publishers of books adopted new technologies at a rapid rate.

The 1970s were a time of rapid progress in the printing trades. Computers entered the industry in many areas. Computers made it possible to set thousands of lines of type in a single minute. Computers

12

Figure 1-18. *An analytical chemist uses a scanning electron microscope for microanalysis to advance knowledge of jet-ink (spray) printing technology. (Mead/Burk Uzzle/Magnum)*

made it possible for presses to put out as many as 100,000 magazines or newspapers in an hour.

Other developments in electronics—in addition to computers—also played important roles in the graphic arts industry. News stories transmitted to newspapers and broadcast stations now move at a rate of 1,200 words per minute. Previously, the rate was around 60 words per minute. Entire volumes of text are transmitted via satellite.

Photographs are reproduced and transmitted over wires electronically. Printing plates are made electronically.

Learning Activities

1. Call your local newspaper. Ask to speak to the managing editor. Tell the editor you are studying graphic arts. Ask if you can receive samples of pasted up pages and platemaking film. Also ask if there are any brochures or printed explanations about how the paper is produced. Request copies of any information available.

2. Visit a local newspaper or printing plant. Ask to see how ''copy'' is prepared for printing. Ask if you can watch a press in operation.

Electronic methods are even changing the way printing is done. In the past, printing has always required contact between paper and some sort of printing plate or cylinder. Newer electronic methods cause ink to be sprayed onto paper (Fig. 1-18). This is known as jet-ink printing. Contact between machines and paper is eliminated. Greater speed and quality will result in future printed products.

Cable and satellite television promise to revolutionize graphic arts further in the future. Systems are being developed that will display information on television screens. It will even be possible to print documents right in your home through attachments to your TV set.

Summing up, there is a lot to be learned about the graphic arts field. Building your understanding of graphic arts can be exciting and interesting.

Vocabulary Checklist

1. creative
2. information
3. writer
4. illustrator
5. designer
6. photographer
7. typographer
8. compositor
9. camera operator
10. stripper
11. platemaker
12. press operator
13. binder

Unit Review

- No matter what job or profession you enter, graphic arts will play a role in your future. Everyone depends upon graphic arts for needed information.

- Positions in graphic arts fall into a number of groups. These include creative, skilled, administrative, and management positions.

- Graphic arts are essential to education.

- The graphic arts industry is an important part of society and of the economy.

- The graphic arts industry has moved ahead quickly because of new technology. Progress is still going on at a rapid rate.

Review Questions

1. Name at least two graphic arts products from which you receive information.

2. Is writing part of the creative or the production area of graphic arts?

3. Is illustration part of the creative or the production area of graphic arts?

4. Is platemaking part of the creative or the production area of graphic arts?

5. What is the job title of people who set type?

6. What is the job title of people who run printing presses?

GRAPHIC ARTS TECHNOLOGY: PAST, PRESENT, AND FUTURE

2

THE BEGINNINGS: SPREADING THE WORDS

There are several definitions of the word *printing*. You may think of it as writing one letter at a time. Another definition is that printing uses machines to place words or images onto paper or another surface. The difference in methods is the key to an understanding of graphic arts technology.

When a person prints a message on paper by hand, the result is a single copy of a message (Fig. 2-1). This is a good way to communicate with one person or a few individuals. You use this method when you write a letter to another person. However, it is not a good method if the writer wishes a message to be delivered to a large number of people.

The second definition of printing involves making large numbers of copies of a single message. This was the basis for the beginnings of mass communications hundreds of years ago. Modern society could not have developed without printing technology.

Without printing, there would be no newspapers, no magazines, and no school books. Neither would there be food packages, or T-shirts with slogans or special designs. There would be no way to commu-

Figure 2-1. *Before the invention of printing, scribes spent years translating books by hand printing. Since only one copy could be made at a time, very few people were able to own books.*

15

nicate ideas among large numbers of people. Printing improves the ability of people to communicate information and ideas.

DEVELOPMENT OF PRINTING: THE FIRST HISTORIC STEP

The Chinese were the first people to use impression printing. Impressions are printed duplicates made from a single original device. The Chinese printed books using large, carved wood blocks for each page. The first printed book using this wood-block method was the *Diamond Sutra.* This book was printed by Wang Chieh in 868 A.D. in China.

Each page was carved with pictures and reading matter. The actual printing was done entirely by hand. Dampened sheets of paper were placed on the inked block. The paper was rubbed until the image was transferred. The pages were printed one at a time. When the book was finished, the pages were pasted end to end to form a roll, or *scroll.*

THE NEXT MAJOR STEP: MOVABLE TYPE

Chinese wood blocks were the first example of using one original of a message to make many copies. Even more important was the invention of movable type. Credit for this development generally goes to Johann Gutenberg of Germany.

In 1452, Gutenberg made single letters from wood. This was 40 years before Columbus sailed to the New World. Gutenberg's wooden letters soon gave way to metal, which would last longer. These single metal *types* could be arranged to spell words and then used to print on paper.

Movable type was the beginning of mass communication. With movable type, it was no longer necessary to carve blocks for printing. Carving blocks

Figure 2-2. *An early print shop showing type cases and hand printing.*

required skilled artists. Anyone who could read could select letters and prepare movable type for printing.

Another advantage of movable type was that it could be reused. When a printing job was complete, the type letters could be placed in boxes and used for other printing jobs (Fig. 2-2). This was actually a first attempt at what we now call recycling.

Under Gutenberg's system, pieces of metal type were brought together and held as a unit in a form. The form was then put on a press. Ink was applied and paper was pressed over the type.

The name "press" for a printing machine also comes from Gutenberg's work. In searching for a way to speed up the job of making impressions from type, Gutenberg borrowed a technique from winemakers. Presses had been used for some time to squeeze juice from grapes. Gutenberg used the same basic device. He just substituted type, ink, and paper for the grapes. Workers would turn a lever on the press to

Figure 2-3. *A page from an original Gutenberg Bible.*

apply pressure. This caused impressions from the type to be transferred to paper.

Gutenberg's first known work was the Bible. It is called the 42-line Bible because there are 42 lines of text on each page (Fig. 2-3). The book was printed two pages at a time by hand on a converted wine press. Gutenberg did his work well. Some of his books survive today. Gutenberg Bibles are among the most valuable books in the world.

The invention of movable type and the printing press were important to the advancement of knowledge. The skill of printing spread rapidly throughout Europe. Books became available to the public for the first time. Printing soon became known as the art form that preserved all other arts.

PAPER AND PRINTING INK: ANOTHER LOOK INTO HISTORY

If type and presses are the means of printing, then paper and ink are the product. The development of paper and ink also had humble beginnings. Today, however, both are highly technical products, with a great variety of uses.

Check Your Knowledge (True or False)

1. The Chinese were the first people to use movable type in printing.

2. The Bible was the first book ever produced on a printing press.

3. Before the invention of the printing press, books were not available to the general public.

The making of paper started with the Moors of North Africa. These people brought papermaking to the West. The first papermaking mill in America was started by William Rottenhouse in about 1690. This paper was made by hand (Fig. 2-4). Papermaking machines were soon developed. The number of mills increased steadily. Most printing paper is made from wood. North America leads the world in papermaking because of its large forests and abundance of water.

Figure 2-4. *In the sixteenth century, paper was made by hand. Only a few pounds a day could be produced by this method. (Paper and Printing Digest)*

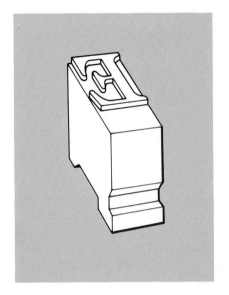

Figure 2-5. *Diagram of a piece of metal type shows how the printing surface of the letter image is raised from the flat surface, or counter.*

RELIEF (LETTERPRESS) PRINTING: THIS IS WHERE IT ALL BEGAN

The earliest printing presses used a relief image carrier. *Relief* means that the image area that does the printing is raised. The raised area is said to be *in relief* from a flat surface. *Carrier* refers to a surface that carries ink to paper or other material. This involves ink transfer from the carrier to paper as pressure is applied. Common examples of relief printing are the rubber stamp and the typewriter.

Letterpress printing is usually done directly from metal or wood types. Wood, linoleum, and metal plates are used to print illustrations. Wood and linoleum plates are prepared by cutting out the design with an engraving tool that has a sharp blade. Metal plates, called photoengravings, are prepared by a combination of photography and chemistry. These plates can reproduce pictures as well as words.

In letterpress printing, the image (relief) area is inked. Paper or another material is placed over the inked image. With slight pressure, the ink is transferred from the raised surface to the paper.

Another form of letterpress printing is called *flexography*. This method uses a flexible rubber plate as the image carrier. The rubber plate is attached to a cylinder on the press. Products such as cellophane, foil, and plastic bags are printed by flexography.

INTAGLIO (GRAVURE) PRINTING: REVERSING A PROCESS

Intaglio (in-tal'yo), meaning to cut in or engrave, is the exact opposite of letterpress. It is also referred to as *gravure*. The images are etched into a metal plate. *Etching* is a chemical process. Chemicals are applied that remove, or dissolve, metal areas. When etching chemicals are applied to a carrier, or printing plate, metal is dissolved. Cavities are formed on the surfaces of the plate. In gravure printing, the actual images to be printed are etched into the surface of the plate. That's why gravure is the opposite of relief printing. The etched images look like tiny cup-shaped cavities below the surface of the plate (Fig. 2-6).

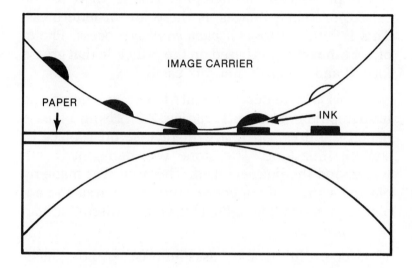

Figure 2-6. *In gravure printing, the image is etched into the plate. Gravure is the exact opposite of letterpress (relief) printing, where the image is raised.*

On a gravure printing press, ink is applied to the entire plate surface. This fills the image cavities. A thin, easy-flowing ink is used. A flexible rubber scraper, called a "doctor blade," removes all the ink from the plate surface. But the ink remains in the image cavities. Pressure from the plate against the paper transfers ink from the image cavities to the paper.

An important feature of gravure printing is the way printed images are formed. The original images to be reproduced are photographed through a fine mesh screen. As a result, the type and illustrations contain a series of tiny dots.

The term *rotogravure* applies to gravure presses that use a rounded plate cylinder rather than a flat plate. Rotogravure presses are usually of the web type. This means they print on paper from a roll.

Figure 2-7. *Alois Senefelder invented the lithographic process in 1798. Lithography led to photo-offset lithography printing techniques.*

Rotogravure presses are extremely fast. They produce color printing of good quality.

PLANOGRAPHIC PRINTING (LITHOGRAPHY): TRANSITION TO MODERN METHODS

Printing is done from a flat (plane) surface image carrier in photo-offset lithography. That is, there are no raised, or relief, images as there are in letterpress. This is referred to as a *planographic* process. Photo-offset lithography is based on the principle that grease (or oil) and water do not mix easily.

Alois Senefelder is credited with inventing the lithographic process in 1798 (Fig. 2-7). Using a grease pencil, he drew an image in reverse on a piece of smooth limestone. The stone was dampened with water, and the images inked. The print was made by placing a sheet of paper over the image area and applying pressure (Fig. 2-8). This was a "direct" lithography process.

Modern lithography uses an offset printing technique. *Offset* printing means that the image to be printed is transferred. In offset printing, the image carrier is prepared on a flat paper or metal plate. The

Figure 2-8. *The basic process of lithography is based on the principle that grease (or oil) and water do not mix. The image is drawn in reverse on the stone with a grease pencil. The stone is dampened with water and the images inked. A sheet of paper is placed over the images and pressure applied. This is a "direct" lithography process.*

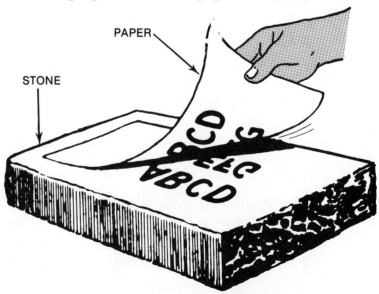

PAPER

STONE

image areas are at the same level as the surface of the plate. The image area is chemically treated to pick up ink but repel water. The non-image areas pick up water but repel ink.

During the printing operation, water and ink are applied to the plate. The printing press has a rubber blanket attached to a steel cylinder. The image is off-set from the printing plate to the blanket. Actual placement of the image on paper is from the offset blanket (Fig. 2-9).

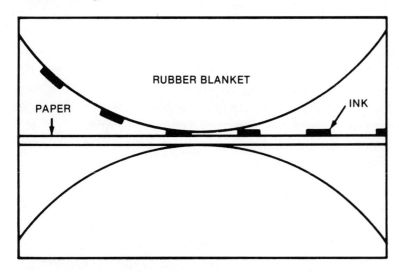

Figure 2-9. *In photo-offset lithography, the ink is transferred from a rubber blanket to the paper.*

SCREEN PROCESS PRINTING: A VERSATILE METHOD

The process known as *screen process* uses a porous (open) stencil as the image carrier. The stencil material is either hand-cut or prepared photographically. The stencil contains the desired design or printing image.

The stencil material is attached to the bottom side of a screen mesh. The screen mesh material can be made of silk, nylon, dacron, organdy, or stainless steel. The mesh is stretched and mounted on a wooden or metal frame.

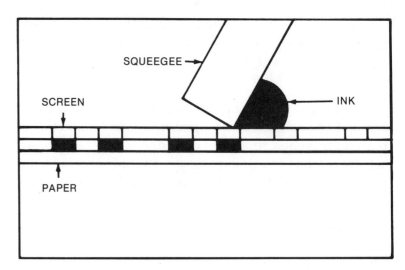

Figure 2-10. *A squeegee forces ink through a screen and onto paper in screen printing.*

Paper or other material is placed under the screen. Ink is poured into the frame and forced through the open areas of the stencil and mesh. A *squeegee* is used for this purpose (Fig. 2-10). The squeegee has a flexible rubber blade attached to a handle.

The screen process has many special features. It is capable of laying down the heaviest film of ink in comparison to the other processes. It can print on many kinds of materials and surfaces. These include paper, glass, wood, metal, plastic, fabric, wallpaper, and cork. Almost any size, shape, and design can be reproduced.

Check Your Knowledge (True or False)

1. Flexography is a form of relief printing.

2. Intaglio is another term for lithography.

3. In photo-offset printing, the image is transferred from the printing plate to the paper.

4. A doctor blade is used in gravure printing.

Production speed of screen printing used to be limited by press styles and ink drying time requirements. New technology has produced automatic presses and faster-drying inks. Modern automatic screen presses can print up to 5,500 copies per hour.

DUPLICATORS AND COPIERS: LIMITED-QUANTITY PROCESSES

Offices in business, industry, government, and schools produce messages for limited distribution. This means that small numbers of copies are needed. The message usually is produced first on a typewriter. Many machines and processes are available for fast and easy duplication of images and text. For limited numbers of copies, these methods are usually less expensive than the four major printing processes already mentioned.

The three major types of office printing equipment are:

1. Spirit duplicator

2. Mimeograph

3. Electrostatic copier.

Spirit duplicator. This method uses a paper image carrier. The carrier can be imprinted on a typewriter or letterpress. Before the imprinting is done, a special backing sheet is placed behind the carrier. This backing sheet looks like carbon paper. The backing sheet places an image on the back side of the carrier sheet. This happens at the same time as the message is imprinted on the front of the carrier.

The carrier sheet is placed on a duplicator machine. As the duplicator turns, a liquid is spread over the back surface of the carrier sheet. The liquid, called *spirit,* dissolves some of the image on the back of the carrier. As the carrier comes in contact with paper, the spirit-dissolved image is transferred.

Spirit duplicating is the least expensive office copying method.

Mimeograph. Mimeographing uses stencils. This method is similar to screen printing. The images are formed in the stencil by hand lettering, drawing, or typing. A stencil is placed over an inked drum. As the stencil comes in contact with paper, ink is forced through the images. The ink creates an image on paper (Fig. 2-11).

Mimeographing used to be popular. But use of this method is declining.

The electrostatic copier. With electrostatic copiers, multiple copies are printed directly from typed, hand-written, or printed originals. The electrostatic copier

Learning Activities

1. Visit one or more printing firms that do offset and letterpress printing. Note the differences in the way impressions are transferred to paper.

2. If you have never seen an electrostatic copier, plan to visit an office that has one of these machines. Note how duplicates are produced directly from the original. Compare the original and several duplicates. Note portions of the copies that are high in quality. Also mark portions that are low in quality.

3. Gather several samples of gravure printing. These might include *TV Guide* or some Sunday newspaper magazine supplements. Look at the printed images with a magnifier. Note the ragged edge around the type and illustrations.

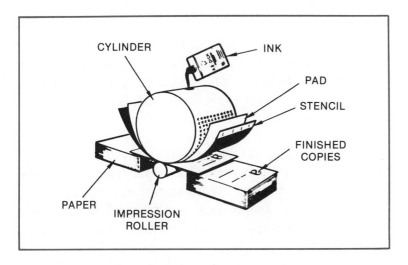

Figure 2-11. *Paper is pressed against a stencil by pressure from the stencil cylinder and impression rollers in mimeograph printing.*

operates on the principle that like electrical charges repel and opposite charges attract.

Technical advances in the electrostatic copier field are being made rapidly (Fig. 2-12). Emphasis in development is on quality and speed. Modern electrostatic copiers are now producing printed copies of high quality that rival offset printing. The speed of copiers is also approaching that of small offset presses. This is a rapidly growing area of offset reproduction.

THE NUMBERS GAME: WHERE SPEED IS VITAL

Basically, the four major printing processes can be considered as parts of a mass communication industry. The office machines—duplicators and copiers—belong in the limited-quantity area of the graphic arts field.

The major printing methods can also be divided according to speed of operation and quantity of product. Here, letterpress, photo-offset lithography, and gravure are separated from screen printing. This is because screen printing has limited production capacities.

Figure 2-12. *Modern, high-speed electrostatic copiers are rapidly making other office copying techniques obsolete. (A.B. Dick Co.)*

The other three processes, however, can use either of two basic production forms: web-fed or sheet-fed. In sheet-fed printing, paper is fed into the press one sheet at a time. This is generally used where a high-quality product is desired and quantity will be relatively small.

In web-fed printing, the paper is fed through the press in a continuous roll. This is the type of printing used to produce mass communication products such as newspapers, magazines, and books (Fig. 2-13). Modern automated presses use computers to improve speed and quality.

Figure 2-13. *Large production jobs such as newspapers and magazines are printed on high-speed web-fed presses like this rotogravure multi-unit press. (Motter Printing Press Co.)*

Each of these kinds of printing is described further in later units.

IMAGES IN PRINTING

In any type of printing, images are transferred from a carrier to paper or another surface. The transferring of images produces an effect similar to what you see when you look in a mirror. In a mirror, images are reversed. Your left hand is on your right in a mirror.

In the process of transferring from your body to the mirror, your image is reversed. The same reversing takes place when an image is transferred from a carrier to paper in printing.

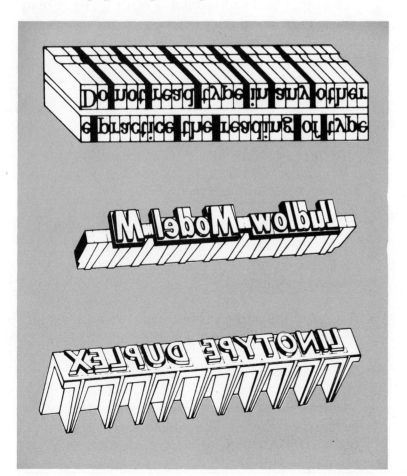

Figure 2-14. *Letterpress printing image carriers are reverse reading. When ink is transferred to the paper or other material, the image becomes a mirror image of the carrier and thus right reading.*

Vocabulary Checklist

1. scroll
2. letterpress
3. relief
4. flexography
5. photo-offset
6. lithography
7. plate
8. blanket
9. gravure
10. intaglio
11. doctor blade
12. rotogravure
13. stencil
14. screen printing
15. squeegee
16. spirit duplicator
17. mimeograph
18. electrostatic copier
19. web-fed press
20. sheet-fed press
21. right reading
22. reverse reading

In printing, however, it is not acceptable to produce a reverse image. It is necessary for people to be able to read and understand printed records. A document that reads correctly when you look at it is called *right reading.* Printed products must be right reading.

To deliver right-reading products, a printing process must be done from a reverse-reading carrier. A *reverse-reading* carrier has an image that is the opposite of the right-reading end product. In effect, the carrier has a mirror image of the final printed item (Fig. 2-14).

Remember that printed items must be right reading. Carriers from which printing is done are reverse reading. Consider how this works in the printing processes you have learned about so far:

- Letterpress printing uses reverse-reading type and plates as carriers.

- Gravure printing uses reverse-reading plates. The image becomes right reading when it is transferred to the paper.

- Offset printing uses right-reading plates. The image is reversed when it is transferred to the blanket. Printing is done from the reverse-reading blanket.

- A spirit-duplicating master has a reverse-reading image on the back of the carrier sheet.

- A mimeograph stencil is reverse reading.

- Electrostatic copiers reproduce copies from right-reading originals. The image is reversed to a drum from which it is transferred to right-reading copies.

- Development of printing made it possible to communicate with large numbers of people.

- The Chinese invented wood block printing in the ninth century.

- Gutenberg's movable type opened the door to modern printing techniques.

- Progress in the production of ink and paper was also vital in the growth of printing technology.

- There are four basic methods of printing: relief (letterpress), photo-offset, gravure, and screen.

- Duplicators and electrostatic copiers increase the ability and ease of printing limited numbers of documents. These machines are widely used in offices.

- Web-fed printing is used where large numbers of a product are required. Sheet-fed presses are slower but are used where highest quality is desired.

- Printing end products are right reading. Right-reading images are created from reverse-reading carriers.

Unit Review

Review Questions

1. Who invented wood block printing?

2. Who invented movable type?

3. What kind of printing uses a raised image to create impressions on paper?

4. What kind of printing is the opposite of letter-press?

5. What kind of printing uses a flat plate and a rubber blanket to transfer the ink to paper?

6. Is a printed end product right reading or reverse reading?

COMMUNICATING WITH GRAPHIC ARTS

3

COMMUNICATION: A BASIC HUMAN NEED

From the very earliest times, people have worked to improve their ability to communicate. The need to communicate information has grown constantly since people began living in groups. As communities and commerce grew, so did the need to communicate information. Throughout history, communication methods have changed. In large part, changes have been aimed at delivering more information more efficiently.

The earliest records of graphic communication are the crude pictures and symbols called *stone carvings*. These were drawn upon walls by cave dwellers

Figure 3-1. *The earliest records of graphic communication are the stone carvings drawn upon walls by cave dwellers. These drawings date back more than 10,000 years.*

(Fig. 3-1). Such carvings and paintings have been found in more than 150 caves in France and Spain alone. This form of communication dates back more than 10,000 years. Cave drawings were made long before the invention of an alphabet.

Another early method of graphic communication was that of *picture writing*. These methods are popularly referred to as *hieroglyphics* (Fig. 3-2). The ancient Egyptians referred to these as sacred writings. Early American Indians also used picture writings to communicate. These picture languages were not really

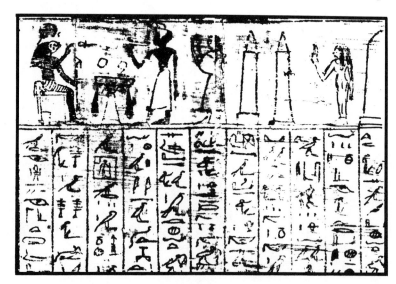

Figure 3-2. *Ancient picture writing is popularly referred to as hieroglyphics. Ancient Egyptians considered these to be sacred writings. The pictures were ideograms representing ideas rather than spoken sounds.*

alphabets even though there were separate characters. They were *ideograms* representing ideas and images. However, the symbols did not represent spoken sounds.

THE FIRST ALPHABETS: AN IMPORTANT CONNECTION

The Babylonians developed an alphabet around 3,000 B.C. They used *clay tablets* to write on. Writing was done with a square-pointed cutting tool called a *stylus*. The message was scribed (cut) into soft, wet clay. As the stylus was pressed into the soft clay, it left a wedge-shaped impression. This wedge- or V-shaped form was called a *cuneiform* (Fig. 3-3). When the message was scribed into clay, the tablet was placed in the sun to dry.

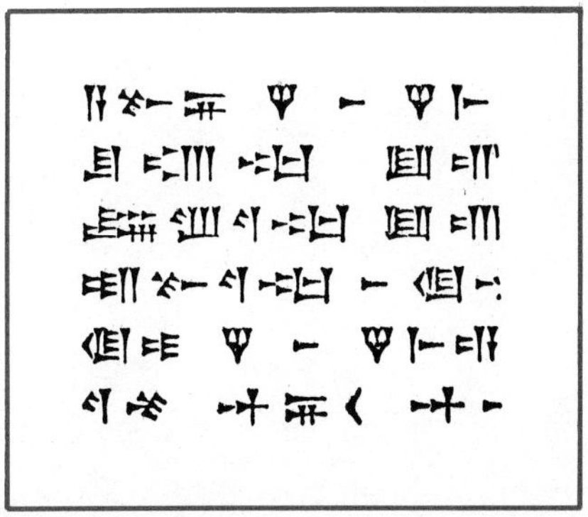

The first alphabet with characters that represented sounds was developed by the Phoenicians around 1300 B.C. These letter forms were the start of our present alphabet. The *Phoenician alphabet* had 22 letters. It was a very important step in the development of communication. Phonetic characters made it possible to write the sounds people used to communicate with each other. The characters could be combined to form words. The words were then combined to form sentences.

Later civilizations improved and refined the Phoenician alphabet. The ancient Greeks took 15 of the Phoenician letters and developed several more letters to make an alphabet of 24 letters. Later, the Romans adopted 18 of the Greek letters and added seven more. The Anglo-Saxons took all of the Roman letters, added two new ones, and later dropped one letter. This led to our present alphabet, which consists of 26 letters.

More than 8,500 years passed between the earliest forms of stone carvings and the development of an alphabet.

COMMUNICATION WITH A PURPOSE: MESSAGES FOR TARGETED AUDIENCES

The audience for graphic communication remained small until the invention of the printing press and movable type. Before that, books and other reading materials had to be printed by hand, one letter at a time. This was a slow process.

The Bible was the most widely published book as European civilization grew. Christian monks trans-

Figure 3-3. *Babylonians developed an alphabet about 3,000 B.C. Messages were scribed with a stylus into soft, wet clay. The stylus left a wedge-shaped impression called a cuneiform.*

lated portions of the Bible from ancient languages. Some spent their entire lives in monasteries, working to hand-print just one copy of the Bible.

The invention of the printing press made the printed message suddenly available to much larger audiences. It also enabled people to create many different types of messages for various purposes. Instead of just printing books, people found it useful to communicate about current events. As the printing industry grew and its methods improved, the mass communication industry was born. Modern society could not have developed without graphic arts.

Graphic arts have made it possible for people to reach selected audiences. Companies wishing to sell a product use advertising to build sales. Targeting audiences has become a vital part of graphic arts communication in modern times. This is because such a wide variety of messages is being delivered. Separate messages must compete for attention.

ELEMENTS OF GRAPHIC ARTS: FROM IDEA TO PRINTED MESSAGE

Regardless of the type of message, the flow of work in graphic arts generally follows a pattern (Fig. 3-4). The process of developing a message includes the following:

1. *Identification of a need.* Every message must be directed to an audience. This includes a news story, an advertisement, or any other type of communication. Someone must desire to communicate a message to a certain audience. All communication starts with a need.

2. *Creating a basic message.* Once the need is known, the message must be created. Decisions might include how to present the message and what type of illustrations, if any, should be used to support it.

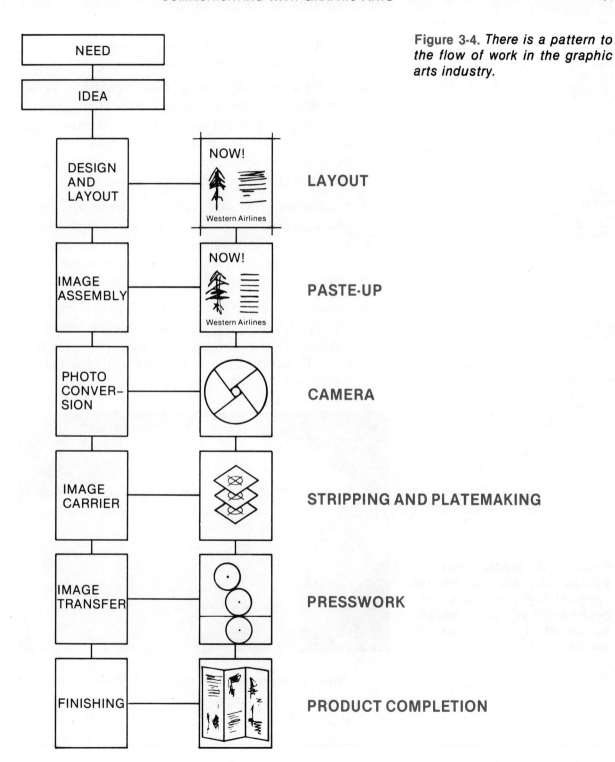

3. *Writing.* A basic message is usually put into words. This is called the *copy.*

4. *Design and layout.* Along with copy, the overall appearance of the message is important. *Layout,* meaning the overall appearance of the message, attracts the audience and helps to hold its attention. Layout blends all elements of a message into a single visual unit.

5. *Illustration.* Messages can be illustrated with photographs, drawings, cartoons, maps, and a variety of other materials. Illustrations may be used to support the copy. Sometimes, an illustration is the main element of a message.

6. *Image assembly.* The copy (Fig. 3-5) is composed into type. The type is checked against the original copy by a proofreader to make sure it is correct. Illustrations are created and positioned within the layout.

Figure 3-5. *Written copy is edited and marked up for typesetting specifications before being sent out to be composed into type. (Stephen B. Simms)*

7. *Photo conversion.* The type and illustrations are combined into a page. Film negatives are made if the printing is to be done by the offset, gravure, or screen methods. In letterpress,

printing plates the same height as the type are prepared.

8. *Image carriers.* These are the plates or letterpress forms used in the printing process. They are described in later units.

9. *Image transfer.* This image is reproduced on paper or other material. All processes involve the transfer of ink to the printing surface.

10. *Binding and finishing.* Some printed products must be bound. Examples are books, magazines, and catalogs. Folding, trimming, sewing, and stapling are terms related to binding. Finishing refers to such operations as collating (arranging pages in order), sorting, wrapping, labeling, and shipping. These processes are described in later units.

As noted, printing processes are described in later units. The remainder of this unit covers the creative aspects of graphic arts preparation.

Check Your Knowledge (True or False)

1. Hieroglyphics is a form of ancient picture writing.

2. The Phoenicians invented the first alphabet with characters that represented sounds.

3. The Greek alphabet had 26 letters.

4. Formulating a basic message is the first step in the graphic arts process.

5. Image assembly involves design and layout.

Figure 3-6. *An editor decides how a story is to be handled in a newspaper or magazine.*

FORMULATING A BASIC MESSAGE: DECIDING ON THE PRESENTATION

Deciding what a message should say often involves activities that can be thought of as *brainstorming*. This function differs from one kind of communication activity to another.

At a newspaper, message development may begin when an editor decides to run a certain story. An *editor* is a person responsible for the content of a publication (Fig. 3-6). The editor decides where a story is to run in the paper, then works with a reporter and explains how the story is to be handled. The editor may also assign a photographer to cover the story. For example, suppose the story deals with the start of construction of a large building. An architect's drawing may be used to illustrate the story. A simple map could be used to help the reader locate the project.

A magazine editor might perform a similar function. Often, editorial decisions are made by a group of editors in conference. Most magazines have *art directors*, who create the basic "look" of the publication.

Figure 3-7. *Editors and staff artists often confer on the presentation of a magazine article.*

Staff artists design layouts for individual pages. Editors, writers, and artists work closely in the development of magazine articles (Fig. 3-7).

At advertising agencies, *account executives* are responsible for message development. These specialists work with clients—the people or companies sponsoring the advertising programs. Copy, art, and production specialists at the agencies prepare advertisements in finished form—ready for publication. The ad copy is then sent to publishers.

Publishers of brochures, newsletters, and other kinds of graphic arts products work in similar ways to develop ideas.

WRITING: IDEAS INTO WORDS

The best ideas have no real value until they are put into words. This is true in every form of graphic arts. A newspaper, for instance, could not run a page of photos without some copy. The minimum requirements would be captions to explain the photos—and a headline to tie it all together.

The same holds true for magazines, advertisements, billboards, brochures, flyers, and other forms of mass communication. The writer must express the idea of the message in words. The message can be extremely brief. Some advertisements rely primarily on illustrations to carry their messages. The written message can be very long, as in a novel or a textbook. Some messages, such as short news stories, have no illustrations.

Most writers, particularly those who work for large publications, specialize in one field. Other writers have to be able to deal with many subjects. A reporter for a small newspaper might cover the police station in the morning and sports later that day.

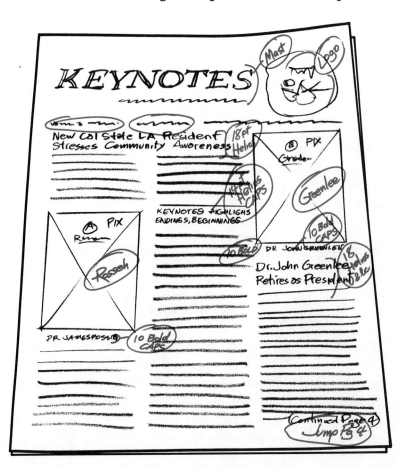

Figure 3-8. *Type can be designed to fit a variety of layouts. An editor or design artist marks up copy to include such instructions to typographers. (Stephen B. Simms)*

When a writer completes a piece of copy, called a *manuscript*, it is usually turned over to an editor. The editor checks the copy for accuracy, spelling, grammar, and style (use of language). Either an editor or a design artist will mark up the copy for typesetting. When copy is *marked up*, typesetting instructions are added. Type selection is based on the layout for a publication or advertisement (Fig. 3-8).

DESIGN AND LAYOUT: PUTTING IT ALL TOGETHER

As with writing, the design and layout functions differ greatly among kinds of publications. However, certain design principles apply to all graphic arts products. The designer, whether artist or editor, seeks a pleasing arrangement of copy and illustrations. The principles used by designers include:

- Proportion
- Balance
- Contrast
- Rhythm
- Unity
- Harmony
- Symmetry
- Variety
- Action.

Proportion. Proportion describes the relationships of various parts on the printed page—their size, width, and depth. Proportion is used to determine the general dimensions of the page itself. An example of a pleasing shape is a page that has dimensions in a ratio of about 2 to 3. Pages in this ratio might measure 6 by 9 inches, or 8 by 12 inches.

A design factor related to proportion is the *optical center* of a page (Fig. 3-9). The optical center is about two units from the top and three units from the bottom of a page. If a single line of type is placed in the exact center of a page, the type appears too low. This is an optical illusion. If the type is moved to the optical center, it will appear balanced on the page.

Figure 3-9. *The optical center of a page is about two units from the top and three units from the bottom of a page.*

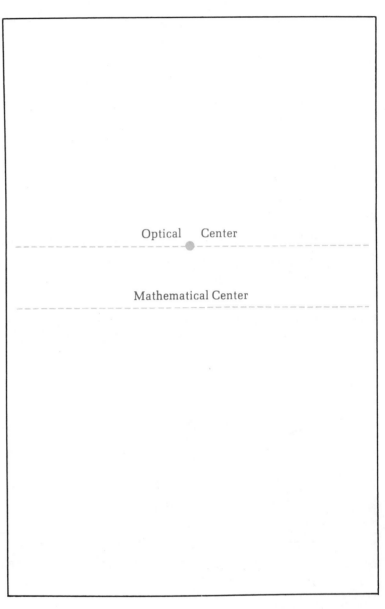

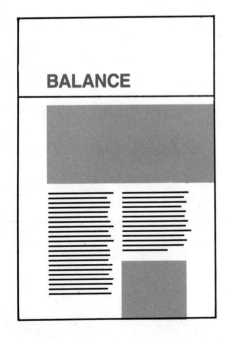

Figure 3-10. *Informal balance allows for placement of images at different locations on a page. This style is more modern than formal balance.*

Balance. In design, there are two basic kinds of balance: formal and informal. In *formal balance,* the images on the page are centered horizontally. An equal amount of each unit is positioned on either side of an imaginary center line. This kind of balance gives a feeling of being strong, orderly, and dignified.

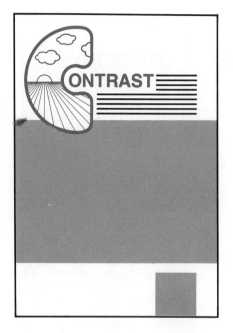

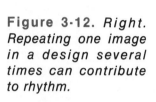

Figure 3-11. Left. Contrast can be achieved by using different sizes and weights of type. Different ink color and shaded backgrounds also can be used.

Figure 3-12. Right. Repeating one image in a design several times can contribute to rhythm.

Informal balance allows for the images to be placed at different locations on the page (Fig. 3-10). This style is considered more modern than the formal style. Informal balance allows more freedom in the placement of the images.

Contrast. Contrast refers to differences in layout elements. Use of contrast can add interest, attraction, and liveliness to a printed page. Contrast is usually achieved by using different sizes and weights of type (Fig. 3-11). Some other ways of producing contrast include using a second ink color, underlining type, and using shaded backgrounds.

Rhythm. In design, rhythm involves use of the same images over and over. This can create interest by setting up a visual pattern that a reader comes to expect.

Rhythm can be achieved by selecting one image in a design and repeating it several times. This could be an ornament, a trademark, or a certain word (Fig. 3-12). Setting type in different shapes for selected paragraphs is another way to achieve rhythm.

Figure 3-13. A design is said to have unity if the type and illustrations fit well together.

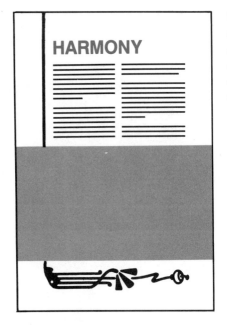

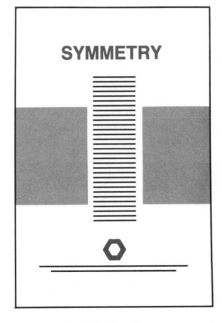

Figure 3-14. *Left. Harmony involves the arrangement of images so that they flow smoothly and do not clash.*

Figure 3-15. *Right. A symmetrical design has type and illustrations occupying balanced positions on a page.*

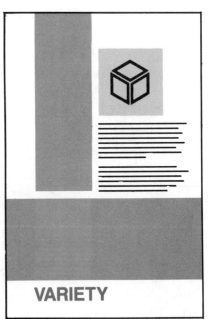

Figure 3-16. *Variety in design is the opposite of symmetry. Variety raises the interest of the design.*

Unity. A design that combines all the images and allows the reader's eye to travel smoothly is said to have unity. This means that type and illustrations fit well together (Fig. 3-13). The images should not appear to be crowded. They should have the look of belonging together. This allows the reader's eye to flow smoothly over the page without confusion.

Harmony. When images are arranged so that they flow smoothly and do not clash with one another, a design has harmony. This includes the choice of typefaces, shapes of the type images and illustrations, and the colors of ink and paper (Fig. 3-14).

Symmetry. When a design is composed of parts, features, or contours that are identical in size and shape, it has symmetry, or is symmetrical. When a design is symmetrical, the type images and illustrations occupy balanced positions on the page (Fig. 3-15). This is often referred to as a "formal" layout.

Variety. A design quality directly opposite to symmetry is variety (Fig. 3-16). Variety is used to raise the interest of the design and to add a spirit of life and action to a page. It is possible for the design artist to create an almost endless variety of designs by using graphic materials in different ways.

Action. Most modern advertising uses the principles of design action. Formal display might be quite pleasing to the eye, but it usually contains no action. Action can be achieved by designing out-of-center balances and unsymmetrical groupings of images. Illustrations containing action can create a feeling of motion and activity (Fig. 3-17).

Figure 3-17. *Action plays an important role in modern advertising design. One way to create a feeling of motion and activity is through the use of illustrations containing action.*

Check Your Knowledge (True or False)

1. Magazine art directors are responsible for the basic "look" of a magazine.

2. Account executives prepare advertising copy in finished form.

3. Typesetting instructions are written on manuscript copy.

4. The optical center of a page is located slightly below the exact center.

5. Harmony involves repetition of certain elements in a graphic arts layout.

PREPARING LAYOUTS: FROM SKETCH TO 'COMP'

Before any piece of graphic communication can be printed, the design artist must prepare drawings called layouts. The layouts use the principles of design covered in the preceding section. A layout is a diagram of a printed product. The layout shows proportions, width of type lines, choices of type styles, and placement of illustrations.

Three steps are generally followed in preparing layouts:

- The first step involves several small, or *thumbnail,* sketches used to decide which design is best.
- The second step involves drawing a rough, full-size layout.
- The final step results in a detailed, full-size, comprehensive layout. This is submitted as a basis for approving a project.

Thumbnail sketches. Thumbnail sketches are small drawings in the same shape and proportion as the job being designed. Several of these drawings may be made—sometimes as many as two dozen. Thumbnail sketches are drawn with pencil. They usually measure about 2 by 3 inches in size (Fig. 3-18).

Many periodicals have standardized formats. Magazine artists often skip the thumbnail sketch. They work with pre-lined dummy sheets. A *dummy* is a layout with enough detail for typesetting and production. Newspaper editors also use standardized dummy sheets.

Rough layouts. After the preferred thumbnail sketch has been selected, a rough layout is drawn. This drawing is the same size as the printed job. Space for type and the location of illustrations are shown on the rough layout (Fig. 3-19). Since the rough layout is drawn in pencil, changes are easy to make.

Comprehensive layouts. The comprehensive layout (referred to as a 'comp') is a detailed drawing of the final printed product. The comp shows the styles and sizes of type and the illustrations in great detail. A comp is generally drawn with colored pencils, felt pens, or tempera paints. The detail is sufficient so that the client or editor can see how the printed job will

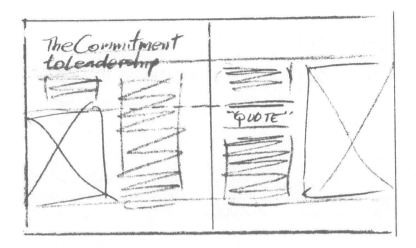

Figure 3-18. *Thumbnail sketches are small drawings in the same shape and proportion as the job being designed.*

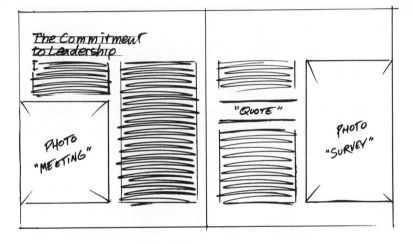

Figure 3-19. *Rough layouts are the same size as the printed job, showing space for type and illustrations.*

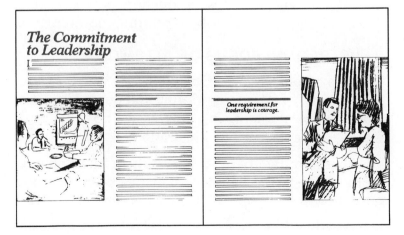

Figure 3-20. *Comprehensive layouts are detailed drawings showing how the printed product will look. Colors, if any, are included by the artist with colored pencils, felt pens, or tempera paints.*

look (Fig. 3-20). The comp is the final step in planning before typesetting begins.

THE LAYOUT DUMMY: EVERYTHING IN ORDER

A layout dummy is a series of design layouts, such as a number of pages for a book, a magazine, or a brochure. The layout dummy is used as a preview of the final printed job, much like a comprehensive layout. The dummy is drawn to show all areas of type and illustrations. A dummy usually includes page numbers, which are known as *folios*.

A layout dummy is useful to production people because it gives a clear picture of how the printed job will fit together. A dummy also contains detailed instructions needed to print the job.

Magazines and other periodicals often use single-sheet master dummies. These are useful for complicated printing jobs. The master dummy or *production schematic* contains simplified instructions for individual pages. Positioning of advertising and stories are shown. The dummy also indicates where color printing is to be used.

Most magazines are printed in sections called *press forms*. A printed section is called a *signature*. The master dummy provides production people with a quick reference for all critical printing requirements.

ILLUSTRATION: FOCUS OF ATTENTION

There is an old saying: "One picture is worth a thousand words." In modern printing and publishing, that is an understatement. In many cases, no amount of words can replace a key illustration.

There are two basic kinds of illustration: photography and drawing. Either or both can be used to present information (Fig. 3-21). Pictures can also be used to set a mood or a style. An example of this is the beautiful western scenery used as the background in some ads.

Illustrations can be simple or complex, depending on the subject of the job to be printed. A page in a magazine, for example, may contain one photograph or many.

Decisions about illustrations can be made before or after design and layout. A design artist may have illustrations supplied at the start. Then the layout is designed for best use of these pictures.

Other layouts are roughed out in advance. Then photography or drawings are ordered to match the layout.

Photos can be altered to fit a layout. The design artist can have a photo blown up (made larger) or reduced in size. Some portions of a photo may not be vital to the main image. These portions may be cut out of the picture that is finally used. This is called *cropping*.

Photographers and illustrators work closely with design artists to help produce the needed pictures. *Composition* of a photo is vital to its effectiveness. Some layouts require sharp images with high contrast. Others need softer images for a more subtle effect. Certain subjects require a clear background. Others benefit from a vague or out-of-focus background.

Photography. Photography is an important method of illustrating graphic arts products. The importance of photography increased greatly with technical and artistic developments of the 1960s and 1970s. In earlier years, cameras were large. Most professional photographs were taken on individual sheets of film.

More recently, improved cameras, lens systems, and films have made it possible for photographers to

Figure 3-21. *Photography and drawings can be used separately or together. This ad combines the two forms of illustration, with action to attract the eye. (Toyota Motor Sales, USA, Inc.)*

use smaller, more flexible equipment. The most popular size of camera today for news pictures and other illustrations is 35 mm. The 35 mm camera is small and portable. The term *35 mm* describes the width of the film used. The film measures just a little more than an inch across. Thus, the cameras themselves can be small and light. A camera is easily carried around the neck of the photographer, on a strap. Total weight is usually under 2 pounds.

Modern 35 mm cameras use advanced lenses and optical systems. This means that different effects can be realized by changing lenses quickly. Many photographers now work with *zoom lenses*. These are lenses that can change the viewing area they cover through use of simple adjustments. With a single lens, a photographer can take closeup photos or can cover large areas of view.

Learning Activities

1. Pick up a magazine. Observe some editorial pages. Note how type and illustrations are blended into a harmonious unit. Are the pages symmetrical or do they feature variety in layout? Look closely at the typefaces used on a page. Are italic or boldface types used for emphasis? Observe how display type is used to attract the reader's attention. Label at least one example each of serif and sans serif typefaces.

2. Visit a photographer's studio if possible. Ask the photographer to explain how the subject matter of a photograph is composed. Ask to see the darkroom to see how photographic film is processed and printed. Look at photos in a local newspaper. Try cropping several photos to see if you can add visual interest.

In addition, most modern 35 mm cameras are of the single-lens reflex type. A *single-lens system* means that there is only one lens on the camera. The image focused on the film is the same as the one seen by the photographer. *Reflex* means that the single image is reflected into a viewfinder used by the photographer. The reflex action is through either a movable mirror or a glass prism that reflects the image. Thus, the photographer sees exactly what is recorded on film.

A further advance in photography has been the building of *exposure meters* into 35 mm cameras. These devices are built into the *viewfinders* that photographers use to arrange and focus pictures. The exposure meters measure the light coming through the lens. The meters then tell the photographer what settings may be used to take a picture. Some exposure meters actually adjust the camera settings automatically.

As cameras have become smaller and more flexible, films have also improved. Today's films are said to combine high speed and fine grain. *High speed* means that the film is sensitive to light. The speed of films is rated on a measurement scale. The films available today are as much as 10 times faster than those that were used in the 1950s. *Fine grain* means that the image is clearer. It is possible to enlarge photos taken on 35 mm cameras by 10 to 20 times and still have quality illustrations.

The net result of improvements in cameras, lenses, and films has been greater popularity for photography. Pictures today are more pleasing and natural than they were years ago. As a result, the use of photographs for graphic arts illustrations has increased.

Drawings and line illustrations. Non-photographic illustrations, or drawings, can be prepared in many ways. Some are true to life. Some utilize image distortion to make their impact (this also can be true with photography). There are cartoons, both humorous and serious. Simple line drawings also have a place in graphic communication. An artist's or architect's rendering (drawing or painting) may be used to show how a structure will look when completed.

All of the above may be printed in simple black and white. This is known as monochromatic printing. *Monochromatic* means only one color of ink is used. The ink can be of any color. One effective way to achieve added color is to use colored *stock* (paper). Combined with an ink of a contrasting color, this method can produce a multi-colored effect.

Color can be added to photographs or drawings by the use of screens in two-color printing. Four-color printing is the most expensive and can be used to reproduce color photography. These processes are explained in units elsewhere in this book.

Check Your Knowledge (True or False)

1. In preparing a layout, an artist first does a full-sized rough copy.

2. A comprehensive layout includes folios.

3. A signature is a printed section of a magazine.

4. Reducing a photo in size is called cropping.

IMAGE ASSEMBLY: HOW TYPE IS USED

The composition of type is necessary for most kinds of printing. Type is made up of individual characters, one for each letter, numeral, and punctuation mark.

These are assembled into words and sentences, in lines of the width called for in the layout.

There are many different type styles in modern graphic arts. Like a person's voice, type styles are used to achieve desired effects. Some type styles whisper; others shout. Different styles create a variety of feelings: warm or cold, happy or sad, eager or unconcerned.

Typefaces have texture or feel, since they create a look or feeling much like fabric. The designer of printing uses the psychology of a typeface to create a mood or style.

Since the early days of printing, type manufacturers have produced hundreds of different typefaces. Many of these were for a special use. The typefaces that have survived fall into several type *classifications.* These can be separated into six groups of typefaces:

1. Roman Oldstyle
2. Sans Serif
3. Square Serif
4. Script and Cursive
5. Textletter, or Blackletter
6. Decorative.

Roman Oldstyle. Types classified as Roman Oldstyle are designed after the lines of the first Roman lettering to appear in printing. Roman Oldstyle faces have full, round serifs. *Serifs* are the fine end strokes of letters. Roman Oldstyle typefaces are soft, round, rich, and warm (Fig. 3-22).

Included under the Roman Oldstyle classification are Transitional and Modern typefaces. The *Transitional* faces resemble Roman Oldstyle very closely (Fig. 3-23). They represent a gradual flattening and refinement of the serifs. There is more contrast in the thickening of the vertical strokes of the letters. Any typeface with a strong contrast between thick and

Figure 3-22. *Goudy Bold is an example of Roman Oldstyle typefaces. It has full, round serifs.*

Figure 3-23. *Baskerville is a Transitional typeface, very similar to Roman Oldstyle.*

Figure 3-24. *Modern No. 20 is an example of a Modern typeface, with round, erect letter forms.*

thin strokes is a natural companion for a Transitional face.

Modern typefaces tend to have flat serifs and contrast in the down strokes (Fig. 3-24). The round, erect letters stand firmly on their bases.

Sans Serif. Most modern layout designs include Sans Serif typefaces. These are the simplest designs of all the typefaces. They are straight up and down and rectangular, with no serifs. They have little or no variation in the weight or strokes of the letters (Fig. 3-25). Sans Serif typefaces include the plain block letters that graphic artists commonly call *Gothic.*

Square Serif. Square Serif typefaces contain strokes of approximately uniform weight and straight serifs of the same weight (Fig. 3-26). There is little or no contrast within the individual letters. Square Serif typefaces are frequently used in headlines of modern

Figure 3-25. *Optima Medium is a Sans Serif typeface. Sans Serif typefaces are simple in design.*

Figure 3-26. *An example of a Square Serif typeface is Beton Bold. Individual letters have little or no contrast.*

printing. They are sometimes used for areas of smaller type copy.

Script and Cursive. Script or Cursive typefaces imitate handwriting or hand lettering. Script is frequently used for invitations to weddings or other social events (Fig. 3-27). Since each letter of a true Script connects, these typefaces should never be *letterspaced* (set with spacing between letters).

Cursive typefaces resemble Script. But the letters do not necessarily connect (Fig. 3-28).

Textletter, or Blackletter. The kind of lettering that had its beginning in the black, angular forms of the medieval scribes was first cast into metal type by Johann Gutenberg. It was called Textletter because it was the text or body letter for most of the first printed books. Later, it was called Blackletter to separate it from the lighter and more open Roman typefaces

Figure 3-27. *Palace Script, as other Script typefaces, imitates handwriting.*

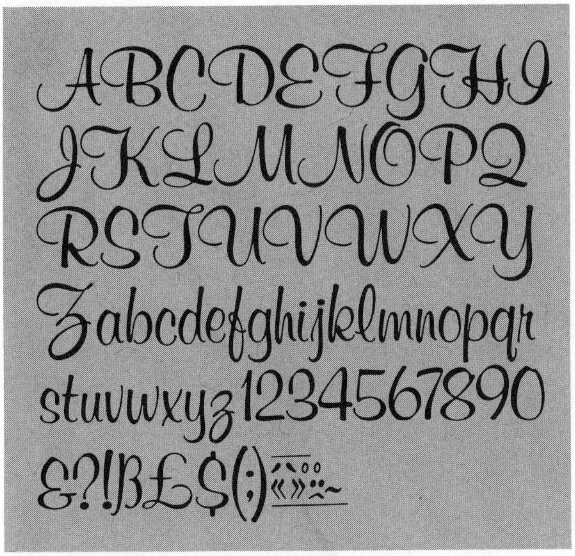

Figure 3-28. *Cursive typefaces, such as Murray Hill Bold, resemble Script, but the letters are not connected.*

Figure 3-29. *Old English is a modern example of a Blackletter/Textletter typeface.*

Figure 3-30. *Ringlet falls under the category of Decorative typefaces.*

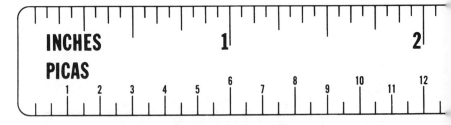

Figure 3-31. *There are six picas to the inch. Each pica measures 12 points. These are the basic units in type measurement. (A.B. Dick Co.)*

Figure 3-32. *A line guage is used to measure type and width of lines. The line gauge is calibrated in picas on one side and inches on the other. The center scale measures lines of agate type. Agate is the smallest type size that can be machine set. Agate lines are often used as units of measurement for advertising copy.*

designed by Nicholas Jensen and other early Italian printers (Fig. 3-29). At a still later date, it was called *Old English.*

Decorative. Decorative typefaces do not fit into any of the previously described classifications. They include types of irregular outline, shaded letters, and outline letters (Fig. 3-30). A line or two of Decorative type can add liveliness to a printed page. Too much can ruin the entire effect.

Type Composition Alternatives. In addition to the wide variety of typefaces available, there are further

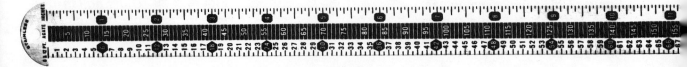

choices among the letters of each. Most typefaces can be composed in any one or all of the following ways:

1. CAPITALS
2. lower case
3. SMALL CAPITALS
4. *ITALIC CAPITALS*
5. *italic lower case.*

Further variety can be achieved with many typefaces by selecting from among several character thicknesses. Some modern typefaces are available in weights ranging from lightface through regular, medium, bold, extra bold, and so forth.

One of the most frequently used methods of emphasizing a word or phrase in copy is to use *italic* type. The slanted letters attract added attention from the reader. By contrast, type that has its strokes in an upright or vertical position is commonly referred to as *Roman.*

A complete set of letters for a given size and style of type, including figures, punctuation marks, and other signs and accents, is called a *font.* All the sizes of one style of typeface combine to make up a *series* of type. The different series of one face of type make up a *family.*

Type Measurement

The printing industry uses a method of type measurement known as the *point system.* The basic unit, called the *point,* is 1/72 inch. Twelve points equal one *pica* (Fig. 3-31). Six picas equal one inch. The tool used for measuring type is called a *line gauge* (Fig. 3-32). It looks like a ruler.

The smallest size in most typefaces is 6 point. Sizes increase by two points at a time to 8, 10, 12, and 14 point. Then sizes go from 14 to 18 point. From there on, each larger size represents a 6-point increase, up to 48 points. From 48-point on, sizes increase by 12 points.

Vocabulary Checklist

1. hieroglyphics
2. ideogram
3. stylus
4. cuneiform
5. alphabet
6. layout
7. optical center
8. proportion
9. balance
10. contrast
11. rhythm
12. unity
13. harmony
14. symmetry
15. variety
16. action
17. thumbnail sketch
18. rough layout
19. comprehensive layout
20. layout dummy
21. photo cropping
22. serif
23. cursive
24. gothic
25. italic

26. Roman
27. font
28. point
29. pica
30. body type
31. display type

Many typefaces also contain larger, smaller, and intermediate sizes. For example, there are sizes in 5½, 7, 9, and 11 point.

Type sizes from 6 to 14 point are generally used for text or body matter. When used in this way, they are called *body type*. Sizes from 18 point up are called *display type*. These larger sizes are generally used for headlines and special emphasis.

Unit Review

Early forms of written communication were very crude. Cave drawings date back 10,000 years, long before an alphabet was invented.

The Babylonians and Phoenicians invented the first alphabets. These were vital steps in the development of communication through graphic arts.

The basic elements of graphic arts represent steps in a work flow process. They include: identification of a need, formulating a basic message, writing, design and layout, illustration, typesetting, photo conversion, plate-making, image transfer (printing), and binding and finishing.

Design and layout blend the copy and illustrations into an attractive page or publication.

Principles used by graphic arts designers are: proportion, balance, contrast, rhythm, unity, harmony, symmetry, variety, and action.

Typesetting and composition are used by the designer to give a printed message style and to create a mood.

1. Name two forms of graphic communication that date back before the invention of alphabets.

2. What ancient people invented the first alphabet to have characters that represented sounds?

3. Name the two major parts of a typical printed page.

4. Designers prepare preliminary drawings for most printing jobs. What are these drawings called?

5. What are page numbers called in book and magazine printing?

6. Sometimes, portions of a photo are eliminated to direct more focus on the main subject. What is this process called?

7. Name the system of type measurement used in the printing industry.

8. How many points equal one pica?

9. How many picas equal one inch?

GRAPHIC ARTS

There are five major types of printing. They are photo-offset lithography, letterpress printing, gravure printing, screen printing, and duplication/copying. Each of these printing methods is explained in this part of the book.

Progress in technology has brought rapid advances in graphic arts. This is especially true in the use of computers in graphic arts jobs. In the following units, you will see how computer technology and electronics have affected the entire graphic arts field. Dramatic advances have been made in all areas of printing, from typesetting through presswork.

Earlier in the book, letterpress printing was described first, mainly because of its historical role. In this part, photo-offset lithography is covered first. This is because offset is now the most widely used printing method.

PROCESSES

Therefore the units in this part cover:

4. *Phototypesetting.* The setting of type and the makeup of type and illustrations into pages ready for photographing are covered.

5. *Photo-Offset Film Making.* This unit describes line photography and halftone photography, including cameras and films to be used, as well as the final steps before platemaking (stripping and opaquing).

6. *Photo-Offset Printing.* Platemaking and both sheet-fed and rotary web-fed printing are explained.

7. *Relief (Letterpress) Composition.* This unit covers the initial steps in relief printing. Included are descriptions of hot metal typesetting, engraving, and plate casting.

8. *Letterpress Printing Presses.* This unit describes platen, flat-bed cylinder, and rotary presses and how they work.

9. *Gravure Printing.* This unit deals with the gravure printing process.

10. *Screen Printing.* Screen printing is covered.

11. *Duplicators and Copiers.* This unit describes a number of methods used for limited-quantity printing and duplicating.

4 PHOTO-TYPESETTING

THE MODERN WAY: A PHOTOGRAPHIC PROCESS

Photo-offset lithography has become the most widely used form of printing for a number of reasons. One of the most important reasons is that it is a photographic process. This means that materials for printing are prepared by creating master art that can be photographed. By contrast, letterpress printing involves mechanical preparation of printing materials.

The photographic process has several advantages. It is faster, step by step, than mechanical composition and engraving. It provides a more precise image to be printed. Finally, the photographic process is more adaptable to electronic and computer technology (Fig. 4-1). For many types of work, offset printing costs less than letterpress.

As outlined earlier, the lithographic process was developed about 300 years after Gutenberg invented movable relief type. Lithography is based on the principle that grease (or oil) and water do not readily mix. Alois Senefelder, using this principle, invented lithography in 1798. He used a grease pencil to draw an image in reverse on a piece of smooth limestone. The stone was dampened with water. Then the image was

inked. A sheet of paper was placed over the image area and pressure was applied. This transferred the image to the paper.

Senefelder's method was a *direct* process of printing. Modern photo-offset lithography is an indirect printing method.

Figure 4-1. *This modern rotary web-fed offset press is an example of how electronic and computer technologies have brought dramatic advances in printing. (Harris Corp., Commercial Press Division)*

THE TYPESETTING REVOLUTION: COLD TYPE AND PHOTOCOMPOSITION

Historically, the composition of type was a slow process. Until late in the nineteenth century, movable type was set by hand, one character at a time. Then the Linotype was invented. The *Linotype* is a large machine that sets a full line of type at a time. The lines are cast using molten (hot, melted) metal. The Linotype revolutionized printing at the beginning of this century.

One of the major advantages of offset printing is its planographic nature. In *planographic* printing, there are no raised, or relief images. The planographic process opened the door for the development of cold-type processes. *Cold-type* composition includes all typesetting processes that do not use molten metal. Cold-type composition is faster and more efficient than hot type. This is true even in the simplest forms of cold type preparation.

Figure 4-2. *The strike-on method of cold-type composition uses machines similar to typewriters. This is an IBM Selectric Composer.*

The two basic cold type composition methods are *mechanical* and *photographic.*

The *strike-on* method is the most popular method of mechanical cold-type composition. Strike-on composition uses machines similar to typewriters (Fig. 4-2). The operator types the copy directly on specially coated paper with an extra-bright white surface. The paper is then trimmed to form galley proofs, which are pasted up on page makeup boards. This process is faster and easier than hot-type composition.

The most important factor in cold-type composition, however, has been its adaptability to technology. The development of *phototypesetting,* also referred to as *photocomposition,* brought major advances in speed (Fig. 4-3). But the really dramatic advances came with the development of *computerized phototypesetting.*

There are phototypesetting machines today that can produce thousands of lines of type in a single minute. The most advanced equipment can compose entire pages of copy, including photographic artwork.

Figure 4-3. *This Comp/Set 510 II is an example of a modern phototypesetting system. (A.M. International, VariTyper Division)*

These newest computerized phototypesetting machines are a far cry from the days of hand-set individual type. The following sections describe the various methods of cold-type composition.

MECHANICAL COLD TYPE: VARYING VERSATILITY

There are four popular methods of preparing cold type by mechanical means. They are:

1. Hand lettering
2. Transfer type
3. Clip art
4. Strike-on.

Hand Lettering

Type that is printed by hand gives some kinds of work a friendly, informal tone. Since it can be drawn to fit into almost any space or design, it is very useful. Pens and brushes are two common tools used for drawing an image. Hand lettering for camera-ready copy should be done with India ink or with black water

Figure 4-4. *The Varigraph Head-writer is one of the most versatile lettering instruments available to layout artists. (Varigraph, Inc.)*

colors. These materials provide the solid black images that are needed.

There are several lettering instruments used to draw display letters. One of the most versatile is the *Varigraph Headwriter* (Fig. 4-4). This instrument uses a special pen and black ink. Mechanical guides assist the artist.

Another type of lettering instrument is a *template* with cutouts in solid plastic sheets used for tracing the images.

Transfer Type

Alphabets of letters are preprinted on transfer sheets of transparent acetate. These are applied directly to the paste-up by rubbing. This is done so that the characters transfer to the desired positions on the paste-up.

Some transfer lettering has an adhesive backing mounted on an acetate sheet (Fig. 4-5). This can be applied to the paste-up by simply cutting out the desired character and pressing it into place.

Transfer type is useful for a few words or lines of type. Transfer type is faster than hand lettering. But

Figure 4-5. *Transfer lettering like this has an adhesive backing. The desired character is cut out, removed from the acetate sheet, and pressed into place on a paste-up. (C-Thru Ruler Co.)*

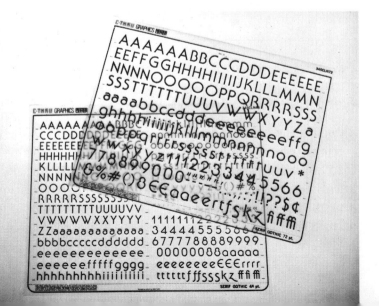

transfer methods are not fast enough if large amounts of type are to be set.

Clip Art

Preprinted artwork, covering almost any subject, is available in *clip art* (Fig. 4-6). Paste-up artists can purchase clip art from many sources. Today's clip art services can be classed with the very best art. Clip-art materials are up to date. Artists are employed by these services to design and draw the original artwork.

Since these materials are used in paste-up, they must be kept clean, undamaged, and easily available. Artists generally keep these materials in filing cabinets or drawers.

Figure 4-6. *Pre-printed artwork, referred to as clip art, is available in almost any subject.*

Strike-On

Strike-on composition includes any type set by a typewriter. Typewriters are available in a wide variety of styles and capabilities. Ordinary standard office typewriters are adequate for small quantities of type composition. These ordinary typewriters can be used only when the right-hand margin is not required to be flush.

To obtain flush left- and right-hand margins, the copy on each line must be *justified.* Several specialized typewriters and typesetting machines have been developed to make the job of justifying typed lines easier. These machines make strike-on copy look more attractive. Ordinary typewriters have characters and spaces of only one width. Justifying typewriters offer a variety of spacing for line justification.

Copy that is being typed for reproduction is prepared on smooth, dull-white paper. It is dull-white because it will become part of a paste-up. The paste-up in turn will be photographed by a graphic arts process camera. A glossy finish would cause reflections

Figure 4-7. *Modern strike-on typesetting machines have interchangeable typing elements, adding to their versatility. (International Business Machines Corp.)*

in photography. For the same reason, a one-time carbon ribbon is used to produce sharp, dense, black images.

An example of a modern strike-on typewriter is the IBM Selectric Composer. The Selectric Composer features a stationary carriage and a moving striking mechanism. The mechanism is fitted with changeable type fonts called *elements* (Fig. 4-7). The elements are available in a variety of typefaces and sizes ranging from 6 to 12 points.

The Selectric Composer also features proportional spacing. This means that the individual characters have varying widths, or units. An ordinary typewriter allows as much space for a narrow letter like "i" as for a wide letter like "w."

A newer version of the direct-impression Selectric Composer is called the Electronic Selectric Composer. This machine has a built-in electronic memory capable of retaining up to 8,000 characters of text entered into the keyboard. The Electronic Selectric Composer

Check Your Knowledge (True or False)

1. Modern photo-offset lithography is a direct printing method.

2. The two basic kinds of cold type composition are mechanical and photographic.

3. Clip art is one method of preparing cold type by mechanical means.

4. Copy set by a typewriter is referred to as strike-on composition.

5. Smooth, glossy paper is best for photographic reproduction.

will play back this text automatically at a speed of 150 words per minute. Another feature of the newer composer is automatic justification of the right-hand margin.

PHOTOGRAPHIC COLD TYPE: THE CHANGING STATE OF THE ART

Cold-type composition produced by the use of photography is called *photocomposition.* Letters are imaged by exposing photographic paper or film. The images are exposed through a film negative, which contains all the characters of a font.

In photography, a *positive* picture has black images on a white background. This is a normal printed image. Positive images are right reading, meaning that the message reads from left to right.

In a *negative* picture, white (or clear) images appear on a black background. Negatives are reverse reading.

After the photographic paper or film is exposed, it is chemically processed. The processing machine automatically develops, fixes, and washes the exposed material. The photographic paper, when dried, is a positive image used in paste-up. Under some computerized systems, the exposed positives form complete pages that are ready for platemaking.

There are many different styles and sizes of photocomposition machines. Two basic types of photocomposition machines are photodisplay and text machines. Photodisplay machines are generally used to compose large display type. Text machines are most frequently used to set smaller, body type.

Photodisplay Machines

Hand operation for character selection and fitting is usually required with photodisplay machines. The

Figure 4-8. *Photodisplay machines usually require hand operation. (Visual Graphics Corp.)*

finished type is either in single-line strips or in multi-line composition (Fig. 4-8).

The principle of operation among these machines is basically the same. The type font, carried on a film strip, grid, or disc, is installed on the machine. The operator manually moves the font so that the character desired is in exposing position. A button is pressed, and a light beam exposes the character onto a photosensitive paper. After the composition has been set, the paper is developed, fixed, and washed. This process is done either in the machine or in a separate processor.

Some photodisplay machines are operated from a keyboard. These machines are much faster than the manually operated ones. A standard typewriter keyboard arrangement is used.

Some of the more popular photodisplay machines include:

- The *StripPrinter* is a machine used to set display-size lines of type manually (Fig. 4-9). A variety of type styles are available, with sizes ranging from 6 to 96 point. The StripPrinter uses a *film strip* font, which contains a single size and style of type. The film strip is inserted through the exposure unit, between the lamp and the photographic paper. The operator lines up the desired character over a preset point on the machine. The exposure is then made by pressing a button. After all exposures have been made, the paper is removed from the machine. It is then developed, fixed, washed, and dried.

Figure 4-9. *The StripPrinter manual display typesetter uses a film strip font containing a single size and style of type. (StripPrinter, Inc.)*

- The *VariTyper Headliner* is a manually operated photodisplay machine (Fig. 4-10). Type is set from plastic discs called *Typemasters* in sizes from 10 to 86 point. Each Typemaster contains one font. The machine does not enlarge or reduce images. The Typemaster disc is about the size of a 33-1/3 rpm record. The type is set on a 35mm paper or film strip. The operator selects the desired character by rotating the disc, which is positioned between the lamp and the photographic paper. Each exposure is made by pressing a button. After exposures are made, the paper is cut and automatically fed into a three-compartment developing tank inside the machine. The exposed paper is developed, fixed, and washed.

Figure 4-10. *The VariTyper Headliner is a manually operated photodisplay machine. (A.M. International, VariTyper Division)*

- The *Photo Typositor* is a manually operated machine that can compose single and multiple display lines. Type can be reduced or enlarged from

25 percent to 200 percent. *Multiple film fonts* are stored on the front reels. This permits mixing of type styles in a single line. Type can be set in a variety of styles, such as backslant, italic, condensed, staggered, and with shadow effects or background tints. Characters are positioned between the lamp and the photographic paper by turning the handwheels on the machine. After each exposure, the character is automatically developed inside the machine. The developed type composition is removed from the machine and then fixed, washed, and dried.

• The *Compugraphic CG series* consists of keyboard-operated display machines (Fig. 4-11). The keyboard is similar to that of a standard typewriter. Type fonts are available in a wide variety of styles and are contained on *film strips*. Each film

Figure 4-11. *One of the most versatile keyboard-operated display typesetting machines is the Compugraphic 7200. (Compugraphic Corp.)*

strip holds two styles. Two film strips can be placed in the machine at the same time. Typeface selections are made by regulating a lens-selection dial. Typefaces are available in eight different sizes for each font. By adjusting the lens, it is possible to set type up to 120 points in size. A visual display unit allows the operator to view the characters. By pressing a button, the line is automatically exposed inside the machine. The exposed photographic paper is then transferred to a lightproof box for processing. The composition can then be cut apart and pasted into position on a paste-up.

Check Your Knowledge (True or False)

1. A photographic positive has black images on a white background.

2. The Varityper Headliner uses a film strip font.

3. A keyboard is used to operate the Photo Typositor.

Phototypesetters

Phototypesetters are made up of three parts:

1. A *keyboard* for input
2. A *computer* for making end-of-line decisions such as hyphenation and justification
3. A *photo-unit* for output or typesetting.

Input unit. The input unit of the phototypesetter is the keyboard. Most phototypesetters use keyboards that are similar to those of standard electric typewriters (Fig. 4-12). Instead of a strike-on character,

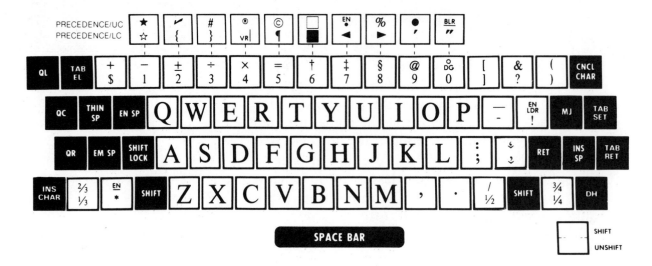

Figure 4-12. *This is a typical keyboard of the Compugraphic CG series. (Compugraphic Corp.)*

each key produces an electrical impulse when pressed.

On some keyboards, the typed line is immediately sent to the computer, where an image is produced. This is called *direct entry.* Another method, called *indirect entry,* stores the typed lines on punched paper tape or magnetic media.

Paper tapes are narrow-width rolls in which holes are punched. Each hole corresponds to a certain keyboard character. The computer can then "read" the holes and produce the correct characters. Corrections can be made on the tape by punching special codes.

Magnetic media may be tapes, discs, drums, or cassettes. These media can be read faster than paper tape. Corrections are easily made at any point on the magnetic record.

Efficiency and speed are gained by the use of magnetic storage. Several operators can enter copy at the same time. The magnetic records can then be placed on a separate computer for high-speed typesetting. In this way, the computer and keyboard devices are more productive.

Computer. The computer is a basic unit of the type-setter. In some phototypesetters, the computer is built in. With others, the computer is separate (Fig. 4-13). The computer's job is to process the unjustified copy and make end-of-line decisions. A format program contains specifications of typesetting. The program

Figure 4-13. *Writing and editing machines in some newspapers are linked to central computers like this one. Massive storage files at left hold billions of characters of information.*

Learning Activities

1. Look at the display advertisements in your local newspaper. Display ads are those that appear on news pages. The category of display ads does not include classified advertisements. Observe the ads that are illustrated by drawings rather than photo-graphs. The drawings may be examples of clip art, particularly if they are general in nature. Look at the larger lines of type in these ads. Can you tell if they are examples of transfer type?

2. Visit an offset printing shop if possible. Ask if you can observe an artist or designer mak-ing up a job using a variety of cold-type methods.

contains the *logic* for typesetting. The program is written in a special language for the computer. The program sets up the basic rules from which the computer can arrange or compose type. The computer automatically hyphenates, justifies, and makes up columns—or even whole pages—of type.

Photo unit. The output from phototypesetters comes from the photo unit. The photo unit is made up of electronic, mechanical, and photographic parts (Fig. 4-14). The type font is carried as a negative image on an *image master*. Depending upon the system, the type font may be a grid, a spinning disc, a spinning drum, or a film strip. In some systems, images are formed by electronically controlled laser (intense light) beams.

In film units, the type is set using high-intensity light flashes through the letters, projecting them onto photographic paper or film. Only the letter image selected passes through a series of prisms, enlarging

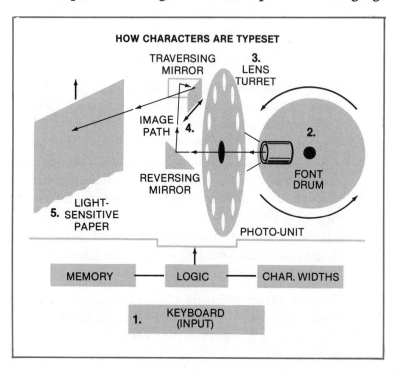

Figure 4-14. *This diagram illustrates how characters are typeset in a phototypesetting machine.*

lenses, and mirrors until it is positioned and exposed on photographic paper. Photo units that use a spinning disc or spinning drum produce type characters at greater speeds than those using grids or film strips. Laser imaging systems are the fastest of all.

When phototypesetting is completed, the film box containing the exposed material is removed from the photo unit. The exposed paper or film is passed through a *processor*. The processor automatically develops and fixes the photographic images, delivering them ready for the paste-up process (Fig. 4-15).

One of the most advanced phototypesetting systems available today is called *Automatic Illustrated Documentation System* (AIDS). Manufactured by Information International, Incorporated, the equipment is capable of composing entire pages of text, line drawings, and halftones (photos). The system was developed for publication printing.

Figure 4-15. *Copy that is ready for paste-up is delivered from a processor, the final step in the photocomposition process. (Visual Graphics Corp.)*

Used with a sophisticated input system and separate computer, the AIDS system can eliminate the need for paste-up. Text, line drawings, and halftones are made up electronically into complete pages. The completed pages can be produced on photographic paper or film. When produced on film, the need for process camera work is also eliminated. Most of the film stripping process also is bypassed. The reasons for this will become apparent in the next section.

Some AIDS computers can produce printing plates directly from computer files. Such systems eliminate film and platemaking, as well as paste-up.

THE PASTE-UP PROCESS: FITTING THE PIECES TOGETHER

After typesetting has been completed, the various elements of a job must be combined. *Paste-up* is the process of physically putting these elements together

Figure 4-16. *Paste-up is the process of placing type and illustrations for a printing job on an illustration board.*

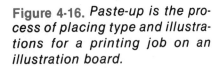

Vocabulary Checklist

1. cold type
2. photocomposition
3. strike-on
4. planographic
5. transfer type
6. clip art
7. justification
8. type element
9. Strip Printer
10. logic
11. image master
12. processor
13. paste-up
14. mechanical
15. line copy
16. halftone copy
17. continuous tone copy

on a piece of white illustration board (Fig. 4-16). The completed board is often called a *mechanical.*

When display copy and body copy are processed on reproduction paper, hot wax is applied to the back of the paper. This allows the layout artist to apply the type to a paste-up board. Before pasting up the type, however, the artist positions any artwork to be used on the job. If photographs are to be used, the artist blocks out spaces according to the layout. Most paste-ups are prepared for what is called *line photography.* Line copy is black and white only. There are no shades of gray.

Photographs and other artwork that contain various shades of gray are called *continuous tone copy* or *halftone copy.* These artwork elements will be explained further in the following section.

The paste-up process is simple but exacting. The artist uses a T-square, triangles, dividers and other instruments to place copy in exactly the right position. The skill of the artist is reflected in the final printed product. Crooked lines or columns of type make a job appear cheap or hurried. Badly prepared layouts can weaken or destroy the impact of the message they carry.

In addition to body and display type, the artist also positions rules, borders, and other line copy on the paste-up. When all copy and line art are in place, the paste-up mechanical is considered camera-ready.

Unit Review

- Photo-offset lithography is a photographic process. It is also planographic, or flat, meaning it has no raised surfaces. Lithography is based on the principle that grease (or oil) and water do not mix easily.

- Cold-type composition, whether mechanical or photographic, is faster and more versatile than the older hot-metal composition.

- Strike-on (mechanical) cold-type composition is rapidly giving way to photocomposition. The most advanced phototypesetting equipment can produce thousands of lines of copy per minute.

- Sophisticated photocomposition equipment can reproduce halftone art and eliminate the need for paste-up entirely. This equipment can produce complete pages of copy.

Review Questions

1. Lithography is based on the fact that water does not mix easily with a certain substance. What is that substance?

2. Name the two kinds of cold-type composition.

3. What is the term for copy that contains no shades of gray?

5 PHOTO-OFFSET FILM MAKING

PHOTOGRAPHIC COPY PREPARATION: HOW IT WORKS

Figure 5-1. *There are two basic kinds of process cameras used in the graphic arts industry, horizontal and vertical.*

As mentioned in the previous section, there are two types of camera copy: line copy and halftone copy. Copy that does not contain shades of gray is line copy. The images are made up of lines and areas of a single tone. Type matter and pen-and-ink drawings are examples of line copy.

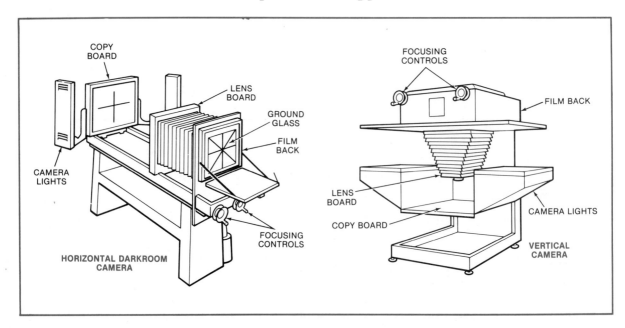

COPY BOARD

LENS BOARD

GROUND GLASS

FILM BACK

CAMERA LIGHTS

FOCUSING CONTROLS

HORIZONTAL DARKROOM CAMERA

FOCUSING CONTROLS

FILM BACK

LENS BOARD

COPY BOARD

CAMERA LIGHTS

VERTICAL CAMERA

The process of copy photography can be illustrated by dividing the subject into four topics:

1. Process cameras

2. Photographic films

3. Film processing

4. Making line or halftone negatives.

Process Cameras

The graphic arts industry uses *process cameras* (Fig. 5-1). These cameras produce film for platemaking and other printing purposes.

There are two basic kinds of process cameras:

- *Horizontal cameras* have all working parts on a flat track or bed. A few large cameras may have parts that hang from an overhead rail. The parts of the camera that hold the copy, the lens, and the film are upright. The camera is called horizontal because the working parts move forward and backward, rather than up and down.

- *Vertical cameras* have an upright bed or track. The working parts move up and down rather than forward and backward.

Both vertical and horizontal cameras do the same thing: They photograph copy to produce film for use in making plates, screens, or other image carriers. Both horizontal and vertical cameras have eight basic parts:

- Copyboard
- Lighting system
- Lensboard
- Bellows
- Ground glass
- Vacuum back
- Copyboard drive
- Lensboard drive.

Figure 5-2. *Copy to be photographed is held in place on the copyboard. (nuArc Company, Inc.)*

Copyboard. As its name suggests, this part of the process camera holds the copy to be photographed (Fig. 5-2). The copyboard has a large, flat surface. The surface often has markings that are used to position the copy. There is a hinged glass cover that holds the copy in place in front of the camera. The copyboard is connected to the track, or bed, of the camera. In this way, the copy can be moved toward or away from the lens. This movement is necessary to adjust the size of the image. The farther away the copy is, the smaller the picture will be. The closer the copy, the larger the picture.

Lighting system. A process camera usually has four extremely bright lights. These lights are positioned to face the copyboard. The lights are focused on the copy (Fig. 5-3). Bright lights are needed because of the nature of the film used. Therefore, copyboard lights usually have superbright, gas-filled bulbs.

On most cameras, the lighting system is mounted so that there is always the same distance between lights and copyboard. The lights are positioned so that no stray reflected light (called *flare*) can enter the lens. As a rule, the lights are positioned at a 45-degree angle to the copyboard.

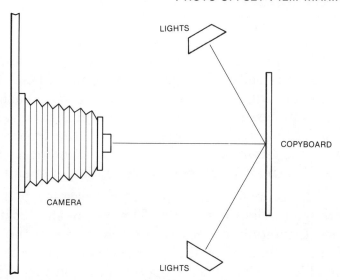

LIGHTS

COPYBOARD

CAMERA

LIGHTS

Figure 5-3. *Bright lights are focused on the copy prior to exposure by the process camera.*

Lensboard. It is necessary to move the camera lens backward or forward in relation to the copy. This is how the picture is focused for photography. To control this movement, the lensboard is mounted on the same track or bed as the copyboard. The lensboard can be moved independently from the copyboard.

The lens is the part of the camera that actually forms the picture (Fig. 5-4). Process camera lenses must be of high quality because exact images are essential. A process camera lens is made of a number of finely shaped glass elements. These elements form an imaging system that is assembled in a lens *barrel.* The lens assembly is then positioned in the center of the lensboard.

Every quality lens needs a method for controlling the amount of light it passes through to the film. On a process camera lens (and also on all other quality cameras), two devices are used. One device, a *diaphragm,* controls the size of the opening in a lens. The diaphragm is a series of metal blades. When a collar that fits around the lens is rotated, the diaphragm blades open or close. This movement changes the size of the opening in the lens through which light passes.

Figure 5-4. *As with any other camera, the lens forms the picture image.*

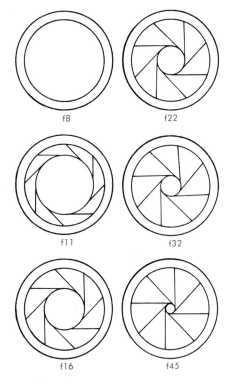

Figure 5-5. *The camera diaphragm is set to open a certain amount for each f-stop, controlling the amount of light permitted to pass through the lens.*

The size of the lens opening produced by the diaphragm is known as the *f-stop* (Fig. 5-5). Stamped on the lens collar is a series of f-stop numbers. Examples are f/8, f/11, f/16, f/22, f/32, and f/45. Each of these numbers represents a different, measured value of light that will be passed through the lens. The larger the f-number, the smaller the opening in the lens. The smaller numbers represent larger openings.

The other device that controls passage of light through the lens is a *shutter*. The type of shutter used most commonly on process camera lenses is the *leaf shutter*. This type of shutter consists of a number of metal leafs. The leafs are operated by a spring. When the spring is operated, the shutter opens or closes, permitting light to pass through the lens. The shutter controls light through the amount of time it stays open. A process camera shutter is connected to a timing device that controls exposure time. The camera operator sets the timer for each photo. The time of the exposure depends, in turn, on the lens opening, the brightness of light, and the copy itself. Special light measuring, or metering, systems are often used to determine the right combination of lens opening and exposure time.

Bellows. A camera bellows assures that the only light that reaches the film is what comes through the lens. The bellows forms a passage for the image to travel in complete darkness from the lens to the film. Since the lensboard moves, the bellows must have the ability to expand or contract (Fig. 5-6). This is called the bellows extension. The bellows is an accordian-like box with folds that can be expanded or moved closer together as the lensboard moves.

Ground glass. The ground glass forms a viewing image for the camera operator to check before the picture is taken. The ground glass is a sheet of glass that

Figure 5-6. *Light travels through the bellows from the lens to the film in complete darkness.*

has been etched on one side. The etched surface has a milky appearance. This etched surface acts as a screen, displaying the image that comes through the lens. The operator can use this image to focus and position the picture to be taken. The ground glass surface must be in the exact position where the film will be placed to take the picture.

The ground glass for a process camera is usually mounted in a hinged frame. The camera operator can open or close this frame like a door as each picture is checked and focused. On most process cameras, the filmholder and ground glass are in darkened rooms. The operator works inside the darkroom.

Vacuum back. The vacuum back of a process camera holds the film. The back is usually made of metal. In the metal surface of the back are a large number of small holes. A motor draws air through these holes and out of the back. This has the effect of holding a sheet of film flat against the back.

To place the film on the back, there is usually a series of lines that act as guides. This pattern of markings is often the same as those on the copyboard. Thus, it is possible for the camera operator to be sure that the copy and film are placed in the correct positions to produce a picture.

The vacuum back is usually hinged at the back of the camera. Typically, the ground glass frame opens in one direction and the vacuum back opens another way. Thus, the operator can move the ground glass out of the way and swing the film into position.

Copyboard drive. The copyboard drive is a mechanism that moves the copyboard on its track. Movement is forward and backward on a horizontal camera, up and down on a vertical unit.

Some cameras have drives that are operated manually. The operator turns handles to move the copyboard. Most large process cameras have electric drives. The operator controls the position of the copyboard by using a set of switches to start and stop a motor.

Lensboard drive. The lensboard drive moves the lensboard in much the same way that the copyboard drive moves the copyboard. Both manually operated and motor-drive models are available.

Check Your Knowledge (True or False)

1. Copy that contains shades of gray is called line copy.

2. Process cameras contain eight basic parts.

3. An f-stop is the size of the lens opening produced by the shutter.

4. The ground glass of a process camera acts as a focusing screen.

5. The vacuum back of a process camera is usually made of metal.

The relative positions of the copyboard and lensboard determine the size of the photographed image. In process camera work, the size of the finished photographic image is usually described in relation to the original copy. This relationship is given as a percentage. If the photographed film is to be the same size as the original copy, the size of the photograph is 100 percent. If the photograph is half the size of the original copy, this is a 50 percent reduction. There are usually settings on the camera bed to help guide operators in setting up the equipment for the reproduction size needed.

Photographic Film

Photographic film consists of a transparent plastic base with a coating that is sensitive to light. The coating is a photographic *emulsion* containing gelatin and silver salts (Fig. 5-7).

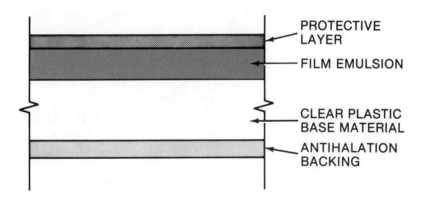

PROTECTIVE LAYER

FILM EMULSION

CLEAR PLASTIC BASE MATERIAL

ANTIHALATION BACKING

Figure 5-7. *Photographic film contains an emulsion that is sensitive to light.*

Film that is sensitive to blue, green, and yellow light is known as *orthochromatic* or *ortho*. Because of this sensitivity, light blue guidelines can be left on the paste-up copy. Since this type of emulsion is not sensitive to red light, red *safelights* can be used for darkroom lighting. So, since ortho film is not sensitive to red, it "sees" red as black. This kind of film is the type used for most line and halftone work.

Panchromatic film is sensitive to all colors (blue, green, and red). Since these colors make up white light, panchromatic film must be processed and handled in complete darkness. The major use of panchromatic film is in color separation work. Color separation is the preparation of film for use in color printing.

Film Processing

Exposure of film on a process camera to cause a latent image in the emulsion is the first step in the processing of film. A *latent image* is an invisible image. To make this image visible, it must be processed with certain chemicals. The procedure for film processing includes four basic steps:

1. Developing
2. Stop bath
3. Fixing bath
4. Washing bath.

Processing trays are positioned in the darkroom sink working from left to right (Fig. 5-8).

Developing. The action of the *developer* involves chemical change of the silver salts in the emulsion. The white areas of the copy *reflect* light through the lens of the camera and expose the film. The black areas of the copy *absorb* (do not reflect) the light and thus produce no exposure on the film.

Figure 5-8. *This is the manner in which processing trays are positioned in the darkroom sink.*

The exposed areas of the film react with the developer to form black metallic silver. The developer

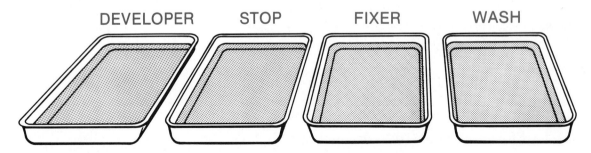

DEVELOPER   STOP   FIXER   WASH

SAFETY TIP

- **Chemicals can cause serious burns and skin irritation. Keep hands away from eyes, nose, and mouth when working with any chemicals such as photographic developer. Wash hands thoroughly with soap and water while the film is being washed.**

does not affect the areas that are not exposed to light. During the development, the *antihalation coating* starts to dissolve. *Halation* is an undesirable spreading or reflection of light on a photographic negative. Halation appears as a halo around highlights. If exposure is correct, a faint image will appear in about 30 to 45 seconds after the film is placed in the developer. Total time for development is generally 2½ minutes at 68 degrees Fahrenheit [20 degrees Celsius].

The developer used for orthochromatic film is known as *lith* developer. It is available in a liquid concentrate or in dry powder form. Liquid developer is mixed with water to the manufacturer's specifications and is stored in two solutions. These are referred to as A and B solutions. When mixed together in equal parts, they form the developer solution. Powdered developer is also mixed and stored in two solutions.

Stop bath. When development is completed, the film is immediately placed in a *stop bath* solution for about 10 seconds. This bath consists of a weak solution of acetic acid and water. Since the solution is slightly acid, it immediately stops the action of the developer. (Development is alkaline, the opposite of acidic.) Water and 28 percent glacial acetic acid are used to prepare the stop bath.

Fixing bath. After stopping the developing action in the stop bath, the film is placed in a *fixing bath*. This

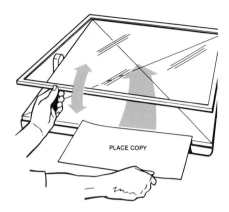

Figure 5-9. *Step 2. Place the line copy on the copyboard.*

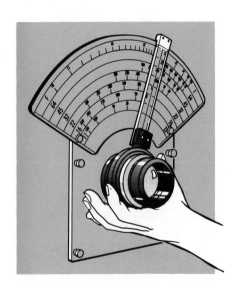

Figure 5-10. *Step 5. Set the lens for the best f-stop.*

dissolves the remaining emulsion in the unexposed areas (black areas of the original copy). It also hardens the emulsion so that it resists scuffing and scratching when the film is dry.

Fixers are available in both liquid concentrate and dry powder forms. Most films used in graphic arts photography fix in about one to three minutes.

Washing bath. After fixing, the film is *washed in running water* for about 10 to 30 minutes. This dissolves the remaining processing chemicals. When washing is completed, the film is squeegeed (stroked with a rubber blade) to eliminate excess water. The film is then hung to dry in a dust-free area of the darkroom. Automatic film drying machines are widely used for this purpose.

Making a Line Negative

To make a line negative, the film is exposed and processed as follows:

1. Clean the copyboard glass of the camera on both sides.

2. Place the line copy on the copyboard (Fig. 5-9). Position it so that the top of the copy is at the bottom. This will allow it to be viewed right side up on the ground glass. The ground glass is an image-viewing screen at the back of the camera.

3. Place the 12-step gray scale (sensitivity guide) next to the piece of copy. This scale will be used as an aid (or aim point) in film processing.

4. Close the copyboard and rotate it into position ready for exposure.

5. Set the lens for the best f-stop, usually f/16 or f/22 (Fig. 5-10). If using f/16, the control setting on the lensboard should match the percentage of enlargement or reduction. If copy is to be photo-

graphed same size, then the pointer is set to 100 on the f/16 scale.

6. Positon the lights (Fig. 5-11). The lights should be pointing toward the center of the copyboard at angles of approximately 45 degrees.

7. Set the exposure time. (The exposure time on any given camera will vary. To find the best exposure time, place a piece of copy on the copyboard containing some Roman type, sans serif type, and fine lines. Cut a piece of film approximately 1 inch wide and 8 inches long. Using a piece of opaque paper or cardboard, step off and expose six or seven 1-inch blocks at 3-second increments. Then develop the piece of exposed film for exactly 2½ minutes at 68 degrees Fahrenheit [20 degree Celsius]. The best time will result in dense black and clear open areas with crisp type and lines. Use a magnifier to examine the images closely.)

8. Determine film size.

9. Open the camera back and position the film on the vacuum back. The square lines on the vacuum back match those on the copyboard (Fig. 5-12). Position the film with emulsion side (light side) facing the lens.

10. Turn on the vacuum pump and close the camera back.

11. Press the timer button to start the exposure.

12. After the exposure is complete, open the camera back and turn off the vacuum pump.

13. Process the piece of film. (Developing time is generally 2½ minutes at 68 degrees Fahrenheit [20 degrees Celsius]. Rock the tray continuously and develop the film until step 4 in the gray scale is solid [Fig. 5-13]. Place the film in the stop bath

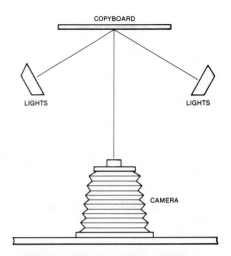

Figure 5-11. *Step 6. Position the lights.*

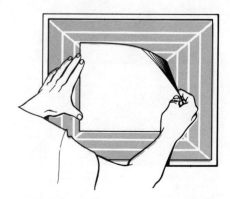

Figure 5-12. *Step 9. Open the camera back and position the film on the vacuum back.*

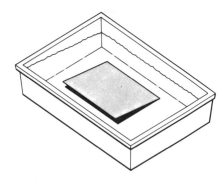

Figure 5-13. *Step 13. Process the piece of film.*

HALFTONE NEGATIVE

Figure 5-14. *Dot patterns on a halftone negative vary with the density (whiteness or blackness) of the original copy.*

for 10 seconds. Then remove the film and fix for 1 to 3 minutes. Wash the film for 10 to 30 minutes. Squeegee the film on the acetate [right-reading] side and dry.)

14. Examine the film negative on a light table.

> ### Check Your Knowledge
>
> 1. Panchromatic film must be processed in complete darkness.
>
> 2. White areas of original copy reflect light through the camera lens to expose the film.
>
> 3. The fixing bath stops the action of the developer.
>
> 4. After fixing, the film is washed in running water.
>
> 5. In making a line negative, the film is positioned with the emulsion side facing the lens.

HALFTONE PHOTOGRAPHY: CONTINUOUS TONES

Photographic prints and paintings by artists contain areas of varying tones of gray. This means that they are made up of black, gray, and white areas. This kind of copy is called *continuous tone* since there are graduations (gradations) in tone.

The purpose of *halftone photography* is to reproduce a black-and-white continuous tone image in a series of dots of different sizes. The size of the dots results from the density (whiteness or blackness) of the original copy. It is this variety in dot size that gives the appearance of different tones Fig. (5-14). This results in a halftone negative.

The halftone negative is used to record an image onto a printing plate. The plate then transfers the image onto paper. The dots are quite small. When viewed with the unaided eye, they give the appearance of a continuous-tone image. A magnified view shows the detail of a halftone's dot formations.

To form a dot pattern, a halftone screen is placed in front of the photographic film. During exposure, light passes through the camera lens and then through the screen before striking the film. The result is a halftone image on the photographic film.

There are two general kinds of halftone screens:

- Magenta
- Gray.

Magenta Screen

The *magenta screen* is colored magenta (a purplish shade of red). Its use is limited to black-and-white original copy. This screen is referred to as a *contact screen* because it is in contact with the film during exposure (Fig. 5-15).

Gray Screen

The *gray screen* is another type of contact screen. It is light gray in appearance. It can be used to photograph colored copy. Its use is similar to that of the magenta screen.

Halftone dot pattern. The *halftone dot pattern* made from a magenta or gray screen involves color sensitivity of both film and screen. The screen acts as a filter, stopping certain portions of light and creating a dot pattern. The individual dots on the screen (white areas) record the gray and black areas of the copy differently.

The emulsion (dull) side of the contact screen is placed in direct contact with the emulsion side of the

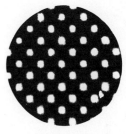

Figure 5-15. *This is an enlarged pattern of a magenta contact screen. (Eastman Kodak Company)*

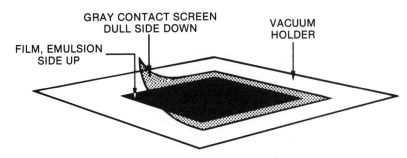

Figure 5-16. *The dull side of the gray screen is placed in direct contact with the emulsion side of the film. The two are held together firmly by the vacuum back of the process camera.*

film (Fig. 5-16). A vacuum back on the process camera is required to maintain proper contact. The emulsion side of the contact screen has printing on the bottom edge. The printing will tell if it is magenta or gray. The readable side of the contact screen is its emulsion. The screen generally curls toward the emulsion side.

Dot values. The *dot values* of a halftone are usually expressed in terms of a percentage comparing black areas to white areas. As an example, a dot value that contains 50 percent black and 50 percent white is a *50 percent dot*. This formation gives the appearance of a checkerboard. A *60 percent dot* contains *60 percent black* and *40 percent white,* and so on (Fig. 5-17).

Screen rulings. Halftone *screen rulings* describe the number of dots in one linear inch of the screen. For example, a 60-line screen contains 60 dots per running inch in any direction. This is considered a coarse screen. A 133-line screen contains 133 dots per running inch. The finer a screen (the more dots per inch), the greater the clarity of the printed product.

Figure 5-17. *Enlargement shows how dot patterns of a halftone vary. At far left is a 5 percent dot value. The pattern in the center has a 50 percent dot value. At far right is a pattern with a 95 percent dot value.*

Describing Halftones

There are three terms used in describing halftones:

   1. Highlights   2. Middletones   3. Shadows.

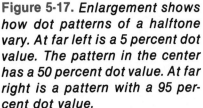

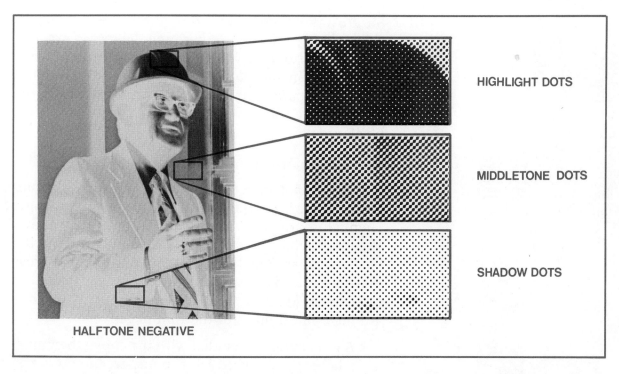

HIGHLIGHT DOTS

MIDDLETONE DOTS

SHADOW DOTS

HALFTONE NEGATIVE

The terms describe both tones in the original copy and their dot values in the halftone negative.

Highlights. The whitest areas of the original copy are called *highlights.* The highlights are the brightest areas of the subject. Highlights are important because they determine the amount of the *first exposure* (called the main exposure) on the camera. The dots in the halftone negative resulting from these tones are referred to as *highlight dots.* In a halftone negative, these highlight dots appear as small transparent openings in large black areas (Fig. 5-18). The printed image of a negative will show the highlight areas as small black dots in large white areas.

Middletones. *Middletones* are the areas of gray on the original copy (usually 50 percent tones). These areas are between the shadows and the highlights. On the printed page, the middle tones are viewed as equal-size black-and-white dots.

Figure 5-18. *Enlargement of dot pattern of a section of the halftone illustrates highlight dots as transparent openings in large dark areas. Middle tones and shadows are also shown.*

Shadows. *Shadows* are the darkest areas of the original copy. Shadows determine the *second exposure* given a halftone. The shadows of the original copy reproduce on the negative as small black dots in a large transparent area. On the printed page, the shadows are viewed as small white dots in a large black area.

Controlling Tonal Values

It is important to remember that these tonal values always refer to the areas of the original copy. Highlights are the whites of the copy. In the film negative, white areas of the original appear as the blackest areas. The highlights in a negative are areas that look the darkest, or densest, on film. Shadows refer to the darkest areas of the original copy. They are the lightest areas of the film negative.

A gray scale is included with the copy when making a halftone and used later to inspect the dot sizes. The idea is to compare the original copy values to the gray-scale values (Fig. 5-19).

The contact screen can produce tones within a certain range of a piece of copy with just *one exposure.* This is its *screen range* and is different for any kind of screen and camera used. The contact screen is limited in the range of tones it can convert into halftone dots. Therefore, a *second exposure* is required. The dot values must be *extended.* This is done by a second exposure known as the *flash exposure.* It forms dots in the film that represent the shadow areas of the original copy. The first exposure is called the *main exposure.* The result of the two exposures is a proper dot pattern over the entire range of the copy.

The proper length for the main exposure depends upon the whiteness of the original copy. With a 133-line magenta contact screen, exposure time should be about three to five times the line exposure

Figure 5-19. *A gray scale is used to check halftones for dot sizes. The original copy values are thus compared to the gray-scale values. (Stouffer G.A. Equipment Co.)*

time. If the whiteness of the original copy is close to that of the gray scale, this is considered a normal exposure. White whites require less exposure and grayer whites need longer exposure.

The flash exposure is made in the darkroom with an *amber light*. This is generally a 00 or 0A Wratten safelight mounted in a safelight lamp. The flash exposure can be made before or after the main exposure with the halftone screen in its original position. The safelight should be about five feet from the film. Test exposures must be made to determine the proper flash exposure time. Test strips of three-second to five-second exposures should show the proper flash time.

Check Your Knowledge (True or False)

1. Continuous tone copy is reproduced by halftone photography.

2. A magenta screen is limited to photographing black and white original copy.

3. Halftone dot values are expressed in percentages of black areas.

4. Highlight dots on a halftone negative appear as small black dots in a large transparent area.

5. The second exposure in halftone photography is called the flash exposure.

Making a Halftone Negative

A series of steps similar to those for line photography can be followed in making halftone negatives. After determining the correct main and flash exposure times, the following procedure is typical:

1. Clean the copyboard glass.

2. Place a piece of black-and-white, continuous-tone copy in the copyboard. Position the copy upside down, with a gray scale beside it.

3. Set the bellows extension and copyboard extension for same size (100 percent) reproduction scale.

4. Set the lens for the same f/stop as used in the line work at 100 percent.

5. Adjust the lamps for proper angles.

6. Set the main exposure time.

7. Select the proper film size. Be sure darkroom safelights are on and white lights off.

8. Open the camera back and position the film.

Figure 5-20. *Step 9. Position the contact screen over the film (emulsion to emulsion).*

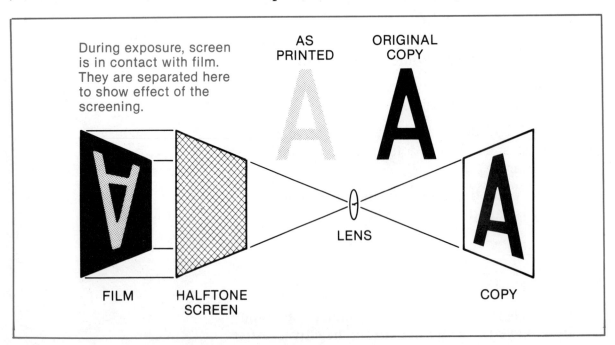

During exposure, screen is in contact with film. They are separated here to show effect of the screening.

AS PRINTED

ORIGINAL COPY

LENS

FILM

HALFTONE SCREEN

COPY

9. Position the contact screen over the film (emulsion to emulsion) (Fig. 5-20). Contact screens must be at least 1 inch larger on all four sides than the film size being used.

10. Turn on the vacuum pump.

11. Close the vacuum back.

12. Press the time buttom and expose the film.

13. Open the camera back but *do not turn off vacuum or remove the contact screen.*

14. Set the flash exposure timer. (Not all continuous tone copy requires a flash exposure. In certain cases, the flash exposure will give the halftone negative better tone reproduction when printed.)

15. Make the flash exposure (if required) with yellow light (Fig. 5-21).

16. Turn off the vacuum and remove the contact screen and film from the camera back. Replace the contact screen in its box.

17. Set the darkroom timer for 2-3/4 minutes (Fig. 5-22). The solutions should be fresh and at 68 degrees Fahrenheit [20 degrees Celsius]. Rock the film throughout the developing period. Do not use the gray scale as a guide in halftone development.

19. After the negative has been stopped, fixed, and washed, squeegee on the acetate side. Hang to dry or place in a dryer.

20. Examine the halftone negative on a light table. The negative should show a 90 percent dot in the highlights and a 5–10 percent dot in the shadows.

After examining the halftone negative on a light table, refer to a halftone problem chart (Figure 5-23). Most of the problems that occur in a halftone negative can

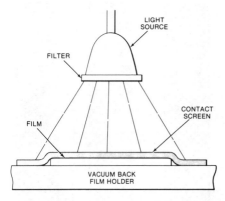

Figure 5-21. *Step 15. Make the flash exposure (if required) with yellow light.*

Figure 5-22. *Step 17. Set the darkroom timer for 2-34 minutes.*

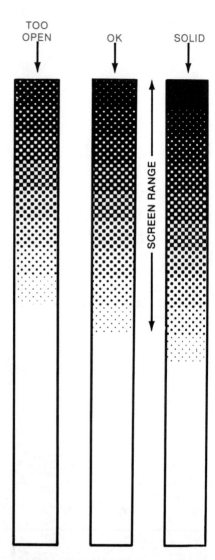

TOO OPEN   OK   SOLID

SCREEN RANGE

Figure 5-23. *Halftone problem charts are used to inspect halftone negatives to determine possible adjustments in exposure times. (Chemco Photoproducts Co.)*

be adjusted by use of the chart. It may be necessary to adjust exposure times to produce a good negative.

Contact Printing

A same-size image on film or paper from either a film negative or a film positive is prepared through *contact printing.* This procedure involves placing a film negative or positive in direct vacuum contact over a sheet of film or photoprint paper. An exposure is made using a beam of light and contacting frame (Fig. 5-24).

To make a *film positive* from a film negative, follow these steps.

1. Place a piece of unexposed Kodalith Ortho Thin-Base film, emulsion side up, on the bed of the contacting frame.

2. Place the film negative over the unexposed film, emulsion side up. Lock the glass frame over the film and bed. Turn on the vacuum motor pump.

3. Exposure to a point-source light is made according to the time recommended for the type of equipment being used.

4. The film is processed according to the manufacturer's specifications.

To prepare a *positive photoprint* from a film negative, place a sheet of photo paper (such as Azo or Velox), emulsion side up, on the bed of the contacting frame. Place the film negative, emulsion side down, over the photo paper. Make the exposure and process the photo paper according to the manufacturer's specifications.

In preparing a *reverse photoprint,* a film positive is used. The procedure is exactly the same as that for a positive photoprint. However, a film positive is used instead of a film negative. The photoprint paper is processed according to the manufacturer's specifications.

STRIPPING: THE FINAL STEP BEFORE PLATEMAKING

Film negatives or positives are used to prepare pre-sensitized offset lithographic plates. The negatives must be assembled and taped in position on a layout sheet of *masking paper.* This paper has a goldenrod color. Masking paper is often called *goldenrod.* The masking paper holds back light rays so that certain areas of the printing plate will not be exposed. This process is referred to as *stripping.*

Before the negatives are taped into position, the masking sheet is hand ruled (Fig. 5-25). The rules show the correct position for each negative. After each negative has been taped in position, the *stripper* cuts away the paper around the negative. This is done to expose the image areas. The assembled sheet of negatives is called a *flat.* The flat is used to prepare an offset printing plate. The platemaking process is covered in the next unit.

The film negative must be placed accurately so that the image will be in the correct position. First, the stripper determines which edge of the masking sheet will match the lead edge of the job. Instructions and a layout usually are provided to guide the stripper. The *lead edge* is the edge of the paper that enters the press first. The lead edge is held by a set of metal fingers called *grippers.* The grippers hold the paper during its cycle on the press.

The lead edge is also the point at which the printing plate is bent to attach it to the plate cylinder. Allowance must be made for this bend in placing the image on the printing plate.

In addition to locating the position of the lead edge, the *gripper margin* must also be marked. This is

Figure 5-24. *A special contact printing point-source light is used to make contact prints from film negatives. (nuArc Company, Inc.)*

Figure 5-25. *The initial step in stripping is to rule the masking sheet (goldenrod) to show proper positions for each negative. (Stephen B. Simms)*

104

SAFETY TIP

- Knives and blades used in the stripping process are extremely sharp. Never place fingers or hands in the path of a blade. When not in use, blades or knives should be stored safely to prevent them from falling off the work area.

the distance between the top edge of the sheet of paper and where the printed image begins. The printed image cannot extend above this line. The stripper locates the lead edge and gripper margin and marks them on the masking sheet with a ballpoint pen. Gripper margins range from 3/16 inch [4.77 mm] for small duplicator-size presses to 3/8 inch [9.53 mm] for larger presses.

In addition to the lead edge and gripper margin lines, the stripper draws other *reference lines.* A vertical line is drawn to indicate the center of the printed sheet. This is called the *center line.* Lines are also drawn to show the outline of the press sheet. If the job is to be trimmed after it is run, lines representing *trim size* are drawn. The stripper may also draw lines to aid in positioning the negatives on the masking sheet. Some masking sheets can be purchased already cut to popular sizes and preprinted with reference lines.

Once the negative has been taped in place on the goldenrod masking paper, image-area *windows* must be cut (Fig. 5-26). This is done by turning over the flat on the light table. The stripper uses a sharp knife or razor blade to cut away the goldenrod paper covering the image areas. A small sheet of clear acetate inserted between the negative and masking paper will protect the negative. Cutting into the negative should

Figure 5-26. *Image-area windows are cut in the mask to expose the image. Windows are at least 1/8 inch larger than image areas. (Direct Image Corp.)*

be avoided because such cut lines will reproduce on the plate.

The windows are cut at least 1/8 inch [3.18 mm] larger than the image areas.

Opaquing

Film negatives often contain scratches and small transparent openings called *pinholes*. These must be covered or they will show up on the offset plate as images. Also, some negatives may contain unwanted image areas. These must be opaqued. *Opaquing* is done after the windows have been cut.

All pinholes and scratches should be opaqued on the right-reading, or base, side of the film negative whenever possible. The negative is examined for pinholes and scratches with its emulsion side down.

Learning Activities

1. Obtain a magnifier of at least four power. Also obtain a sheet of printed material that you are sure was printed by the photo-offset method. Look at any photographs or gray artwork through the magnifier. Observe the tiny dots that make up the image. Note that the dots in the highlight (bright) areas of a photo appear as small black dots in a large white area. Dots in the shadow (dark) areas appear as small white dots in large black areas.

2. Visit an offset printing firm or newspaper, if possible. Ask if you can view the darkroom area and watch the process camera being operated. Also ask to visit the stripping area and watch flats being prepared on the light tables.

1. copyboard
2. lighting system
3. lensboard
4. bellows
5. ground glass
6. vacuum back
7. copyboard drive
8. lensboard drive
9. emulsion
10. orthochromatic film
11. panchromatic film
12. latent image
13. stop bath
14. fixing bath
15. gray scale
16. magenta screen
17. gray screen
18. contact screen
19. dot pattern
20. highlights
21. middletones
22. shadows
23. flash exposure
24. safelight
25. contact print

26. reverse photoprint
27. masking paper
28. stripper
29. flat
30. lead edge
31. grippers
32. gripper margin
33. trim size
34. pinholes
35. opaquing
36. windows.

A fine art brush is used to apply opaquing paint (Fig. 5-27). Care must be taken to avoid getting opaque solution on the image areas of the negative.

Figure 5-27. *Pinholes and scratches in negatives are covered by opaquing. The opaquing paint is applied to the base side of the film (right-reading side) with a fine art brush.*

- Line photography is used for copy that does not contain varying shades of gray. Copy that does contain shades of gray is called continuous tone or halftone copy. Halftone copy is photographed through a screen that creates a dot pattern of the image.

- Film processing involves exposure of film on a process camera and developing the film.

- Contact printing involves placing a film negative or positive in direct vacuum contact over a sheet of film or photoprint paper. An exposure is made using a beam of light. Contact prints are same-size prints.

- Stripping is the final step before plates are made. The negatives are masked and placed in exactly the right position so that image areas line up properly.

- Opaquing is the process of covering up pinholes and scratches in film negatives. The opaque solution is applied with a fine artists brush.

Unit Review

1. What is the process in which offset film negatives are positioned prior to plate-making?

2. Pinholes and scratches in film negatives are covered up with a solution. What is this process called?

3. Look at a halftone negative or print through a magnifier. What type of pattern do you see in the image areas?

Review Questions

6 PHOTO-OFFSET PRINTING

PLATEMAKING: GETTING READY FOR THE PRESS RUN

Photo-offset lithography is a planographic (flat) printing process. This means the image area is on the same *plane*, or surface, as the non-image area. The image carrier, or plate, used in offset printing is called a *lithographic plate.*

During platemaking, the platemaker exposes the negative to a metal or plastic offset plate. The platemaker completes the process by developing the images on the exposed surface, using special chemicals. (Paper plate masters are also used for small jobs. These do not require an exposure. This is because the images are formed on the master by a typewriter or grease-based crayons.)

Lithographic plates are made from many kinds of materials. Aluminum and zinc are widely used. Plates are also made from stainless steel and other alloys. For short press runs, direct-image paper masters can be used on small presses. Plates are referred to as *additive working* or *subtractive working*. With the additive plate, lacquer is applied to the images. In the case of subtractive plates, the emulsion is removed from the nonimage areas.

Presensitized plates consist of a base and a light-sensitive coating. The coating reacts photographically when exposed to light. Care must be taken not to scratch the coating when removing plates from their packages. Plates are handled by their outer edges. They should not be bent or creased in any way. The plates are exposed to ultraviolet light in a *platemaker*. This is done under subdued room light or in a room with yellow light.

The platemaking unit has a vacuum frame that consists of a rubber blanket and a glass cover. The blanket is bordered by a rubber sealing gasket. It is connected by a rubber hose to a vacuum pump.

The plate is placed *emulsion side up* on the rubber blanket in the frame. The goldenrod flat is then positioned over the plate with the emulsion side of the negative *down* in direct contact with the emulsion of the plate. The lead edge of the goldenrod flat is aligned with the lead edge of the plate. The flat is also aligned along the left-hand edge of the plate (Fig. 6-1).

A platemaker's *gray scale* is used to determine the correct exposure time. The gray scale has 21 different densities. The gray scale is usually laid along the tail edge of the flat.

The glass on the top of the platemaking unit must be checked for cleanliness before each exposure. When the plate and flat are in position, the glass cover is locked. The vacuum blanket compresses the plate and flat to produce a tight contact. Then the frame is rotated upside down (Fig. 6-2). The plate and flat are exposed to the ultraviolet light source.

The timer is set for the recommended time, and the exposure is started. After exposure is complete, the vacuum frame is rotated back to its normal position and the vacuum turned off. The glass frame is opened carefully. After removing the flat and the

Figure 6-1. *stripped-up flat is positioned on the plate by aligning the lead edge first and then aligning the left-hand edge.* (Stephen B. Simms)

Figure 6-2. *The vacuum frame of the platemaker is rotated before the exposure is made inside the unit. (nuArc Company, Inc.)*

Figure 6-3. *After exposure, the plate is treated with a desensitizing gum. Then the image is hardened by applying the developing lacquer in a circular motion. (Stephen B. Simms)*

plate, the glass frame is closed, locked and moved or tilted to avoid glass breakage.

After exposure, the plate is developed with chemicals. The first step in processing a plate is to remove the unexposed coating. A *desensitizing gum* is rubbed over the entire surface of the plate. A small cellulose sponge is used for this purpose. The sponge is moved back and forth across the plate. The plate surface must be left moist before the second step of processing is begun.

Developing lacquer is then applied to the plate (Fig. 6-3). The lacquer is poured onto the surface of the plate in a small pool, about 1½ inches in diameter. A clean cellulose sponge is used with a circular motion to develop the images to a ruby-red color. (Some plates contain coatings that turn blue when developed.)

The plate is then rinsed with tap water in a plate sink (Fig. 6-4). This removes all the excess chemicals. If the plate is going directly to the press, no further preparation is necessary. If the plate is to be stored for a period of time, it must be preserved. This is done to protect it from oxidation, dirt, and handling.

A thin coating of *gum arabic* solution is applied to the surface of the plate. This is done with a lint-free cotton pad or disposable paper wipe. The gum is wiped on the plate in the direction of its length. The buffing action is continued until the plate is completely dry.

DIRECT PLATEMAKING: SCIENCE MARCHES ON

The days of preparing negatives, stripping, and then exposing plates with film may be numbered. Electronic processes are rapidly replacing film with direct platemaking.

This may be done directly in the camera, using specially treated plates in place of the film. In this case, halftone art is pasted up along with line art and the two are photographed together.

The most advanced methods now utilize laser scanners.

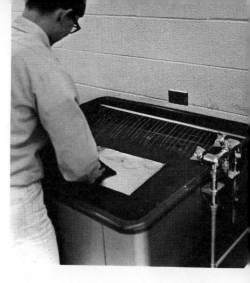

Figure 6-4. *After the plate has been developed, it is rinsed in tap water to remove any excess chemicals.*

Check Your Knowledge (True or False)

1. Aluminum is a common material used in the manufacture of lithographic plates.

2. The presensitized plate is placed emulsion side down in the platemaker.

3. The emulsion side of the negative is placed in direct contact with the plate's emulsion.

PHOTO-OFFSET LITHOGRAPHY PRINTING: TRANSFERRING THE IMAGES TO PAPER

As a reminder, photo-offset lithography is a planographic (flat) printing process. It is based on the principle that grease and water do not readily mix. The images on the plate are receptive to the grease-based ink used in offset lithography. The nonimage (clear) areas of the plate accept moisture but do not attract ink.

In the actual printing process, the plate (attached to a cylinder) is dampened first with water and then by ink. The image area repels the moisture (does not become wet) and accepts the ink. The nonimage area, which is moist with water, repels the ink. The image is then transferred from the plate to a rubber *blanket* on another cylinder. The rubber blanket then transfers the image onto the paper (Fig. 6-5).

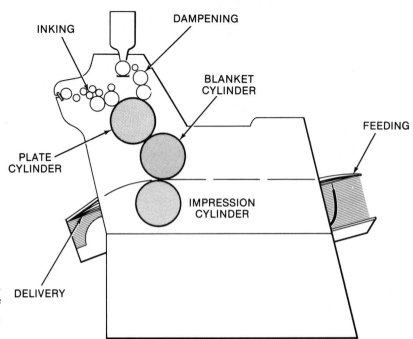

INKING

DAMPENING

BLANKET
CYLINDER

FEEDING

PLATE
CYLINDER

IMPRESSION
CYLINDER

DELIVERY

Figure 6-5. *This diagram illustrates a simplified view of how a small offset press operates.*

Press Sizes and Types

Small offset presses, up to a sheet size of about 11 by 14 inches, are generally referred to as *duplicators.* Units that print on sheets larger than 11 by 14 inches are known as *presses.*

All offset presses are divided into five main units. These are:

1. Main printing
2. Inking
3. Dampening
4. Feeder
5. Delivery.

The operation of each of these units is automatic, once the press is set up and running. These units are included on duplicators and presses alike.

Main printing unit. The main printing unit generally includes three cylinders (Fig. 6-6). These are:

1. Plate cylinder
2. Blanket cylinder
3. Impression cylinder.

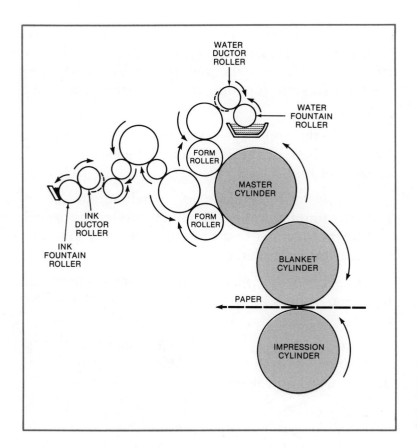

Figure 6-6. *Typical arrangement of inking and dampening units is shown here. The illustration shows a press that prints on only one side of the paper.*

The *plate cylinder* contains the offset plate, which, when inked, transfers the image to the blanket cylinder.

The *blanket cylinder* transfers the image from the plate to the paper.

The *impression cylinder* transports the paper in contact and under pressure with the blanket cylinder.

Inking unit. The inking unit generally consists of:

- Three to four metal vibrating rollers
- Four or more rubber rollers
- Two to four rubber form rollers.

The *ink fountain* contains a series of thumbscrews (keys). These screws push against a thin blade to control ink transfer to the fountain roller. The press operator fills the fountain with ink before running a job.

When the press is in operation, the metal *fountain roller* revolves in the fountain. It picks up a small amount of ink.

The *ductor roller* picks up a small amount of ink from the fountain roller. The ductor roller rocks back and forth, touching first the fountain roller and then the distributing roller.

The *distributing roller* is in constant contact with the other rollers as it receives ink from the ductor roller.

The *oscillating (vibrator) rollers* move back and forth sideways as they rotate. They assist in spreading ink evenly to all rollers.

Form rollers receive the evenly spread ink from the oscillating rollers and then ink the image on the plate. Duplicators generally contain two form rollers, while larger presses have three or four form rollers (Fig. 6-7).

Dampening unit. The *dampening unit* is similar to the inking unit. However, the ductor and form rollers are usually covered with a cloth material known as

Figure 6-7. *The main printing unit of an offset press usually contains three cylinders. On a perfecting press, there is no impression cylinder. Instead, the two blanket cylinders act as impression cylinders as the paper web is fed through.*

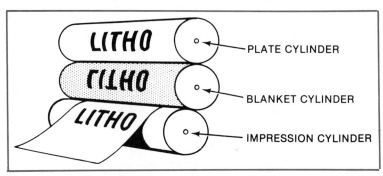

molleton. Cloth molleton covers are similar to gloves that fit tightly on the rollers. The fountain roller rotates in a container of water mixed with *etch*. The etch is a mild acid. The mixture is called *fountain solution*. The etch, when mixed with water, keeps the nonimage areas of the printing plate from inking up. The fountain roller transfers a thin film of fountain solution to the ductor roller. The ductor roller then transfers the solution to a distribution roller, which transfers it to the form roller.

The fountain solution must be prepared carefully so that a proper balance is made with the ink.

Feeder unit. The paper is loaded into the *paper feeder* on a paper table. The paper feeder is a part of the feeder unit (Fig. 6-8). The paper feeder table rises automatically as the sheets of paper are fed into the press. The height of the stack is regulated to remain at the same height throughout the press run. A vacuum pump inside the press provides air through plastic

Learning Activities

1. If possible, visit an offset printing firm. Ask if you can observe the platemaking and printing operation. Try to view some original copy that has been printed. If possible, observe the copy in the various stages it went through. These would include typeset galleys, paste-up mechanical, film negative, printing plate, and finished product.

2. Make a list of all the steps involved in offset printing, as covered in this unit and the preceding two units. Or, draw a simple diagram showing these steps. For each step, indicate whether the image is right reading or reverse reading.

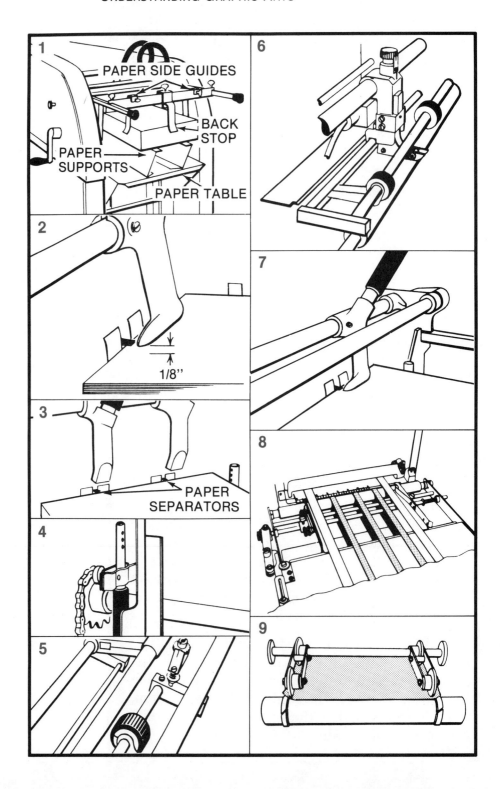

1 PAPER SIDE GUIDES
BACK STOP
PAPER SUPPORTS
PAPER TABLE

2 1/8"

3 PAPER SEPARATORS

Figure 6-8. *Loading and feeding of paper on a sheet-fed offset press is illustrated here.*

1) Build paper stack a ream at a time, positioned squarely with back stop and side guides.

2) Paper stack should rise to 1/8 inch below bottom of suction foot. Let paper table rise last inch automatically.

3) Flexible separators under each suction foot should project 1/8 inch over edge of paper.

4) Face air blowers diagonally toward lead edge of sheet. Adjust height so that middle hole in blower is even with top of paper stack when air pump is off.

5) Place top pullout rollers as close to center as possible on either side of suction feet. Use a test strip of stock you are running to check for light, even tension between rollers.

6) Double sheet eliminator should be adjusted whenever you change paper stocks. Lower paper stack and disengage pile height control. Turn on press and feeder pump. Insert 1-inch test strip under detector. Turn adjusting screw until trip gauge does not open. Insert two paper strips under detector and turn adjusting knob until gate does not open. Then turn knob half the number of clicks back to the setting of one sheet.

7) Position suction feet to split sheet evenly. Start with minimum suction and increase until sheets feed consistently when press is running.

8) Run one sheet down to stop fingers on feed table. Line up conveyor tape evenly under the sheet. Line up metal strap over conveyor tapes. Square side guides. Adjust sheet jogger. For good registration, side guide must be square with paper.

9) Run sheet halfway into jogger (paper receiver). Center ejector wheels over non-printing area. Align rings 1/8 to 1/4 inch outside of ejector wheels. (If paper curls up, align rings inside.) Run sheets into jogger and adjust side to fit sheet.

tubes at the front of the paper stack. The air is regulated so that it will separate the top five to six sheets of paper. This makes it easier for the sheets to be picked up.

A set of *suction feet* drops down against the front edge of the top sheet of paper on the pile. The feet lift the sheet to the edge of a feedboard. The suction stops automatically for a moment, releasing the sheet to a pair of rubber *forwarding rollers*. These rollers deliver the sheet of paper onto a set of moving *conveyor tapes*.

The conveyor tapes carry the sheet to the end of the feedboard, where it is stopped by a set of pins known as the *front guides*. A *side guide* then pushes the sheet into the correct position sidewise. The action of the side and front guides squares the sheet. All sheets of paper enter the printing unit in exactly the same position.

Grippers, which are contained in a gap in the impression cylinder, automatically take hold of the sheet. The sheet is then drawn around the impression cylinder and forced against the blanket to receive the impression. The sheet then moves to the delivery unit.

Delivery unit. The job of the delivery unit begins as the grippers release the sheet to a set of *transfer cylinder grippers.* These grippers close on the edge of the sheet just as the impression cylinder grippers open to release it. The transfer cylinder grippers consist of several *gripper fingers.* When the sheet is released by the transfer cylinder grippers, it passes over a rubber *ejector roller.* The ejector roller propels the sheet into the receiving tray.

Most offset duplicators are equipped with a tilted *paper receiving tray.* This unit includes *paper guides* and a *paper retainer,* which directs the sheets into the tray. On some duplicators, the left paper guide moves back and forth to square the sheets when the press is operating. The front paper guide can be adjusted for any depth of paper being run.

Figure 6-9. *Webs of paper can be seen at the top of this multi-unit perfecting offset press. Each unit prints a single color product from its own roll of paper. (Rockwell International, Graphic Systems Division)*

WEB OFFSET PRESSES:
WHERE THE BIG JOBS ARE RUN

Presses that are fed from a roll of paper are known as *web* presses (Fig. 6-9). These presses are used for work requiring long runs, such as newspapers and magazines. The method of feeding and the design of these presses differ from those of *sheet-fed* presses. They operate on the same principles as smaller offset presses and duplicators, however.

MULTICOLOR OFFSET PRESSES:
EVERYTHING ON A SINGLE RUN

Many offset presses are *single-color.* This means they have only one printing unit and can print only one color at a time. If a second or third color is required on a job, the sheets are allowed to dry after the first color has been printed. The sheets are then fed through the press again to print the next color. This process is repeated until all the colors for the job have been printed.

Presses capable of printing more than one color in a single pass through the press are known as *multicolor presses.* These presses consist of several single printing units connected in a row to form one press. Each unit can run a different plate and a different color of ink.

PERFECTING OFFSET PRESSES:
COVERING BOTH SIDES OF A SHEET

Most sheet-fed presses print on only one side of the sheet at a time. To print on the reverse side, it is necessary to let the ink dry. The paper is turned over and run through the press a second time. Presses that are capable of printing on both sides of the sheet are known as *perfectors.* These presses may be either sheet-fed or web-fed, and they may be a single-color or multicolor.

Vocabulary Checklist

1. blanket
2. ink fountain
3. ductor roller
4. form roller
5. dampening unit
6. molleton
7. fountain solution
8. suction feet
9. paper guide
10. paper retainer
11. web offset press
12. perfector.

Unit Review

- Offset plates are flat. They are made from several different kinds of metals. For short press runs, direct-image paper masters can be used on small presses. The most common kinds of plates are presensitized with a light-sensitive coating, which reacts photographically when exposed to light. After exposure, the plates are developed with chemicals.

- Electronic equipment is rapidly replacing the film processing and stripping methods with direct platemaking. This can be done either through the copy camera or with laser scanners.

- An offset press has five major units. These units are: main printing, inking, dampening, feeder, and delivery.

- In offset printing, the plate is dampened with water and then with ink. The image area repels moisture but accepts ink. The nonimage area accepts moisture and repels ink. The image is transferred from the plate to a rubber blanket. The blanket then transfers the image to the paper.

- Small offset presses, those that print sheet sizes of about 11 by 14 inches or smaller, are called duplicators. Larger presses are called presses.

- Larger press runs, such as for publications, are done on web-fed presses. These are often multi-unit presses that can print two, three, or more colors on a single run.

- Presses that print on both sides of the paper at the same time are called perfector presses.

1. Does the image area of an offset plate accept moisture or repel it?

2. There are three cylinders in the main printing unit of an offset press. One is the plate cylinder and one the blanket cylinder. What is the third cylinder called?

3. What is a press called that prints on a continuous roll of paper?

4. What type of press prints on both sides of the paper at once?

7

RELIEF (LETTERPRESS) PROCESSES

RELIEF (LETTERPRESS) PRINTING: GUTENBERG'S IDEA IS BASICALLY UNCHANGED

The printing process known as *letterpress* involves the transfer of ink from a raised (relief) surface through direct pressure. The basic concept is the same as that used by Gutenberg in the fifteenth century. Gutenberg had borrowed a technique from winemakers. Presses had been used for some time to squeeze juice from grapes. Gutenberg substituted type, ink, and paper for the grapes. Workers would turn a lever on the press to apply pressure and create printed impressions.

The process has been greatly refined and speeded up during the past 500 years. But the basic principle remains the same. The image to be printed is on a raised

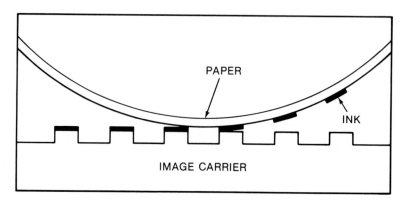

Figure 7-1. *Letterpress (relief) printing involves transfer of ink from a raised surface (image carrier) to paper through the application of pressure.*

122

surface. The image area is inked and a piece of paper is then placed over the inked image. When pressure is applied, ink is transferred from the relief (raised) surface to the paper (Fig. 7-1).

This unit deals with the processes leading up to letterpress printing. Topics include hot metal composition, engraving, and platemaking.

HOT METAL COMPOSITION: THE OLDEST TYPESETTING METHOD

Metal type used in letterpress printing is the oldest method of type composition. Type metal is an alloy. An *alloy* is a metal formed by combining two or more basic metals. Type metal alloys are formed from lead, antimony, tin, and copper. The alloy that results has properties that are ideal for typecasting. Type metal is easy to melt and easy to handle in a molten state. This is important because, since the 1890s, typecasting has been done on automatic machines. When cast and cooled, type metal has properties that create clear, sharp forms. This results in readable, attractive printed images.

After the typeface has been designed, a brass *matrix* is created for each character. A matrix is a mold or die. A separate matrix is needed for each design, size, and style of typeface required. The matrix is placed into a casting machine. Molten metal is forced into the matrix. Each character is automatically ejected from the casting unit. The entire casting operation is automatic and results in a complete set of alphabet characters for any given size and style of type.

The term *hot metal* includes all the methods used to set metal type into lines and pages. Some very large types are made of special hardwood. *Wood type* is generally classified as hot metal. The main ingredient

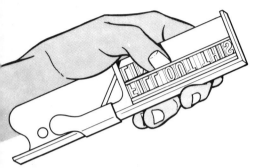

Figure 7-2. *Hand-set type is assembled in a composing stick.*

of metal type is molten metal. The two methods of hot-metal composition are:

- Hand set
- Machine set.

HAND-SET TYPE: UNCHANGED OVER THE YEARS

Hand-set type is composed with individual metal or wood characters assembled into single lines. The process has not changed much since Gutenberg's time.

A *composing stick* is held in one hand (Fig. 7-2) while the individual type characters are selected from a type case. The *type case* is a drawer that has a standard arrangement of small compartments for each character and a variety of spaces (Fig. 7-3). The characters are assembled in the composing stick until they make up a full line. Different spaces are then used to justify the line (Fig. 7-4). To *justify* a line means to fill it out to the desired width. Spacing used within a line of type is called word spacing or letter spacing. Justified type has both left and right margins aligned vertically.

The type case is the historical source of some of the most common terms in typesetting and printing. All capital letters and special characters were stored

Figure 7-3. *Type is stored in type cases. This is a California job case arrangement. (Zellerbach Paper Co.)*

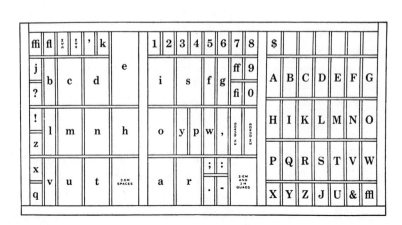

in the upper case, and lower case letters were stored in another case located below the upper case. This brought the designations of *upper case* for capital letters and *lower case* for lower case letters. Today, however, both the upper and lower cases of Gutenberg's time have been combined into a single case. It is called the *California job case*.

If spacing is required between lines of type, strips of metal, called *leads* and *slugs*, are inserted (Fig. 7-5). This is referred to as line spacing or *leading*. Leads are usually two points thick. Slugs are generally six points thick. A *lead and slug cutter* is used to cut these materials to any pica measure (width).

A slug is placed in the composing stick to start the process of typesetting. The compositor keeps adding lines of type until the stick is full. Usually, between two and three inches of type can be held in place. By this time, the stick, with the weight of the type building up, gets quite heavy. The amount of type held in a stick—two to three inches—is sometimes called a *stick* of type. When the composing stick is full, the type is transferred to a shallow three-sided tray called a *galley*. The compositor then continues to set type until the galley is full or the job is completed.

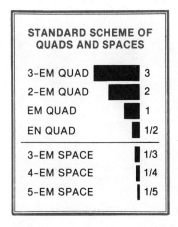

Figure 7-4. *Quads and spaces are the basic units of word spacing in typesetting. The em quad is square—its width is the same as the point size of the type. The en quad is one-half the width of the em quad. In other words, in 10 point type, the em quad is 10 points by 10 points square, and the en quad is 5 points wide by 10 points high. Em spaces are fractional parts of em quads. A 3-em space, for instance, is one-third the width of the em quad. The 3-em space is the standard space used between words in ordinary composition.*

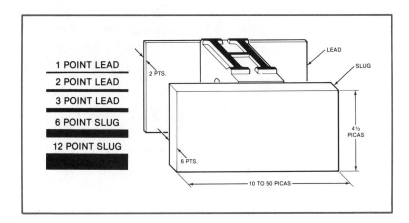

Figure 7-5. *Leads and slugs are inserted to provide spacing between lines of type (referred to as line spacing). These materials are cut to the desired pica measure (width) with a lead and slug cutter.*

Figure 7-6. *When type has been properly arranged in a galley, it is tied up with string. This is called a form, and it is now ready to be proofed. (American Typefounders, Inc.)*

Figure 7-7. *After the type has been set, it is kept in the galley, which is a metal tray. A proof is taken by inking the type, placing a sheet of paper on the inked form, and turning a cylinder over the form. Such proofs are generally called galley proofs. (Zellerbach Paper Co.)*

The printer arranges or *makes up* the job in the galley according to the layout specifications. This may include adding lines of display type, rules, decorative elements, or photoengravings. A *photoengraving* is a metal plate with the image in relief. These illustrations and photographs are also called *cuts*. Cuts are mounted on wood blocks that raise their printing surfaces to the same height as the type. Photoengraving techniques are described later in this unit.

When properly arranged in the galley, the type is *tied up* with string (Fig. 7-6). A piece of string wound around the type several times holds it firmly and securely. When type and related printing elements are tied up and ready to be proofed or printed, they are called a *form.*

After a type form is tied up, a proof is taken. A proof is a print of the type prepared for proofreading. The galley containing the type form is placed on the bed of a *proof press.* The type is inked with a small rubber roller called a *brayer.* A sheet of paper is placed on the inked form, and a proof is made by turning a cylinder over the type form. Proofs made in this manner are called *galley proofs* (Fig. 7-7).

The galley proofs are read carefully for errors. Proofreaders' marks are fairly standardized throughout the United States (Fig. 7-8). The corrected proof is sent to the *compositor*, who makes necessary corrections. A *revised proof* is then prepared and checked against the original proof. Both proofs are then submitted for approval.

When the metal type is no longer needed for a job, it is returned to the case. The leads and slugs are sorted and placed in the storage racks. The process of returning type to its proper compartments in the case is called *distribution*. When a type form has been printed, it is called a *dead form*. All type that is ready

Insert period ⊙	Caps—used in margin *Caps 2.*
Insert comma ⋀	Caps—used in text ═
Insert colon ⁚	Caps & small caps—used in margin *c + sc.*
Insert semicolon ⁏	Caps& small caps—used in text ═
Insert question mark ?	Lower case—used in margin *lc.*
Insert exclamation mark !	Lower case—used in text /
Insert hyphen ⸗/	Wrong font *wf.*
Insert apostrophe ⱽ	Close up ⌒
Insert quotation marks ⱽ ⱽ	Delete ℯ
Insert 1-en dash $\frac{1}{N}$	Close up and delete ⌐ℯ
Insert 1-em dash $\frac{1}{M}$	Correct the position ℊ
Insert space #	Move right ⌐
Insert lead *ld)*	Move left ⌐
Insert virgule *shill*	Move up ⊓
Superior ⌄	Move down ⊔
Inferior ⋀	Aline vertically ‖
Parentheses (/)	Aline horizontally ═
Brackets [/]	Center horizontally ⊐⊏
Indent 1 em ▫	Center vertically ⊔⊓
Indent 2 ems ▭	Push down space ↲
Paragraph ¶	Use ligature ⌒
No paragraph *no ¶*	Equalize space—used in margin *eq. #*
Transpose—used in margin *tr*	Equalize space—used in text √√
Transpose—used in text ⌒	Decrease space √
Spell out *sp.*	Let it stand—used in margin *stet*
Italic—used in margin *ital*	Let it stand—used in text ....
Italic—used in text ──	Dirty or broken letter ⊗
Boldface—used in margin *bf*	Carry over to next line *run over*
Boldface—used in text ⌒⌒	Carry back to preceding line *run back*
Small caps—used in margin *s.c.*	Something omitted—see copy *copy out*
Small caps—used in text ═	Question to author *Qu? ⊙*
Roman type *rom*	Caret—general indicator used to mark ⋀ exact position of error in text

Figure 7-8. *This is a chart of standard proofreaders' marks used throughout the printing industry. There are some variations, but these are the most commonly used marks. The marks are used in the publishing and advertising agency fields. Proofs should be prepared with margins adequate for the insertion of proofreading marks and corrections. (Compugraphic Corp.)*

for distribution is called *dead matter*. To *kill* a type form is to return or distribute all its parts to the proper storage compartments and racks.

Check Your Knowledge (True or False)

1. A composing stick is used with some typesetting machines.

2. Leads and slugs are used for line spacing in hot metal composition.

3. When type is arranged on a tray, it is called a galley proof.

MACHINE-SET TYPE: A REVOLUTION IN ITS DAY

Machine-set type can be produced on any of three machines:

1. Linotype   2. Monotype   3. Ludlow.

The three machines differ in the way they function. However, they all have some basic characteristics in common. All three machines cast type by injecting hot metal into matrices. Under all three systems, the metal is generally used just once. After the job has been printed, the metal type is cleaned. Then the metal is remelted and used again to cast new type. The differences among the typecasting machines lie in the way typecasting is done and in the kinds of type that result.

Linotype. A Linotype machine casts single complete lines of type (Fig. 7-9). The type line consists of characters and spaces on a single body rather than characters on individual bodies.

Figure 7-9. *This cutaway view of a Linotype machine shows how brass type matrices are returned to their magazine by the elevator and distributor. Molten metal is injected into the matrices to form a solid line of type called a slug. (Mergenthaler Linotype Co.)*

The operator sits at a keyboard similar in appearance to that of a typewriter. At the touch of a key, a matrix is released into an assembler. When all the matrices for a line are assembled, the line is automatically spaced out by *spacebands*. These are wedge-shaped spacers that spread the words to fill the line. Left and right justification result from this spacing. Molten metal is forced into the line of matrices, forming a solid line of type, or *slug*.

After the slug is cast, the matrices are automatically carried to the top of the Linotype by means of a conveyor called an *elevator*. Then, as they proceed along the top of the machine, they are dropped in proper order into a storage compartment called a *magazine*. Each type size has its own magazine.

The slug is delivered to a tray called a *galley* in front of the machine near the operator. If the operator makes an error, the entire line is reset.

Monotype. The Monotype system uses two machines —a keyboard and a caster. The keyboard machine punches a roll of paper tape as the operator presses the keys. The tape is then run through the caster, which casts single characters properly spaced in lines of preset width. A complete set, or font, of type in the form of a matrix (mold) is placed in the caster. One complete matrix must be used for each size and style of type desired.

Since the pieces of type are individual characters, single letters can easily be removed and corrected by hand. Monotype is well suited to setting complicated forms such as timetables and columns of financial figures.

Ludlow. The Ludlow is used to cast lines of type from matrices that are set by hand in a special composing stick (Fig. 7-10). The justified line is then inserted into the Ludlow machine and mechanically cast into a single slug. The slug formed by the Ludlow is T-shaped. The face of the type is on the wide end of the "T." To give the typeface added strength, slugs are used to support the overhanging parts.

The Ludlow system is similar to hand-set type, but new lines of type can be cast at any time from the brass matrices. Any number of cast slugs can be

Figure 7-10. *The Ludlow machine casts slugs of type from hand-set matrices. Lines that are justified in a special composing stick are inserted into the Ludlow machine and cast mechanically. (Stephen B. Simms)*

produced from one line of matrices. The individual matrices are returned to their proper storage compartments after use. The type cases used for Ludlow matrices are similar to those used for hand-set type.

TYPESETTING TRADITION: THE SIGNIFICANCE OF HOT METAL

The days of hot metal, both hand set and machine set, are drawing to a close. Rapid advancements in phototypesetting are making hot metal obsolete. In many areas of the country today, it is difficult to find hot metal equipment in operation.

Typesetting was a slow and difficult process until the late nineteenth century. It was then that a German-born U.S. inventor, Ottmar Merganthaler, introduced the Linotype. His brilliant mechanical device revolutionized typesetting overnight. The Linotype and a similar machine, the Intertype, were the primary methods of typesetting for almost 75 years. Eventually, the sciences of photography and electronics combined to displace the Linotype. Today, computer-controlled phototypesetting is the most widely used method.

Letterpress printing followed the same path as hot-metal typesetting. Phototypesetting is tied mainly to offset printing. As computerized phototypesetting replaced hot metal, offset replaced letterpress as the main printing technique.

However, hot-metal techniques have given the printing industry many of its traditions. Many terms widely used in printing originated with hot-metal typesetting. Much of this language and terminology of printing still survives. Use of these words for newer techniques makes more sense when you have the knowledge to relate back to the older methods. Expressions such as "upper case" have little meaning in phototypesetting unless you understand their origins.

Some of the hot-metal terminology, of course, has no application in modern phototypesetting. Two of the more colorful examples are "printer's devil" and "hell box." *Printer's devil* is the traditional term for a print shop apprentice. The printer's devil, usually a young person, was expected to perform a variety

Learning Activities

1. Go to your local post office. Ask to examine rubber stamps used in marking mail. Is a rubber stamp right reading or reverse reading? Note the relief images on a rubber stamp. Look closely at the surface of a rubber stamp after it has been inked but before it has been used to print an image. Make several impressions with different pressures placed on the rubber stamp. Look at the images you have created. See if you can figure out how pressure and inking affect the images.

2. Examine a typical typewriter in your school office. Note how the type images are raised so that only the characters touch the ribbon. This forces the inked or carbon side of the ribbon against the paper. If your school office has a typewriter equipped with a type element, ask to view it closely. Note how the surfaces of the characters are raised above the exterior base of the ball.

3. If possible, visit a printing firm that has letterpress equipment. Ask if you can examine some individual pieces of type. Note how the image of the type is raised above the base. If the firm has a hot metal machine such as a Linotype, ask if you can watch it in operation. Note how each line of type is cast individually.

of chores. Responsibilities included cleaning up the shop and running errands. The *hell box* is a large box for broken and discarded type. The term came from the fact that the contents of the box went into a fiery furnace for remelting. The terms tied together: The printer's devil took care of the hell box.

LETTERPRESS PLATES: LOCKING UP A FORM

For letterpress printing, all of the raised surfaces of type and illustrations must be at the same height. This is necessary to produce an impression on paper. The height from the bottom of a piece of type or type slug to its face is 0.918 inch. This is standard for all letterpress type. The measurement is known as *type high* (Fig. 7-11).

When all of the type and illustrations to be included in a job are ready, they are assembled into a form. A letterpress printing *form* consists of all of the type and illustration elements needed to print a job.

The type form is locked up in a metal frame called a *chase.* The chase holds the type firmly in place on the press. The type is locked up on a metal table called a *stone* (Fig. 7-12).

The surface of the stone must be perfectly clean before placing the type form on it. The surface is wiped with a clean cloth. Even a small piece of dirt can cause a character or line of type to be raised above the type-high level. An out-of-level character may then punch into the paper when printed on the press.

Type is removed from the galley by carefully sliding the form onto the stone. The chase is then placed over the type form with one of the longer sides nearest the compositor. The side nearest the compositor will be the bottom of the chase. The side away

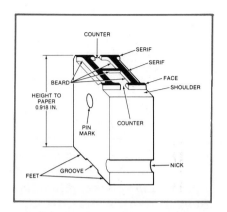

Figure 7-11. *Each piece of foundry type is exactly .918 inch high. The face of the character, which carries the ink, is a mirror image of the symbol to be printed. This illustration shows the parts of a piece of foundry type.*

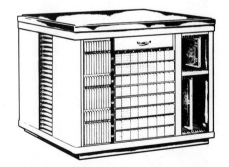

Figure 7-12. *The imposing table (stone) contains storage for furniture, chases, reglets, and galleys. (Hamilton Industries Div.)*

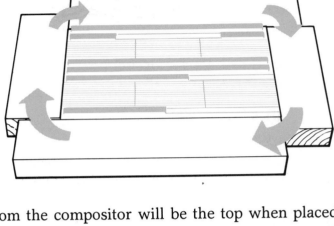

Figure 7-13. This illustration shows the first four pieces of furniture placed around the type form using the chaser method. Note that the pieces of furniture overlap somewhat in this method.

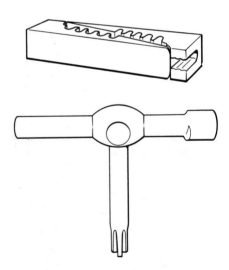

Figure 7-14. The quoin (top) is a metal device that acts like a wedge to hold the type form firmly inside the chase. The quoin key is used to tighten the quoins.

from the compositor will be the top when placed in the press.

When the type form is properly positioned in the center of the chase, it is surrounded with furniture (Fig. 7-13). *Furniture* is hardwood that has been cut to accurate pica widths.

Quoins (pronounced coins) and a quoin key (Fig. 7-14) are used to lock the form in the chase. *Quoins* are metal devices that act as a wedge to hold the form firmly inside the chase. A *quoin key* is used to tighten the quoins. Quoins are placed near the form, at the top and right sides of the chase. The quoins are positioned so that they press the form toward the lower left corner of the chase frame (Fig. 7-15). Reglets are inserted between the quoins and furniture to protect the surfaces of the furniture. *Reglets* are strips of wood 6 or 12 points thick.

When the furniture, reglets, and quoins are in place, the string is removed from the form. The quoins are tightened by pressing firmly together with your fingers. A *planer* is used to level the form (Fig. 7-16). The flat side of the planer is placed on the surface of the type form. The planer is tapped firmly several times with the quoin key. This should level the type form with the quoins just finger tight.

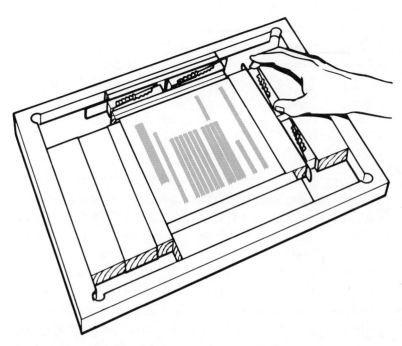

Figure 7-15. *Quoins are positioned at the top and right side of the form. The quoins are first tightened with the fingers.*

After the form is planed, it can be locked up tightly. The quoin key is used to tighten each quoin separately. Each is turned very slightly, in sequence, until all are turned equally tight. They should not be overtightened.

The lockup is then tested to see that all the material is perfectly tight in the chase. This is called

Figure 7-16. *After inital tightening, a planer is used to level the form. The form can then be locked up tightly with the quoin key.*

Check Your Knowledge (True or False)

1. A Linotype machine produces one line of type at a time.

2. A Ludlow operator casts type using a keyboard.

3. The chase is the frame into which a type form is locked up.

4. Quoin keys are used to level a type form.

Figure 7-17. *The locked-up form is then tested for "lift." If there are any loose type lines, they are rejustified. The locked-up form is then ready for the press.*

testing for *lift* (Fig. 7-17). It is done by raising one edge of the chase slightly and resting it on a quoin key. The printer presses a finger on parts of the form to check its tightness. Any loose type lines are rejustified. The lockup is now ready for the press.

PHOTOENGRAVING: A MAJOR STEP FORWARD

Photoengraving is the process by which original relief image carriers are produced by photographic, chemical, and mechanical means. Commercial photoengraving dates back to about 1880 in the United States. Earlier, illustrations had to be prepared by hand in wood or metal engravings. The photengraving process, combined with the development of mechanical hot type composition in the 1890s, revolutionized the publishing industry. The two processes greatly increased the quality and production capacity of newspapers, magazines, and other printed products.

Photoengraving did not change much from the 1880s until the middle of the twentieth century. Slow, technical hand work was required to produce a high-quality engraving. Photoengraving was slow because multiple steps were necessary to prepare a plate.

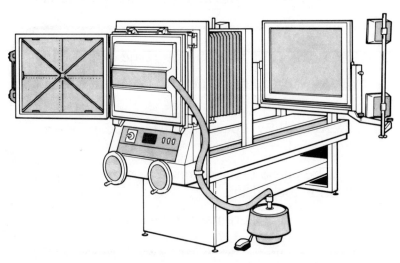

Figure 7-18. *Step 1. A process camera is used to photograph copy as the first step in photoengraving.*

More modern methods can produce quality photoengravings in minutes rather than hours. The key to this increased speed and quality has been one-step etching. One-step etching eliminated the need to etch a plate several times.

Photoengravings are made from zinc, copper, or magnesium. Zinc is the oldest of the photoengraving materials. Magnesium is the newest. Halftone engravings are generally done in copper because of that metal's finer grain.

PRODUCING A PHOTOENGRAVING: THE STEP-BY-STEP PROCESS

The following steps are used to prepare a photoengraving:

1. Copy is photographed with a process camera (Fig. 7-18). This is the same type of camera used to prepare film for offset platemaking. Use of a process camera is described in Unit 4. Illustrations of solid tones are considered line copy. Photographs are halftone copy.

2. Negatives are stripped into position on a flat (Fig. 7-19). The negatives are turned over (*flopped*). Flopping the negatives produces the necessary reverse-reading image when the film is used to make a photoengraving.

Figure 7-19. *Step 2. Negatives are stripped into position on a flat, just as in offset printing.*

3. The metal to be used for the plate is coated with a light-sensitive solution. This is done in a machine called a *whirler*. The light-sensitive solution is poured on the metal while it is revolving. The whirling action distributes the solution evenly over the metal. The solution is dried by a heating element in the whirler. (This step is unnecessary when presensitized metal is used.)

4. The high-contrast negatives are placed in contact with the coated metal. Negatives and metal are

138

placed in an exposure frame. An exposure is made under a bright light. The light-sensitive solution hardens as light rays pass through transparent areas of the negative.

5. The coated metal is developed by exposure to special chemicals. Areas that have been exposed to light are retained. The light-sensitive coating on unexposed areas of metal is washed away by the chemicals. The image is further hardened by chemical means or by heat, making the image resistant to etching.

6. The metal is placed into an etching machine and clamped to a base in a horizontal position. Liquid etching solution is sprayed or splashed against the surface of the metal. The nonimage area is washed away, leaving the image standing out in relief.

7. Larger nonimage areas of the metal are routed (cut away). A radial-arm router is used (Fig. 7-20). The router rotates rapidly. The rotating cutter removes unwanted metal. This step prevents large nonimage areas from reproducing during proofing or printing operations.

8. The final step in production is called finishing. A skilled engraver inspects the image area. The engraver uses hand tools and spot etching to refine the image.

9. The metal relief image carrier is proofed in a reproduction proofpress. Then the plate is

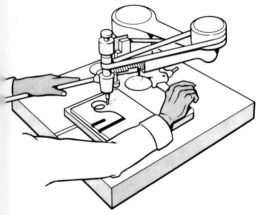

Figure 7-20. *Step 7. A radial-arm router is used to rout metal from nonimage areas of the plate.*

blocked or mounted. In this step, the metal plate is fastened to a block of wood or metal to make the image type-high (0.918 inch). The photoengraving is then used directly on a press.

TYPES OF LETTERPRESS PLATES: SINGLE ENGRAVINGS FOR THE PRESS

In some letterpress printing operations, the entire page of type and illustrations is prepared as a single engraving. These are either flat engravings for cylinder presses, or curved engravings for rotary presses. By using full-page plates, the original type matter does not wear out in the printing operation.

Line Engraving

A line engraving is a photoengraving made from an illustration having solid blacks and pure whites. It may have sharp black lines on a white background or white lines on a black background. There are no gray tones.

Halftone Engraving

A halftone engraving can be used to print with one color of ink. The result is a printed image that looks as if it had been printed in various tones of that color. The tones may vary from black to white. The use of halftone engravings permits the printing of photographs, paintings, and some types of drawings.

Stereotype

A stereotype is a metal printing plate. The procedure involves pouring molten metal into a mold called a *matrix,* or *mat* (Fig. 7-21). The matrix is made by pressing a piece of thick paperboard over the typeform. The pressure forms an exact impression of the typeform in the slightly damp paperboard. The mat is

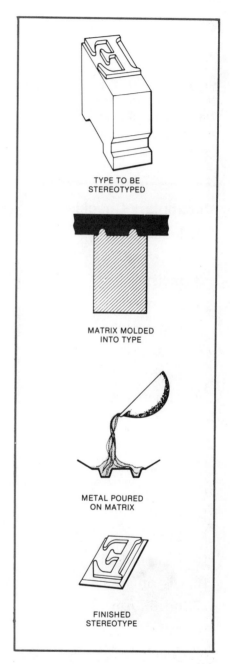

TYPE TO BE STEREOTYPED

MATRIX MOLDED INTO TYPE

METAL POURED ON MATRIX

FINISHED STEREOTYPE

Figure 7-21. *This sequence illustrates the basic steps in preparing a stereotype plate for letterpress printing.*

140

Figure 7-22. *This is a stereotype flat casting for a cylinder press. Halftones and type are included together in a single stereotype casting.*

Vocabulary Checklist

1. letterpress
2. relief
3. matrix
4. hot metal
5. composing stick
6. type case
7. justify
8. upper case
9. lower case
10. slug
11. leading
12. galley
13. cuts
14. brayer
15. compositor
16. distribution
17. dead form
18. kill
19. Linotype
20. Monotype
21. Ludlow
22. elevator

dried in an oven. When dry, the mat is placed in a casting machine and molten metal is poured in. This forms a relief printing plate. Stereotypes can be prepared as flat plates for cylinder presses (Fig. 7-22) or curved for use on rotary presses.

Electrotype

An electrotype is another kind of relief image carrier similar to a stereotype. In the case of electrotypes, the surface is usually treated with a coating of chromium or nickel. This hardens the surface of the plate. Electrotypes last longer—creating more impressions—when they are used on a press.

Linoleum Block

The linoleum block is one of the simplest forms of letterpress platemaking. Since it is a hand-cut process, it is not used in commercial printing because of the time involved. Linoleum-block impressions are used by many artists for preparation of prints in limited quantities. Linoleum blocks are sometimes used to print posters or decorative prints.

A linoleum block is prepared by cutting into a flat surface of linoleum (Fig. 7-23). Linoleum is a coated material used for floor covering. Special types of linoleum are used for decorative or printing purposes. The image area is left raised on the block. Nonimage areas are cut away.

THE RUBBER STAMP: IT IS REALLY A LETTERPRESS PLATE

The rubber stamp is a good example of a letterpress plate. A mold is made from metal type. The mold is used to make a rubber relief printing surface. In operation, the rubber printing surface is inked and then pressed on paper to transfer the image. Generally, an inked pad is used to transfer ink to the printing surface. Some rubber stamps are self-inking with reservoirs contained in their handles.

23. magazine
24. Ottmar Merganthaler
25. form
26. stone
27. chase
28. printer's devil
29. hellbox
30. quoin
31. reglet
32. planer
33. stereotype
34. electrotype

Figure 7-23. *A linoleum cutting tool is used to outline the design area on a linoleum block. Nonprinting areas are then removed with a larger blade to a depth of about 1/16 inch.*

Unit Review

- Relief, or letterpress, printing involves the transfer of ink from a raised surface through direct pressure.

- The manufacture of metal type for letterpress printing is the oldest method of movable-type composition.

- The term *hot metal* includes all methods used to set metal type into lines and pages.

- A type case is a compartment storage unit for type characters. In Gutenberg's day, capital letters and special characters were stored in the upper case. Lower case letters and figures were stored in a lower case. This is where the terms *upper case* and *lower case* originated. The two cases were eventually combined into a single drawer called the California job case.

- Spacing between lines of type is called leading or line spacing. In hot metal, this refers to the insertion of metal leads, or slugs, to space out lines. Spacing within a line of type is referred to as word or letter spacing.

- Machine-set type can be produced on any of three machines: a Linotype, a Monotype, or a Ludlow machine. The Linotype casts a single line of type called a slug. The Monotype casts single type characters, similar to hand-set type. The Ludlow machine casts a single line of type and is used mainly for display type.

- A galley is a tray into which a column of type is delivered by a Linotype. The term *galley* is also used to designate a column of copy on proofs—a *galley proof.*

- Hot metal is rapidly becoming obsolete. This is because newer methods of phototypesetting are faster, more versatile, and less expensive.

1. In printing, what is the common term for capital letters?

2. Lines of type are usually filled out to a desired width. What is this process called?

3. What is the term that means returning type to its proper compartments in the case?

4. The Linotype machine casts a single line of type. What is this line called?

5. What was the traditional name given to print shop apprentices?

6. What is the name of the metal frame in which a type form is locked up?

7. What is the name of the table on which the form is locked up in the metal frame?

8. The type form is surrounded with pieces of hardwood. What is this hardwood called?

Review Questions

8 LETTERPRESS PRINTING PRESSES

THREE TYPES OF PRESSES

There are three types of letterpress printing presses. They are:

1. Platen   2. Flat-bed cylinder   3. Rotary.

The basic printing operation is the same for all three (Fig. 8-1). It involves the transfer of ink from a raised surface through direct pressure. The image to be printed is on the raised surface. The nonprinting area is lower than the printing surface. The image area is inked, and a piece of paper is then placed over the inked image. By means of pressure, the ink is transferred from the relief surface to the paper. The differences between the presses basically lie in the way paper and the impression carrier are brought together.

THE PLATEN PRESS: LIKE A CLAM SHELL

The platen press operates on the same principles as a clam shell opening and closing (Fig. 8-2). The chase holding the type fits snugly against the solid *bed* of the press. The carrier is held in place with a spring clamp at the top of the chase.

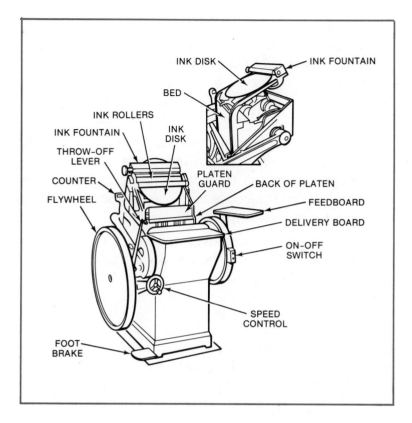

Figure 8-1. *The main parts of a hand-fed, power-operated platen press are illustrated here.*

The *platen* is the flat metal surface that moves toward the type to make the impression. As the press revolves, the platen returns to the open position for receiving the next sheet. Rollers ink the type each time the platen opens.

The *throw-off lever* at the left side of the press controls whether a sheet is to be printed. The lever is pushed toward the rear of the press when no printing is desired. When the lever is moved back, the platen strikes the type at each revolution of the press.

The *feed board* at the right side of the press holds the paper to be printed. The paper is taken from the feed board, one sheet at a time, and fed into the press. As the sheets are printed, they are removed and placed on the *delivery board.*

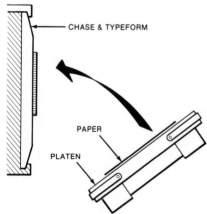

Figure 8-2. *The platen press operates like a clam shell opening and closing. The platen presses the paper against the inked type to transfer the image.*

The *flywheel* balances the press and gives it a steady, even motion. The flywheel is used to turn the press over by hand to take a trial impression. It is also used when washing the press, to move the rollers up and down. On most presses, the flywheel revolves toward the rear of the press, counterclockwise.

Grippers are sometimes used to hold the paper flat against the platen when printing. They must be moved and positioned so they strike on margins of the sheet and not in image areas. Type can be smashed if grippers are placed improperly.

The *ink rollers* pass over the type twice—down and up—between each impression. They bring an even distribution of ink from the revolving *ink disc* above. While printing a job, ink can be added to the lower left side of the disc.

Preparing the Platen Press: Makeready for a Printing Job

There are several steps to be followed in setting up and operating the platen press:

1. *Oil the press.* There are a number of oil holes located on the press. A little oil should be dropped into each of these before every job. Follow the instructions in the press manufacturer's operating manual. Do not oil too heavily. Wipe up excess oil with a clean cloth.

2. *Ink the press.* Check the ink rollers and ink disc to be sure they are clean and dry. Place a very small quantity of ink on the lower left side of the ink disc (Fig. 8-3). Start the press and let it run at a moderate speed until the ink is evenly distributed over the ink disc and rollers. Remember that it is easier to add ink if too little is applied at first than to remove it later. Do not ink the press too heavily. Always apply ink before the chase is placed in the press. To add ink during the run, put a very

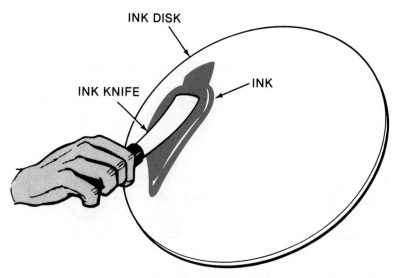

Figure 8-3. *Step 2. Ink the press.*

small quantity at a time on the lower left side of the ink disc.

3. *Insert the chase.* Turn the flywheel to run the rollers down to their lowest position. Place the chase in the bed of the press so that it rests on the supporting ledges, called *lugs* (Fig. 8-4). The quoins should be at the top and right sides of the chase.

4. *Adjust grippers.* Sight across the grippers and see if they will safely clear the type. If not, loosen the bolts and move the grippers to the outside edges of the platen. They may then be set in proper position after the press is set up.

5. *Prepare the tympan.* The platen is covered with a *drawsheet* and *packing.* Together, these are called the *tympan* (Fig. 8-5). A complete tympan generally consists of one or two sheets of pressboard and three or four sheets of book paper. The pressboard and book paper are held under the drawsheet. The packing should be slightly smaller in width than the platen. A piece of tympan paper is used to hold the packing on the platen. The tympan paper should be nearly as

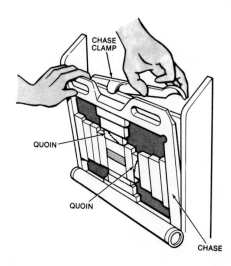

Figure 8-4. *Step 3. Insert the chase.*

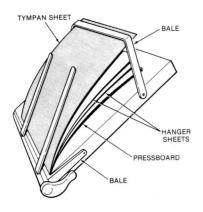

Figure 8-5. *Step 5. Prepare the tympan.*

wide as the platen. It must be long enough to fit under the *bales* located at the top and bottom of the platen. The tympan acts as a cushion against the paper being printed. The paper can thus be pressed firmly and safely against the type. Be sure that the drawsheet is uniformly tight and that the tympan is flat and firm.

6. *Take a trial impression.* After the tympan is prepared, take a trial impression on the tympan. Pull the throw-off lever to the *on* position (toward you). Turn the press over by hand by pushing the flywheel away from you. After printing on the drawsheet, push the throw-off lever to the *off* position. Be sure to return the press to its neutral position with the ink rollers at the bottom.

7. *Locate the paper.* The faint image on the tympan acts as a guide for locating the paper. Using a line gauge, measure and mark the desired margin requirements at the *bottom* (top of the sheet to be printed) and *left* of the impression. Draw guidelines parallel to the type at these two margin locations.

8. *Locate the gauge pins.* The *gauge pins* are small pin-like metal guides used to hold the paper in position on the tympan during printing. Three gauge pins are installed—two at the bottom (top of the sheet to be printed) and one at the left (Fig. 8-6). The gauge pins are usually positioned 1 inch in from the ends of the sheet on the bottom guidelines. The gauge pin on the left guideline is positioned about halfway up from the bottom guidelines.

   Position a piece of paper against the gauge pins. Take a trial impression by pulling the throw-off lever to *on* and turning the press over by hand. After printing on the paper, push the throw-off lever to *off* and return the press to its neutral position.

Remove the printed sheet and check it for proper margins and alignment. Use a line gauge for this measurement. It may be necessary to adjust the gauge pins slightly to obtain the desired position.

9. *Adjust the packing.* Examine the last printed sheet. The image should be sharp and clear. The back of the sheet should not appear embossed (punched). Add or remove packing sheets to gain uniform image impression.

10. *Adjust the ink.* If the image appears light, it is necessary to add more ink. Add a small quantity of ink to the lower left corner of the ink disc. Start the press and allow the ink to distribute evenly. Take an impression and check the ink coverage by lightly rubbing a finger over the printed image. The image will smear if there is too much ink. If the ink is too heavy, remove some from the ink disc with a clean cloth and a little solvent.

11. *Set the gauge pins.* Take a final trial impression. Check margins and print quality carefully. Set the gauge pins by pressing the sharp front toes

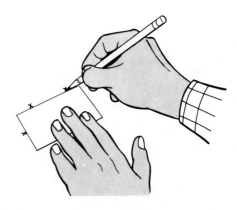

Figure 8-6. *Step 8. Locate the gauge pins.*

Check Your Knowledge (True or False)

1. Paper is fed into a platen press one sheet at a time.

2. The first step in makeready for a platen press is to ink the press.

3. A tympan consists of a drawsheet and packing.

4. In taking a trial impression, a platen press operator uses the flywheel and the throw-off lever.

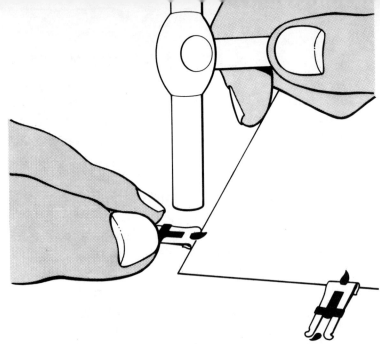

Figure 8-7. *Step 11. Set the gauge pins.*

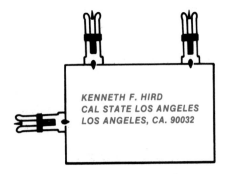

KENNETH F. HIRD
CAL STATE LOS ANGELES
LOS ANGELES, CA. 90032

Figure 8-8. *Step 12. Position the gripper and gripper fingers.*

into the tympan (Fig. 8-7). A small drop of sealing wax can be placed at the back of each gauge pin to hold it firmly.

12. *Position the gripper and gripper fingers* (Fig. 8-8).

13. *Set the counter to zero,* ready for printing an impression.

Feeding the Platen Press: Strictly a Hand Operation

A stack of paper to be printed is placed on the feed board and "fanned out" like a deck of playing cards. The edges of the sheets project slightly over one another. This separates the sheets and makes it easy to pick them up one at a time.

The operator picks up the sheets with the right hand. A single sheet is fed down to the gauge pins with a swinging motion. The sheet is fed to the *lower* gauge pins first and then slid into exact position against the *left* gauge pin (Fig. 8-9).

As the sheet is printed, it is removed from the tympan with the left hand. As each sheet is removed, it is placed on the delivery board. Sheets are stacked in small piles. Freshly printed sheets can become

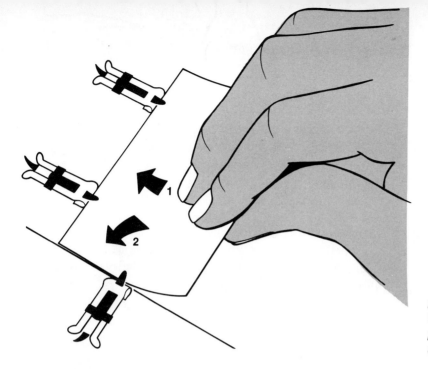

Figure 8-9. *In feeding the platen press, the sheet is first positioned against the lower gauge pins. It is then slid into position against the left gauge pin.*

setoff if they are stacked too high. *Setoff* means that ink from one sheet is transferred to the bottom side of another sheet. Printed sheets should be spread out on a drying rack in very thin piles until the ink is completely dry. Care also should be taken not to touch the freshly printed images.

Washing the Platen Press: Necessary After Each Run

The ink must be removed from the platen press (and any other kind of press) after each run. Ink must not be allowed to dry on the ink disc and rollers. The procedure outlined below is recommended when washing a platen press:

1. Remove the chase before washing the press. Place the chase on the stone and wash the typeform with a clean cloth and solvent. Wash the furniture and chase to remove all traces of fresh ink.

2. Remove the tympan and packing from the platen. Close the bales. Put the gauge pins in their proper storage area.

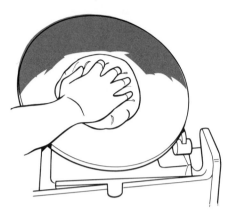

Figure 8-10. *Step 3. Using a small quantity of solvent on a clean cloth, stand at the left side of the press and begin washing off the ink disc.*

3. Take a clean cloth and drop a small quantity of solvent on it. Stand at the left side of the press (alongside the flywheel) and begin by washing off the ink disc (Fig. 8-10). CAUTION: Do not place solvent cans or cloths on the feed board or delivery board.

4. Use your left hand to turn the flywheel until the rollers are on the ink disc. Move the rollers over the ink disc, wiping them as they roll upward (Fig. 8-11). Use a clean portion of the cloth and continue the operation as the rollers descend from the ink disc. Finish cleaning each roller as it turns free of the ink disc. Then wipe off the ink disc again with a fresh part of the cloth. Repeat this operation with another clean cloth and some solvent, and the press will be thoroughly clean.

5. Wipe the bed of the press with a clean cloth and some solvent. The bed must be kept clean at all

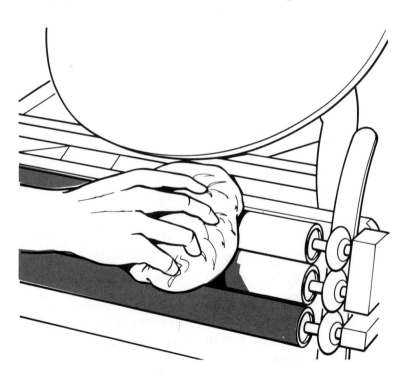

Figure 8-11. *Step 4. Move the rollers over the ink disc, wiping them as they roll upward.*

SAFETY TIPS

The following cautions should always be observed when working around a platen press:

- **If a sheet misses the gauge pins or does not touch the side gauge pin, do not reach after it. This is dangerous. Allow the press to open again, and then make the needed adjustment.**

- **If a sheet falls through the press, let it go until the press has been stopped. Never reach into the press after the platen begins to close for the impression.**

- **Do not leave a press unattended while it is running.**

- **Only one person should operate a press at a time.**

- **When working with solvent, place all solvent-soaked cloths in a fireproof**

times, since a true impression depends upon the condition of this surface.

6. Be sure to leave the press with the rollers at the bottom. Flat spots will develop on the rollers if they are left on the ink disc.

7. Clean the type and the ink knife.

FLAT-BED CYLINDER PRESS: PRINTING BY ROLLING CONTACT

The flat-bed cylinder press operates with the type form held in a large flat bed of the press (Fig. 8-12). The bed moves backward and forward on a track beneath an impression cylinder. Sheets of paper are fed in at the top and are carried around the cylinder. Each sheet receives its impression by a rolling contact

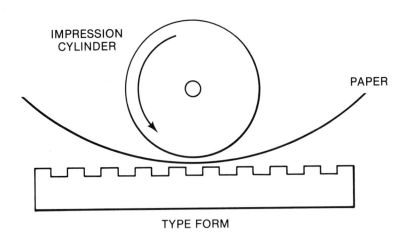

IMPRESSION
CYLINDER

PAPER

TYPE FORM

Figure 8-12. *On a flat-bed cylinder press, the cylinder, as it turns, presses the paper against the type form. The bed containing the type form moves back and forth on a track beneath the cylinder.*

with the type. Only a small area of the cylinder actually touches the type at one time.

Most cylinder presses have a two-revolution design. This means that the cylinder prints while it is making one revolution. Then the cylinder is raised during the second revolution to allow the type to make its return trip on the flat bed. Inking rollers ink the type during its return trip. The printed sheets are delivered to the front of the press.

THE ROTARY PRESS: FOR THE BIG JOBS

The rotary press uses an impression cylinder to press the paper against a printing plate cylinder (Fig. 8-13). The printing plates for a rotary press are curved to fit the shape of the printing cylinder.

Most rotary presses print on both sides of the paper in a single run through the press. In this case the paper passes between two curved printing plates. As explained in the chapter on offset printing, this type of press is called a *perfector*.

Rotary presses generally print from a roll of paper and are known as *web-fed*. The term *web* describes any continuous roll of paper.

Presses that print from single sheets of paper are known as *sheet-fed*.

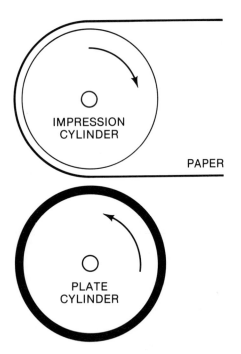

IMPRESSION
CYLINDER

PAPER

PLATE
CYLINDER

Figure 8-13. *On a rotary press, an impression cylinder presses the paper against a printing plate cylinder. Most rotary presses are web-fed.*

MIXING TECHNOLOGIES:
COLD TYPE AND LETTERPRESS

As phototypesetting replaced hot-metal composition, printers with letterpress equipment were faced with problems. Large presses are very expensive. For example, a daily newspaper in a large city has several million dollars invested in its presses. Through the years, most newspapers installed rotary letterpress units. This led to a complex situation: Newspapers could save money and improve service by changing from hot-metal composition to computerized photo-typesetting. But many newspapers did not want to discard their rotary letterpress printing equipment. Thus, methods were developed for combining photo-typesetting and letterpress printing.

In a modern newspaper, reporters and editors work at machines linked into computer systems. The reporters actually write their stories on video screen units connected to computers. A reporter's story can

Learning Activities

1. Visit a letterpress printing firm or newspaper, if possible. Ask to see the press or presses in operation. Look at how the paper and the impression carrier are brought together and determine whether it is a platen press, a flat-bed cylinder press, or a rotary press.

2. While visiting a letterpress printing firm or the print shop in your school, ask to see how type is locked into a chase. Then ask to see a chase in position on the press. Note how ink and paper are applied to the form to create printing impressions.

Vocabulary Checklist

1. platen press
2. flat-bed cylinder press
3. rotary press
4. throw-off lever
5. feed board
6. flywheel
7. grippers
8. ink roller
9. ink disc
10. tympan
11. drawsheet
12. packing
13. bales
14. gauge pins
15. web
16. sheet-fed

be recalled from the computer by an editor. Any needed changes can be made and headlines written by the editor. Then the story is released for typesetting. Phototypesetting is controlled automatically by the computer.

Planographic (flat) images result. But letterpress printing requires relief type and plates. To use phototypesetting originals on letterpress printing equipment, relief carriers are created. The most popular technique developed for newspapers was an electronic system that produces flexographic carriers. As you will remember, flexography is a relief printing method that uses rubber carriers. Special machines convert paste-up mechanicals to flexographic plates. These rubber plates are then wrapped around cylinders of rotary letterpress units. This approach, in effect, mixes the technologies of offset and relief printing.

Another type of relief printing plate currently being used by newspaper and magazine publishers is made of photosensitive polymer. A film negative is made from the page paste-up. The negative is then used to expose a light-sensitive photopolymer plate. Etching of the plate results in relief images.

Unit Review

- Letterpress printing is in a decline, giving way to the more modern photo-offset method. Many daily newspapers have made large investments in modern letterpress presses, however. Many dailies, therefore, now use a combination of advanced photocomposition and letterpress printing.

- Most letterpress printing operations use a single engraving (plate) for a full page of images. These plates may be flat for cylinder presses, or curved for rotary and web-fed presses.

- Types of letterpress plates include: line engravings, halftone engravings, stereotypes, electrotypes, and simple linoleum blocks.

- The rubber stamp is a simple but good example of a letterpress printing plate.

- There are three types of letterpress printing presses: platen, flat-bed cylinder, and rotary. The basic printing operation is the same for all three.

- Rotary presses generally print from a roll of paper and are known as web-fed. Most rotary presses also print on both sides of the paper on a single run. This is called a perfector press. Presses that print from single sheets of paper are known as sheet-fed.

Review Questions

1. In letterpress platemaking, molten metal is poured into a mold. What is this mold called?

2. Which type of letterpress printing press operates like a clam shell opening and closing?

3. If a press prints from a continuous roll of paper, what type of press is it?

9 GRAVURE PRINTING

THE GRAVURE PRINTING PROCESS: THE THIRD METHOD FOR BIG JOBS

The printing process known as *gravure* is the exact opposite of letterpress (Fig. 9-1). It is also referred to as *intaglio* (pronounced in-tal' yo), which means to cut or engrave. The images are etched (eaten away) into the metal plate image carrier. The etched images look like tiny cup-shaped cavities below the surface of the plate. Plates are generally made of copper and are either flat or curved, depending on the type of press to be used.

On a gravure printing press, ink is applied to the entire plate surface. The ink fills the image cavities. The type of ink used is very thin. A flexible rubber scraper, called a *doctor blade,* removes all ink from the plate surface—leaving ink in the image cavities. Pressure from the plate against the paper transfers ink from the image cavities to the paper.

One important characteristic of gravure concerns the printed images. The original camera copy must be photographed through a fine mesh screen. As a result, the type and illustrations contain a series of tiny dots. The outlines of the type, seen under magnification, appear ragged.

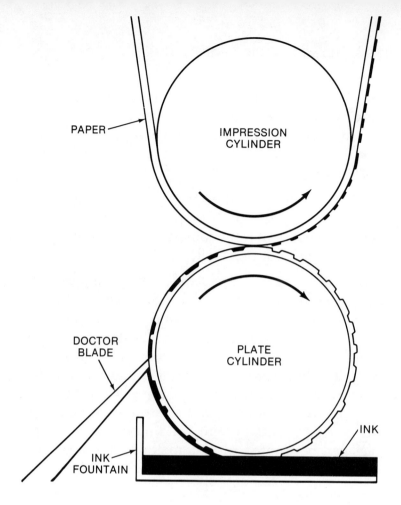

Figure 9-1. *Diagram shows how ink is transferred from image cavities in printing plate to paper in gravure printing. Doctor blade removes ink from the surface of the plate. Gravure is the exact opposite of letterpress.*

Rotogravure

Rotogravure applies to gravure presses that use rounded plate cylinders rather than flat plates. Rotogravure presses are usually web fed, meaning they print from a roll of paper. This method is many times faster than printing from single sheets. Rotogravure presses are not only fast, but they produce large quantities of color-printed images of high quality. This is why rotogravure has been used for many years as the printing method for Sunday newspaper magazine supplements.

GRAVURE PLATES: ENGRAVINGS AND ETCHINGS

Gravure plates are divided into *engravings* and *etchings.* Engravings are prepared by cutting an image into

Figure 9-2. *This is a sample of drypoint engraving.*

metal or plastic. This is generally done by hand with engraving tools. Etchings are prepared by an acid process that etches or cuts into the metal plate.

Drypoint Engraving

Drypoint engraving is the least expensive and simplest form of gravure printing (Fig. 9-2). Prints made by this process generally consist of lines only. Solid image areas are not practical.

A clean, scratch-free piece of plastic about 0.05 inch (1.4 mm) thick is needed for the plate. A *stylus* is used to cut the lines that will print. The stylus makes a groove, or furrow, in the plastic. The design grooves are cut so that a burr is made on one side of the groove. The burrs are cutaway ridges that act to retain the ink in the grooves during printing. However, the burrs wear out rapidly from the extreme pressure applied during printing. Only a limited number of copies can be printed by this method. If a very fine line is desired, the burr is removed.

Preparation of a drypoint engraving involves a series of operations:

1. A suitable design consisting of fine lines is drawn or traced full size on paper.

2. With a piece of carbon paper placed under the drawing, carbon side up, the design is traced.

3. The reversed design is taped behind a piece of transparent plastic. The plastic should be slightly larger than the design.

4. A stylus is used to cut the lines into the surface of the plastic. The deeper the line is cut, the darker the image will print. A twisting wrist action produces a burr on one side of the line, making a darker image. A shallow line without the burr

will print lighter. Shadow areas can be made by crosshatching the lines.

5. When the design has been cut, the drypoint plate is printed on an etching press.

COPPER GRAVURE PLATES: HOW THE PROCESS WORKS

The image carrier for most gravure printing is an etched metal cylinder coated with copper. (Most gravure printing is done on rotary web-fed presses as opposed to flat-bed cylinder presses.) The copy preparation steps leading up to the platemaking process in gravure printing are the same as for offset printing. In other words, the same steps outlined in Unit 4 apply here, right up to the process camera stage. It is in the processing of paste-up copy that the differences begin.

In gravure printing, the original paste-up copy is photographed on a graphic arts process camera

Learning Activities

1. Pick up a copy of the color magazine supplement in your Sunday newspaper. Obtain a magnifier. View the type copy through the magnifier. Do the edges have a slightly ragged appearance? Are the photographs more clearly reproduced than in the other sections of the newspaper?

2. Obtain a piece of clear plastic about 0.05 inch (1.4 mm) thick and a stylus cutting tool. Prepare a suitable line drawing. Transfer the design to the plastic and cut the lines into the plastic following the directions outlined in this unit. Make printed copies on an etching press or similar press.

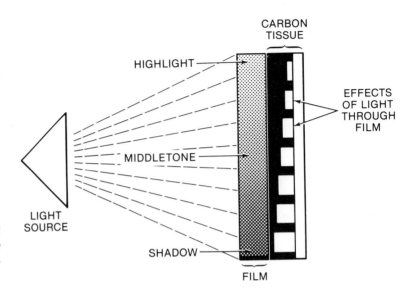

Figure 9-3. *When light strikes the carbon tissue, the tissue becomes hardened and insoluble to etching solution bath.*

through a gravure screen. A *film positive* is then made from the negative. The positive is exposed on sensitized *carbon tissue*. All copy, including type, is screened for gravure platemaking. The carbon tissue consists of a gelatin layer on a paper base. The gelatin becomes sensitive to light when treated chemically, and it receives the image during exposure (Fig. 9-3).

The gelatin coating of the exposed carbon tissue is placed in *direct contact* with the copper-plated cylinder. Hot water is used to develop the tissue, which melts and *washes away* the unhardened gelatin areas. The areas that were exposed to light *remain* on the plate surface and act as an acid resist. The paper backing is removed, and the gelatin is allowed to harden. The cylinder is then placed in an *etching bath*.

The etching bath *dissolves* all the areas of bare copper to form the printing image. All the areas *protected* by the gelatin acid resist are unaffected by the etching bath. The *depth* of the image is controlled by etching time: The longer the plate is left in the acid, the deeper the inking cavities will be.

Once etched, the cylinder is given a thorough washing in water. This removes all remaining etching solution, including the acid resist. The cylinder is given a thorough examination and made ready for printing.

THE GRAVURE PRINTING OPERATION: HOW AN ENGRAVING AND ETCHING PRESS WORKS

There are two types of gravure presses. The first type is a small hand-operated *engraving and etching press*. It is suitable for small quantities of printing from a plate that is usually cut by hand methods.

The second type of press is a *rotary web-fed*. Copper plates are used on web-fed gravure presses.

The engraving and etching press is used to print the drypoint engravings and metal etchings described earlier in this chapter. The press is hand-operated. This makes the printing process slow.

Check Your Knowledge (True or False)

1. Rotogravure presses are usually web-fed.

2. Drypoint engravings are made from plastic.

3. Gravure printing differs from offset printing in that a process camera is not used in gravure.

The printing process requires that the engraved plate be inked and placed on the bed of the press. Excess ink is removed from the surface of the plate. The plate is then covered with a damp sheet of paper. A felt blanket is placed over the sheet of paper. The impression roller of the press causes the ink to be transferred to the paper.

The following steps describe a typical printing operation on an engraving and etching press: (Fig. 9-4):

1. Paper is prepared in advance of printing. Soft, uncoated paper is used. The paper should be about two inches larger than the design on all four sides. The sheets are dipped in a container of

Figure 9-4. *Side view shows paper and plate going through an engraving and etching press.*

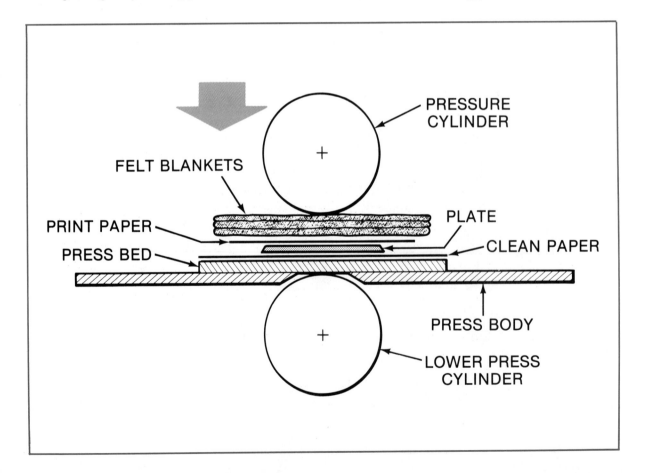

water. They are immediately stacked, alternating one wet sheet with one dry sheet. The sheets can be left stacked overnight between two pieces of heavy glass.

2. Black letterpress ink is prepared for printing. A few drops of linseed oil are added to the ink on a mixing tray. The ingredients are mixed thoroughly with an *ink knife*. The ink knife is similar to a putty knife.

3. Ink is applied to the plate with a piece of soft cloth. The ink must be forced into the engraved lines. A clean cloth is then used to wipe the ink from the entire plate surface, leaving the image areas filled. The plate is then cleaned with a cloth once again, using the heel of the hand for pressure.

4. A piece of dampened paper is placed over the plate. The plate is placed on the bed of the etching press. A felt blanket is placed over the paper. The press impression pressure is adjusted and the bed is run under the impression cylinder.

5. The blanket is removed, and the printed sheet is placed between two white blotters until dry. The process is repeated for additional copies.

6. The plate is cleaned with a mild solvent to remove all ink. Lacquer thinner should not be used, since it may melt parts of the plastic.

ROTOGRAVURE WEB-FED PRESSES: HIGH-SPEED PRINTING CAPACITY

Rotogravure printing is particularly useful for high-quality color reproduction involving very large press runs (Fig. 9-5). It is also a high-speed printing process. Finally, the copper plates can withstand very long press runs. This eliminates the need to stop the presses to change plates.

Figure 9-5. *Rotogravure printing is desirable for high-quality color reproduction involving very long press runs. Press speed and long life of copper plates more than compensate for the time-consuming plate-making process. (Motter Printing Press Co.)*

Vocabulary Checklist

1. gravure
2. rotogravure
3. intaglio
4. doctor blade
5. engravings
6. etchings
7. drypoint engraving
8. stylus
9. burr
10. film positive
11. carbon tissue
12. gravure screen
13. etching bath
14. engraving and etching press
15. rotary web-fed press
16. ink knife
17. gravure cylinder
18. impression cylinder
19. ink pan

The platemaking process is more time-consuming than that for offset or letterpress printing. This disadvantage is more than compensated for on very long press runs by rotogravure's press speed.

The parts of a gravure rotary web-fed press include four major units:

Gravure cylinder. This is the cylinder on which the images to be printed are etched.

Impression cylinder. This cylinder brings the roll of paper into contact with the gravure cylinder.

Doctor blade. This flexible blade removes excess ink from the surface of the gravure cylinder.

Ink pan or fountain. It is from the pan or fountain that the gravure cylinder picks up a coating of the thin ink used in gravure printing.

- Gravure printing is the exact opposite of letterpress. It is referred to as intaglio, meaning to cut or engrave. The images are engraved (cut) or etched (eaten away) into the metal plate.

- On a gravure plate, ink is applied to the entire surface. It is then wiped off by a doctor blade, which leaves ink in the etched image cavities.

- In gravure printing, original camera copy must be photographed through a fine mesh screen called a gravure screen.

- Rotogravure refers to gravure presses that use rounded plate cylinders rather than flat plates. They are usually of the web-fed type.

- There are two basic types of gravure plates: engravings and etchings. Engravings are prepared by cutting images into metal or plastic. Etchings are made through an acid process that etches or cuts into a metal plate.

- Drypoint engraving is the simplest and least expensive form of gravure printing. This method is used for line reproduction only, since solid image areas are not practical.

- The image carrier for most gravure printing is an etched metal cylinder coated with copper.

- Copy preparation for gravure printing is the same as that for offset lithography. The processes become different when paste-up copy is ready to be photographed by the graphic arts process camera.

- There are two types of gravure presses. The engraving and etching press is a small, hand-

Unit Review

168

operated press. The other type of press is the rotary web-fed. Copper plates are used on web-fed gravure presses.

- There are four major units in a gravure rotary web-fed press: the gravure cylinder, the impression cylinder, the doctor blade, and the ink pan or fountain.

Review Questions

1. What is the name of the flexible rubber blade that removes ink from the surface of a gravure plate?

2. Name the simplest form of gravure printing.

3. What is a small, hand-operated gravure press called?

4. What is the proper name for a gravure press that prints from a roll of paper?

5. On a rotogravure press, what is the cylinder called that brings the paper into contact with the gravure cylinder?

SCREEN PRINTING 10

THE SCREEN PROCESS: HOW IT WORKS

The printing method known as *screen process* uses a porous (open) *stencil* as its image carrier. The stencil material is either hand-cut or photographically prepared. The stencil contains the desired design or printing message.

The stencil material is adhered (attached) to the bottom side of a *screen mesh*. The screen mesh material can be silk, nylon, dacron, organdy, or stainless steel. The mesh is stretched and mounted on a wooden or metal frame called a screen frame.

Printing is done on paper or other material placed under the screen. Ink is poured into the frame and forced through the open areas of the stencil and mesh. A squeegee is used for this purpose. A *squeegee* is a device with a flexible rubber blade attached to a handle. When a squeegee is moved along a surface, ink is forced to flow in front of the rubber blade. When the surface is a porous screen, some of the ink is forced through the screen (Fig. 10-1).

The screen process method is versatile. It is capable of applying the heaviest film of ink when compared with the other processes. Screen printing can be done on many types of materials and surfaces. These

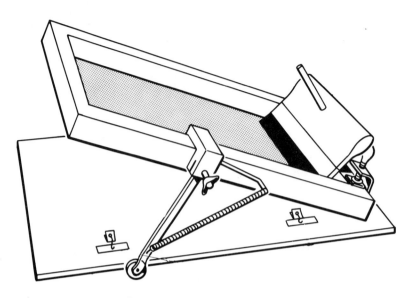

Figure 10-1. *Screen printing uses a porous (open) stencil as its image carrier. The stencil is attached to the bottom of a screen mesh, which is stretched and mounted on a frame. Printing is done on paper or other material placed beneath the screen.*

include paper, glass, wood, metal, plastic, fabric, wallpaper, and cork. Almost any size, shape, and design can be printed (Fig. 10-2).

For many years, the production speed of screen process printing was limited by press designs and ink drying times. Inserting materials for printing was slow. Use of a squeegee was also slow. New technology, however, has brought automatic presses and faster-drying inks. Today, automatic screen process units can print up to 5,500 copies per hour.

HAND-CUT PAPER STENCILS: FOR SHORT PRESS RUNS

Hand-cut paper stencils are used for very short screen printing runs. The design should consist of a simple silhouette. Designs that have open areas such as in the letters P and Q should be avoided.

Ordinary brown heavy-weight kraft paper can be used for the stencil. The stencil paper is cut to fit the inside dimensions of the frame. The design is taped in

Figure 10-2. *Screen process can be used to print on a wide variety of surfaces, such as glass. (Atlas Silk Screen Supply)*

a fixed position on a light table. The piece of kraft paper is then taped over the design. A sharp stencil knife is used to cut out the design areas on the kraft paper that are to print (Fig. 10-3).

Adhering a Paper Stencil

Four steps are followed in adhering a paper stencil to a screen:

1. The cut stencil is positioned on the bottom of a clean printing frame (Fig. 10-4).
2. Several spots of glue (or rubber cement) are applied on the screen mesh around the entire stencil area (Fig. 10-5). The glue serves to hold the stencil temporarily.

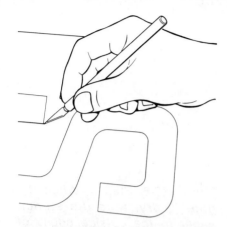

Figure 10-3. *The design is cut into the paper stencil with a sharp knife. The design is drawn to actual size in the desired location as it will appear on the printed sheet.*

Figure 10-4. *Step 1. Position the cut stencil on the bottom of a clean printing frame.*

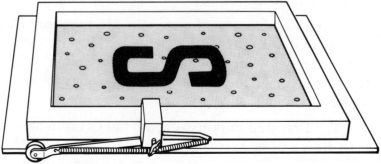

Figure 10-5. *Step 2. Apply several spots of glue (or rubber cement) to the screen mesh around the entire stencil area.*

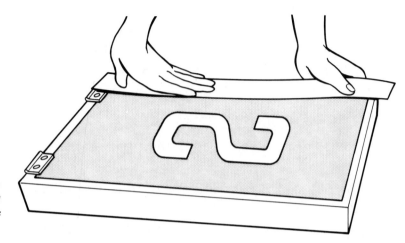

Figure 10-6. *Step 3. When the glue is dry, tape the stencil paper to the outside edges of the frame with kraft tape.*

3. When the glue is dry, the stencil paper is taped to the outside edges of the frame with kraft tape (Fig. 10-6).

4. The top four edges and inside of the frame are taped.

HAND-CUT FILM STENCILS: TWO TYPES, SIMILAR PREPARATION

There are two kinds of hand-cut film for screen process printing:

1. Aqua film   2. Lacquer film.

Aqua film is adhered to the screen mesh with *water*. It requires the use of a *lacquer-base ink*.

Lacquer film is adhered to the screen mesh with *lacquer thinner*. It requires a *water-soluble ink*.

Aqua and lacquer film stencils are prepared in a similar manner. These films have two layers. One is a thin layer of water-soluble or lacquer gelatin called the *film* layer or the *emulsion*. This layer is joined to a plastic backing sheet.

The first step in preparing a hand-cut film stencil is to draw a design. This may consist of artwork or let-

ORIGINAL   FILM

Figure 10-7. *Film is taped to the original design with the gelatin side up.*

tering. The drawing is taped to a light table or other smooth, hard surface. A piece of stencil film is cut 3 inches (75.6 mm) wider than the size of the drawing on all four sides. With the emulsion side up, the film is taped over the center of the drawing (Fig. 10-7).

A sharp knife is then used to cut the image, *without cutting through the backing sheet* (Fig. 10-8). The backing sheet should not be cut because the film edges become rounded. A groove is formed when the backing is cut. The adhering liquid collects in the groove. The film can dissolve when this happens. This causes a fuzzy image outline. A backing sheet that has been indented or cut by the knife will not adhere to the screen mesh.

The film is removed from the image areas that are to be printed (Fig. 10-9). A knife is used to lift a corner of the film to be removed. The unwanted film is peeled from the backing sheet. A small piece of masking tape can be used to assist in lifting the unwanted film.

The film emulsion must be kept clean and dry while cutting. Any kind of moisture will quickly dissolve aqua film. A piece of clean white paper should be placed between the film and the operator's hand during the cutting operation. This keeps moisture from the operator's skin away from the film.

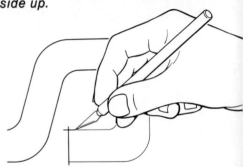

Figure 10-8. *A sharp knife is used to cut through the gelatin coating. Light pressure is required on the stencil knife to avoid cutting the backing.*

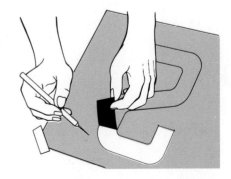

Figure 10-9. *The emulsion is removed from image areas, using a knife to lift a corner of the area to be removed.*

Figure 10-10. *A clean cloth is used to adhere the film to the bottom of the screen with the adhering liquid. The liquid may be water or lacquer thinner, depending on the type of film used.*

Water-soluble film is adhered to the bottom of the screen with *water*. Lacquer film is adhered with *lacquer thinner* (Fig. 10-10). In either case, the screen should be cleaned thoroughly with the proper solvent to remove any hardened ink. A new screen should also be washed to remove the protective coating of *sizing*. (Sizing is a glue-like material used to give form and stiffness to fabrics.) The film will not adhere until all sizing is removed. A mild detergent and warm water are used to remove the sizing. The screen is then rinsed with hot water and allowed to dry.

Adhering an Aqua Film Stencil

The following steps are recommended in adhering an aqua film stencil to a screen mesh:

1. Obtain two small, clean pieces of cloth. Wet one cloth with water.

2. Wet the entire screen with water on both sides of the mesh.

3. Working on a flat table surface, place the stencil *emulsion side up* on top of several sheets of clean

SAFETY TIPS

- **Stencil knives are extremely sharp and should be handled with care. Never place fingers or hand in the path of the knife blade. Store the knife safely when not in use.**

- **Solvents used in screen printing are highly volatile and contain toxic fumes. Be sure the work area is well ventilated. Keep solvent-soaked cloths in an approved safety container.**

newsprint. The newsprint should be *slightly smaller* than the inside dimensions of the screen mesh.

4. Position the screen frame over the stencil. Bring the screen frame down on top of the stencil. The *emulsion side* of the stencil will be against the *bottom of the screen.*

5. Beginning at the upper left corner of the stencil, press the dampened cloth against the top side of the stencil. Work from top to bottom, making about three 1-inch-wide swaths. Use the dry cloth immediately to pat the stencil dry. Continue this procedure until the entire stencil is adhered. A properly adhered stencil appears dark.

6. Lift the screen frame and turn it over. Use the dry cloth to wipe the backing sheet of the stencil.

7. Turn the screen frame over again and blot up excess moisture with a sheet of clean newsprint.

8. Dry the film with an electric fan, or allow the stencil to dry overnight.

9. Once the stencil is completely dry, peel off the backing sheet.

Adhering a Lacquer Film Stencil

Similar procedures are followed in adhering a lacquer film stencil to a screen mesh:

1. Obtain a container of lacquer thinner and two small pieces of clean cloth. Wet one cloth with lacquer thinner.

2. Working on a flat table surface, place the stencil *emulsion side up* on several sheets of clean newsprint.

3. Position the screen frame over the stencil. Bring the screen frame down on top of the stencil. The *emulsion side* of the stencil will be against the *bottom of the screen.*

4. Beginning at the upper left corner of the stencil, press the dampened cloth against the top side of the stencil. Adhere only a small portion of the stencil at a time. Work quickly, since the lacquer thinner evaporates rapidly. As the thinner is applied in small sections, use the dry cloth to pat the section dry. A properly adhered stencil appears dark.

5. Continue this procedure until the entire stencil is adhered.

6. Dry the adhered stencil. Use an electric fan or allow the stencil to dry overnight.

7. Once the stencil is completely dry, peel off the backing sheet.

PAPER AND LIQUID MASKS: KEEPING NONPRINTING AREAS CLEAR

To prevent the flow of ink in unwanted (nonprinting) areas of the screen, a mask must be prepared. A *mask* is something that covers an unwanted or nonimage area of the screen mesh. Two methods are generally

Check Your Knowledge (True or False)

1. In screen printing, a squeegee is used to force ink through the screen.

2. Aqua film requires a water-soluble ink.

3. Water-soluble film is adhered to the bottom of the screen with water.

4. The emulsion side of the stencil rests against the bottom of the screen.

used to mask the nonprinting areas of the screen. These are:

1. Paper masks   2. Liquid masks.

Paper masks are prepared in the following manner:

1. A piece of kraft paper is cut to the same size as the outline of the cords on the bottom of the frame. These cords hold the screen material in place.

2. The kraft paper is placed on the bottom of the frame over a light table. The area to be cut out is marked. The outline should be about 1/2 inch (12.7 mm) away from the design on all edges (Fig. 10-11).

Figure 10-11. *Step 2. Place the kraft paper on the bottom of the frame over a light table. Mark the area to be cut out.*

Figure 10-12. *Step 4. Attach the paper to the screen with kraft tape.*

3. The kraft paper is placed on a piece of cardboard on the light table. The marked area is cut out with a knife.

4. Kraft tape is used to attach the paper to the screen (Fig. 10-12). The top edges and inside edges are taped to protect them from ink. In addition, the four inside edges of the screen mesh are covered with kraft tape. The tape is extended outward about 1½ inches (38.1 mm).

Liquid masks are made for both aqua and lacquer films. *Water mask* should *not* be used with *water-base inks. Lacquer mask* should *not* be used with *lacquer-base inks.* Select the liquid mask suitable for the type of film stencil and ink being used.

Liquid mask can be applied to the nonprinting areas of the screen with a 1-inch (25.4 mm) brush (Fig. 10-13). Two thin coats are applied to the nonprinting areas of the screen mesh on the bottom of the frame. The first coat is allowed to dry before a second coat is applied.

Kraft tape can be used to protect the top edges and inside edges of the frame. The four inside edges of the frame are also covered with kraft tape. The tape is extended outward about 1½ inches (38.1 mm).

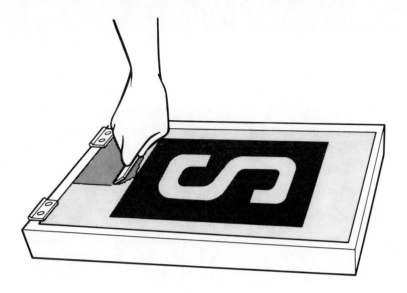

Figure 10-13. *Nonimage areas of the screen are coated with a water or lacquer mask.*

INDIRECT PHOTOGRAPHIC STENCILS: STARTING WITH A FILM POSITIVE

The indirect photographic stencil method requires a film positive of the image. A *film positive* is an image on photographic film. The image is positive because it is made from a negative. Often, a two-step process is needed to make a film positive. First, the original paste-up or artwork is photographed on a process camera. This produces a negative. The negative is then printed against another sheet of film to produce a film positive.

As an option, an *autopositive* film may be used. This is a film material that produces images that match the originals. Photographing a positive image produces positive film. Contact printing with a film negative produces another film negative.

Another method used to prepare a positive involves drawing on a piece of acetate or vellum. This requires black India ink. Transfer type can also be used.

With these procedures, any of the typesetting and composition methods covered in earlier units can be used. If a continuous tone photograph is to be reproduced, a halftone positive must be made.

The image areas of the film positive must be *opaque,* and the nonprinting areas must be *transparent.* A film negative image is not acceptable because the image area is transparent and the nonimage areas are opaque.

PHOTOGRAPHIC STENCILS: REPRODUCING FINE DETAIL

There are two methods of making stencils photographically. Both methods reproduce very fine detail, including halftones. The methods are called indirect and direct.

The *indirect method* uses a photographic positive to prepare the stencil. The stencil is then transferred to the screen fabric.

In the *direct method,* the stencil is exposed and processed on a light-sensitive (coated) screen. The indirect method is faster than the direct method.

Indirect stencil method. A piece of photographic stencil film is exposed, developed, and adhered to the

Learning Activities

1. If possible, visit a printing firm with screen printing facilities. Ask to see how a stencil is prepared and how it is adhered to the mesh screen. If possible, observe a printing operation.

2. Look in your kitchen cupboard. There should be numerous examples of screen printing. Metal cans such as spice tins, aluminum lids for home canning jars, and a variety of plastic wrappings are typical examples of screen printing. Bring some examples to show your class.

screen. There are several types of photographic stencil film. The film consists of a light-sensitive emulsion on a plastic backing. The film is light-sensitive but does not require complete darkness. It should be handled under subdued light, using special photographic safelights.

The photographic stencil can be exposed on a platemaker. The platemaker is equipped with a light source and a vacuum frame. The film positive and photographic stencil material are held in tight contact during the exposure.

Direct stencil method. As the name implies, direct photographic stencils are prepared directly on the screen fabric. The screen fabric is first coated with a light-sensitive emulsion. The emulsion is then exposed to a light source through a film positive (Fig. 10-14). The light passing through the clear areas of the film hardens the emulsion below. Where the film positive is opaque, the emulsion under these areas remains soft. After exposure, the areas of the stencil

Figure 10-14. *The screen fabric is coated with a light-sensitive emulsion. The emulsion is then exposed to a light source through the film positive.*

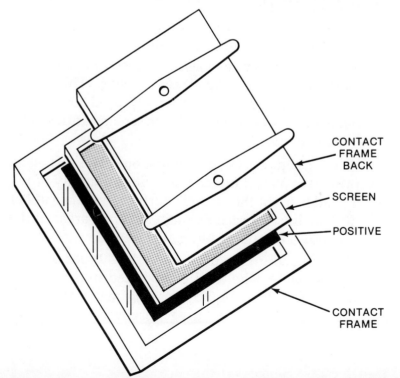

CONTACT FRAME BACK

SCREEN

POSITIVE

CONTACT FRAME

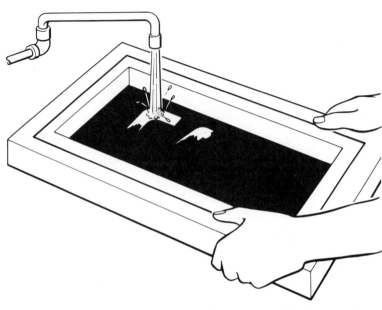

Figure 10-15. *The photographic direct stencil is developed by holding the frame with the stencil under running water.*

that remain soft are washed away with hot water. This forms the clear image area openings in the stencil (Fig. 10-15).

SCREEN PROCESS PRINTING: A SIMPLE METHOD

Screen process (porous) printing is a stenciling technique. A heavy film of ink is applied through a mesh screen in the form of a design. The *screen process* was formerly known as *silk screen printing.* This name originated because silk was widely used to support the stencil. In recent years, other screen fabrics have been developed.

The screen process is a simple one. The surface to be printed is placed under a stencil. A quantity of ink is moved across the stencil surface with a rubber blade. The ink is forced through the open areas of the stencil and onto the printing surface below.

The procedure for printing various types of stencils is the same. The kind of ink used must not dissolve the stencil or liquid masking material. Hand-operated screen presses are generally used for short

Figure 10-16. *Larger screen presses, such as this cylinder-type screen-printing press with automatic feed and delivery, are used for longer press runs.*

press runs. The screen printing industry uses power-operated screen presses (Fig. 10-16).

THE HAND-OPERATED SCREEN PRESS: ITS BASIC PARTS AND FUNCTION

The basic parts of a hand-operated screen press (Fig. 10-17) consist of:

1. Frame
2. Fabric
3. Base
4. Side kick
5. Squeegee.

Frame. The screen printing frame is generally made from wood. Soft pine is ideal for this purpose.

Fabric. Nylon, dacron, and stainless steel are materials used to make screen fabrics. Fabrics are manufactured with weaves of various sizes. These sizes are referred to as *mesh counts*. The mesh count indicates the number of openings per square inch of fabric. For example, a coarse mesh fabric would be 6XX. A closely woven fabric for fine detail printing

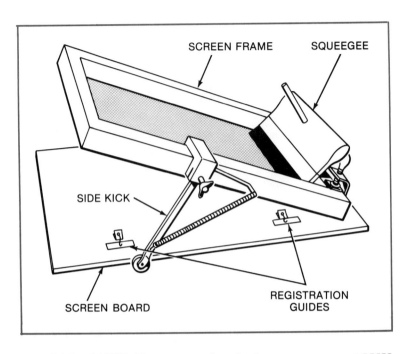

Figure 10-17. *This illustration shows the major parts of a hand-operated screen press.*

would be l8XX. For general printing purposes, 12XX mesh is used.

Base. The base provides a flat surface for the printing operation. The base is slightly larger than the screen frame.

Check Your Knowledge (True or False)

1. Water mask should never be used with water-base inks.

2. Image areas of a film positive must be transparent.

3. There are two methods of making stencils photographically.

4. Silk screen printing refers to a process that involves stencils made of silk material.

Side kick. The side kick is a device used to hold the frame up when sheets are being loaded onto the base and when printed sheets are being removed.

Squeegee. The squeegee is a rubber blade attached to a handle. It is used to force ink through the open areas of the stencil and mesh. The blade shape to be used is determined by the type of printing being done.

A *square-edged* blade is used for printing on flat surfaces.

A *square rounded-edge* blade is used for depositing extra-heavy ink.

A *single-sided bevel edged* blade is used to print on glass.

A *double-sided bevel-edged* (V-shaped) blade is used to print on uneven surfaces.

A *round-edged* blade is used to print on textiles.

A *double-sided bevel-edged* blade is used for printing on ceramics.

OPERATING A SCREEN PRESS: THE PRINTING PROCESS

The procedure used to print various types of stencils is the same. Before starting, the operator positions a screen with the stencil adhered to the screen mesh. The masking or block-out has been completed. The following steps are then followed in preparing the press and completing a production run:

1. The work area is covered with newspapers to protect the surface from ink and solvents.

2. The printing base is placed on the work surface. All tools and materials required for printing are placed on the work surface.

3. The screen frame is attached to the base. A side kick is attached to the frame.

4. A squeegee with a square-edged blade is selected. The blade should be slightly wider than the design to be printed.

5. A sheet of clear acetate is obtained. The acetate sheet should be about 2 inches (50.8 mm) wider on all four edges than the paper area to be printed. The acetate is taped to the surface of the base in the center of the image design area. One piece of masking tape about 1 inch (25.4 mm) long is used to secure the acetate sheet at the edge.

6. Using an ink knife, the operator places a quantity of the desired type and color of ink on the inside of the screen frame. Enough ink is deposited so that when it is pulled in front of the squeegee, it will cover the design completely. The ink should be the consistency of thick syrup. A thinner may be required to thin the ink.

7. The screen frame is lowered on the plastic sheet.

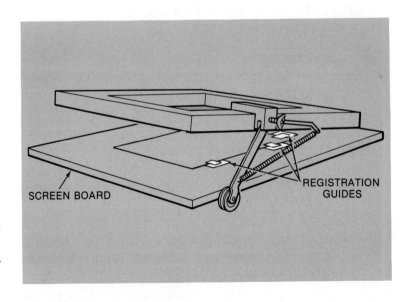

SCREEN BOARD

REGISTRATION GUIDES

Figure 10-18. *Step 12. Tape two registration guides on the long side of the paper being printed. Tape one guide on the short side.*

8. The squeegee is tilted at a 30-degree angle and placed behind the ink. Downward pressure is applied as the squeegee is pulled along the entire open area of the stencil.

9. The screen frame is carefully raised about 6 inches (150 mm) and the squeegee is returned to its starting point.

10. The squeegee is rested against the end of the frame. The frame is raised and supported with the side kick.

11. A piece of paper is positioned under the printed area of the clear acetate according to the location of the stencil image desired. The location is marked while the operator holds the paper firmly in position. The sheet of acetate is removed.

12. Two registration guides are taped on the long side of the paper being printed (Fig. 10-18). One guide is taped on the short side. (It is advisable to apply a small amount of spray adhesive to the base after the sheet is positioned. This will hold each sheet securely to the base. Otherwise, the sheets may stick to the underside of the frame during the printing operation.)

13. A sheet of paper is positioned against the registration guides.

14. The screen frame is lowered, and the squeegee is drawn across the screen. Ink is forced through the screen, printing the image (Fig. 10-19).

15. The printed copy is removed and placed on a screen printing drying rack, beginning at the *bottom shelf* (Fig. 10-20).

16. Another sheet of paper is positioned against the registration guides. The printing operation is repeated. More ink is added to the frame as needed.

RUBBER SQUEEGEE FORCES INK
THROUGH STENCIL AND MESH

Figure 10-19. *Step 14. Lower the screen frame and draw the squeegee across the screen.*

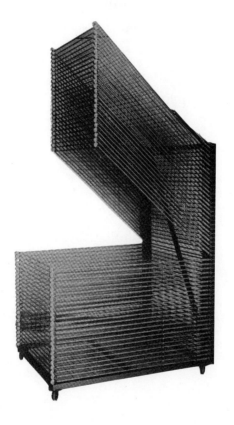

Figure 10-20. *Step 15. Remove the printed copy and place it on a screen printing drying rack, beginning at the bottom shelf.*

Vocabulary Checklist

1. stencil
2. screen mesh
3. squeegee
4. aqua film
5. lacquer film
6. emulsion
7. screen frame
8. sizing (fabric)
9. base
10. side kick
11. paper mask
12. liquid mask
13. indirect photographic stencil
14. film positive
15. autopositive
16. direct photographic stencil
17. screen process printing
18. mesh count
19. blockout

THE CLEANUP OPERATION

When the printing operation is complete, the screen, squeegee, ink knife and all other tools must be cleaned. If the stencil is to be used again for printing, only the ink is removed from the screen frame. In removing ink, water is used for water-base inks. Lacquer thinner is used for lacquer-base inks. Mineral spirits are used for oil-base inks. The screen is placed on newspapers with the mesh against the newspapers. The ink is removed from the screen with a small piece of cardboard. The ink knife should never be used for this purpose. It may damage the fabric.

Once the ink has been removed from the screen, the blockout (cut stencil) is dissolved. The following procedures are used for removing blockout from different types of screens.

Aqua film stencil. The screen is placed in a sink under warm running water. The stencil is thoroughly dissolved by rubbing it with the palm of the hand.

Lacquer film stencil. Several layers of newspapers are placed on a flat surface (Fig. 10-21). The screen is placed on the newspapers with the mesh against the newspapers. A quantity of lacquer thinner and a clean cloth are used to dissolve the stencil. The layers of newspapers are changed and the process repeated until the stencil is completely removed.

Photographic indirect stencil. The screen is placed in a sink under hot running water. A screen brush is used to dissolve the stencil completely.

Photographic direct stencil. A special solvent is required. (Refer to the film stencil manufacturer's recommendations.)

After the stencil is removed, the screen is checked by holding it up to the light. Clogged areas and dry ink

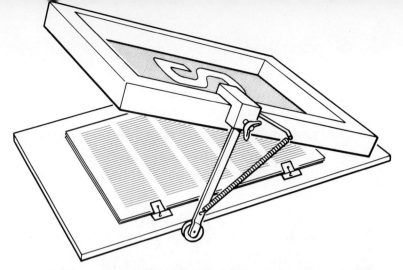

Figure 10-21. *Layers of news-paper are placed on a flat surface prior to dissolving a lacquer film stencil.*

should be completely removed. There may be a slight tint or stain in the area where the stencil was adhered to the mesh. This is caused from use. It does not affect the openings in the mesh.

Unit Review

- The screen printing process uses a porous (open) stencil as the image carrier.

- The stencil material is adhered to the bottom side of a screen mesh. The mesh can be made of silk, nylon, dacron, organdy, or stainless steel.

- The screen method is versatile. It can print on a variety of surfaces, including paper, glass, wood, metal, plastic, fabric, wall-paper, and cork. Almost any size, shape, and design can be screen-printed.

- Automatic screen presses can print up to 5,500 copies per hour. Better presses and faster-drying ink have eliminated the traditional problem of screen printing: lack of production speed.

- Hand-cut paper stencils can be used for very short press runs.

- There are two kinds of hand-cut film for screen printing. Aqua film is adhered to the screen mesh with water. Lacquer film is adhered to the screen with lacquer thinner.

- Two kinds of masks are used to prevent the flow of ink in the nonprinting areas of the stencil. These are paper masks and liquid masks.

- There are two methods of making stencils photographically. They are called indirect and direct. Both produce very fine detail, including halftones.

- In screen process printing, the surface to be printed is placed under a stencil. A quantity of ink is moved across the stencil surface with a rubber blade. The ink is forced through the open areas of the stencil and onto the printing surface below.

- Basic parts of a screen press are: screen frame, fabric mesh screen, base, side kick, and squeegee. Different shaped squeegees are used for printing on various surfaces.

Review Questions

1. What was the common name used to describe screen process printing until a variety of screen fabrics was developed in recent years?

2. What liquid is used to adhere aqua film to the screen mesh?

3. What kind of ink is required when aqua film is used?

4. What kind of ink is required when lacquer film is used?

DUPLICATORS AND COPIERS

11

LIMITED-QUANTITY PROCESSES: OFFICE DUPLICATION AND COPYING

Most offices produce limited-quantity messages. These messages are usually prepared initially on a typewriter. Many machines and processes are available for fast, easy, and inexpensive duplication of graphic information.

Office duplicating processes require an image carrier such as a *stencil* or *master*.

Office copying processes are methods that do not require an intermediate image carrier. Rapid advances in electronics and computer technology are causing the older duplicating methods to be phased out. High-speed office copiers have capabilities undreamed of as recently as the 1960s.

Of the office duplicating methods, the most familiar are the *spirit duplicator* and the *mimeograph*.

SPIRIT DUPLICATORS: LEAST EXPENSIVE METHOD

The spirit duplicator process is the least expensive of the office duplication methods (Fig. 11-1). This process uses a *spirit master* as an image carrier. The spirit master is included in a three-part set:

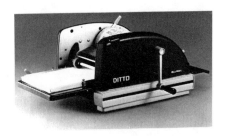

Figure 11-1. *Spirit duplicators are the least expensive of office duplication machines.*

1. Paper master sheet

2. Aniline dye carbon sheet

3. Protective tissue insert.

The paper master is usually a sheet of heavy white paper. The aniline dye carbon sheet is placed against the back of the master sheet. When the master is not in use or has been prepared, the tissue insert prevents accidental transfer of the dye material to the master. To use a master, the protective tissue is removed.

The most popular aniline dye carbon paper is purple. However, many other colors are available. It is possible to transfer images of multiple colors to a single spirit duplicator master. For example, a message can be typed with a purple carbon sheet in place. Then, part of an illustration can be drawn with a red carbon sheet as backing. Additional colors—green, blue, yellow, orange, and others—can also be used. This is a unique feature of the spirit duplicator process: Multiple colors can be reproduced from a single image carrier.

The image to be reproduced is typed or drawn on the front of the paper master sheet. A ball-point pen is used for drawing. Pressure transfers the images to the back of the master. The image on the back of the master is reverse reading. The typed or drawn image on the front of the master is right reading.

Typing or drawing errors can be removed by scraping the aniline dye carbon image from the back of the paper master. A small unused piece of carbon sheet can then be used under the master to make any corrections.

The aniline dye carbon sheet is usually discarded after the image is placed on the carrier.

Actual printing is done on a spirit duplicator machine. A spirit duplicator machine has a supply, or reservoir, of alcohol. This is where the name of the process comes from: alcohol is a spirit fluid. As the spirit master rotates on a drum, the reverse side, containing the reverse-reading carbon image, is coated with alcohol. This softens in the carbon impression. The aniline dye dissolved by the alcohol is then transferred to paper passing through the duplicator. Since the carbon image is reverse reading, the printed impression is right reading.

MIMEOGRAPH DUPLICATING: SIMILAR TO SCREEN PRINTING

The mimeograph duplicating method is similar to screen process printing. The image carrier is a stencil made of a special wax-coated material.

The mimeograph stencil is made from a porous tissue paper that is coated on both sides with a wax-like material. The stencil master is made up of three parts:

1. Stencil sheet made of wax-coated porous tissue paper

2. Cushion sheet

3. Backing sheet.

Images are formed by typewriter or stylus directly on the stencil. In typing on a stencil, the typewriter ribbon is not used. This enables the metal keys to cut through the wax coating, exposing porous tissue areas to permit the passage of ink.

A mimeograph *stylus* is a metal writing instrument with a hard edge. When it is pressed against the stencil in writing or drawing, the wax coating is moved aside.

When a stencil is being prepared the cushion sheet provides a soft backing to permit imaging. The

Figure 11-2. *The completed stencil is attached to the cylinder on the mimeograph machine. (A.B. Dick Co.)*

backing sheet provides protection to prevent damage to the underlying surfaces from the typewriter keys or stylus.

Typing or drawing errors can be corrected using *correction fluid.* The fluid is brushed over each letter of the error in a light coating. The fluid is allowed to dry for 30 seconds before making the correction.

The completed stencil is attached to a cylinder on the mimeograph machine (Fig. 11-2). The inside part of the stencil cylinder is coated with thin ink. During printing, the ink flows through tiny holes in the stencil cylinder. The ink is caught by a cloth pad wrapped around the cylinder—behind the stencil. As sheets are fed into the machine, an impression roller presses them against the stencil on the stencil cylinder. The ink flows from inside the cylinder, through the cloth pad, and through the stencil openings onto the paper.

OFFSET DUPLICATORS: SMALL LOW-COST PRINTING PRESSES

Small, table-top offset presses are sometimes used in offices in the same way as duplicators. Often, these machines are called offset duplicators. Such units are practical in offices using direct-image offset plates. These are plates on which typewritten copy can be placed directly. Special grease-based ribbons must be used. The plates can then be etched and the small presses can be used as duplicators.

Offset duplicators are basically the same as the offset presses covered in Unit 6. Thus, there is nothing special you need to know about this process.

ELECTROSTATIC COPYING (XEROGRAPHY): TECHNOLOGY OF THE PRESENT

The *electrostatic copier* does not use a stencil or master. Multiple copies are printed directly from typed, handwritten, or printed originals. The electrostatic

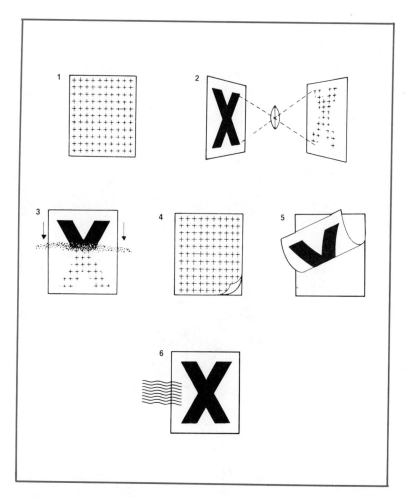

Figure 11·3. *Basic xerography consists of six steps: (1) A photoconductive surface is given a positive electrical charge. (2) The image of a document is exposed on the surface, causing the charge to drain away from the surface in all but the image area, which remains unexposed and charged. (3) Negatively charged powder is cascaded over the charged image area, making a visible image. (4) A piece of plain paper is placed over the surface and given a positive charge. (5) The negatively charged powder image on the surface is electrostatically attracted to the positively charged paper. (6) The powder image is fused to the paper by heat. (Xerox Corp.)*

copier applies the principles of electrical and magnetic force (Fig. 11-3). Electricity is used to create a magnetic image on an electrically charged surface. Imprinting is done with a ferrous (iron-based) material called a *toner*. The toner is attracted to the magnetic field. The toner image is then transferred to paper.

In using a copier, an original document is positioned face down on a platen or plate. Light reflected from the original copy is measured by a photoelectric cell. This automatically regulates the degree to which the lens opens or closes. To save space within office

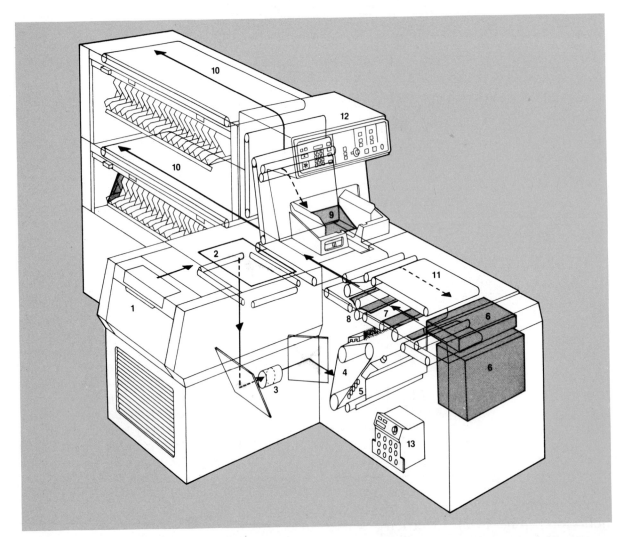

Figure 11-4. *Cutaway view of Xerox 9400 copier shows how document moves from document handler (1) to the platen (2). Here it is exposed by lamps and mirrors through a lens (3). This focuses the image (in the same or selected reduced sizes) onto the photoreceptor belt (4). Magnetic rollers (5) brush the belt with dry ink, which clings to the image area. A sheet of copy paper moves from either the main or the auxiliary tray (6) to the belt. Here the dry ink is transferred to it (7). The copy then goes between two rollers (8), where the dry ink image is fused to it by heat and pressure. A copy of a single-page document emerges in the receiving tray (9). Copies of multi-page documents go to the sorter (10) for collating into as many as 999 sets. If the sheet is to be copied on both sides, it returns by conveyor (11) to the auxiliary tray to repeat the process. This machine also has a control console (12) with lighted instructions guiding the operator on all jobs. A maintenance module (13) allows easy adjustment and testing of the unit's systems. (Xerox Corp.)*

copiers, the image of the document moves through a series of mirrors on many units (Fig. 11-4).

The first mirror carries the image of the document to the lens. On compact copiers, space is saved by using smaller mirrors that reflect only a portion of the image at any moment. To cover the image of the full document, some mirrors oscillate. This means the mirror rocks back and forth to take in the image area in a sweeping motion. In other compact copiers, the document is placed on a moving platen. The platen actually travels across the surface of the mirror, moving the document.

The image from this first mirror is reflected through the lens. The lens regulates the amount of light and also focuses the image for reproduction. From the lens, the image travels to a stationary mirror.

The fixed mirror reflects the image to a selenium-coated drum. Selenium is a metal that has special electrical properties. Selenium accepts and changes

Check Your Knowledge (True or False)

1. Mimeograph is the least expensive form of office duplicating.

2. The tissue insert in a spirit master is used only to prevent accidental transfer of dye material to the paper master.

3. A mimeograph stencil is usually prepared on a typewriter.

4. Ink flows from inside the cylinder on a mimeograph machine.

Figure 11-5. *Tabletop xerograph machines have become popular in recent years. (A.B. Dick Co.)*

electrical charges very quickly. Thus, the drum can form or release charges rapidly. This means that images can be formed and changed rapidly for reproduction. When charged, the drum becomes sensitive to light. The image of the document creates a magnetic field. The magnetized image, in turn, attracts the ferrous toner. The toner image is transferred to paper under contact with a pressure roller. Once the image is transferred, the magnetic charge on the drum is released. Then the drum is recharged—ready for a new image.

As it leaves the copier, the imprinted paper passes over a heating element called a *fuser*. Fusing is the melting and combining of materials. In this case, the fuser melts plastic-based portions of the toner. The toner image is fused onto the paper.

Xerography is another name for electrostatic copying (Fig. 11-5). Great advances have been made in xerography in recent years. Some machines can now reproduce copies as large as a newspaper page. Many machines now have automatic sorters and collaters.

Figure 11-6. *Reproduction of halftone and color originals is possible in the new electrostatic copiers. (Xerox Corp.)*

Learning Activities

1. Visit your school's administrative office. Ask if you can observe the staff operating a duplicating machine. Ask if someone will demonstrate how stencil or master image carriers are prepared.

2. If possible, visit a small printing firm (such as an instant printing shop) where customers can have small numbers of copies made from originals on copiers. Ask if you can watch some copies being printed. Check to see if the copier has the capacity for collating multiple copies. Check the quality of the photocopies and compare them to the original.

The most advanced machines have capacities as high as 50 stations (receiving trays) for collating multiple copies.

Some of the newer high-speed copying machines are so fast that they recycle multiple copies. For example, an operator might wish to make 10 copies of a six-page memo. On older machines, the operator would make 10 copies of the first sheet, and so on. High-speed copiers make a single copy of each of the six sheets and then run them through repeatedly. The individual groups of sheets are stapled and placed in stacks automatically.

Xerographic printers also have been linked to computers. No original copies are required in computer methods. Instead, the computer is programmed to produce a layout. The layout may consist of type only, or it may include illustrations. A number of type fonts are available in the computer. This selection allows the programmer to mix and match typefaces. In computer xerography, a laser is used to scan the drum internally. The laser operates much faster than the optical exposure method.

Full color reproduction also is possible in some special applications. Three drums are used in color xerography (Fig. 11-6). The newest equipment can separate colors from reflective or transparent artwork. *Reflective copy* is artwork, such as photographic prints, which must be photographed by reflected light. Transparent art, also called *transmission copy,* is photographed by transmitted light. Transmitted light means that the light flows through the copy rather than being reflected off it. An example of transmission copy is a color photo transparency or slide. Color xerography units can produce color enlargements from 35 mm color slides as well as reproducing from color prints.

Vocabulary Checklist

1. stencil
2. spirit master
3. spirit duplicator
4. mimeograph
5. aniline dye carbon sheet
6. stylus
7. correction fluid
8. electrostatic copier
9. toner
10. xerography
11. fuser
12. reflective copy
13. transmission copy.

**Unit
Review**

- Office duplicating and copying processes are designed to print limited numbers of impressions. Many machines are available for fast, easy, and inexpensive duplication.

- Duplicating processes require preparation of an intermediate image carrier such as a stencil or a master. Electrostatic or xerographic copying methods reproduce directly from original copy.

- The spirit duplicator process is the least expensive of the office copying methods. Spirit duplicators use intermediate image carriers called spirit masters. Images are transferred to paper in the form of an aniline dye. A solvent is used to moisten and transfer the dye from the back of the image carrier to the impression sheets.

- Mimeograph duplicating is similar to screen process printing. A wax-coated stencil is used. Images are formed (cut) in the stencil by typewriter or stylus. In printing, ink flows from a cylinder through a cloth pad and through the stencil. An impression roller presses the paper sheets against the stencil, which is attached to a stencil cylinder.

- Electrostatic copying, also called xerographic copying, is rapidly replacing all other forms of office printing. Electrostatic copying transfers an image to an electrically charged drum. The image, in effect, becomes an electromagnet. Ferrous (iron) materials in a toner are attracted to the magnetic image. The toner image is then transferred to paper.

- Many highly advanced xerographic machines are now being used in the business world. Some have the ability to sort and collate large numbers of originals as they are copied. Some high-speed copiers are so fast that collating is unnecessary. These machines copy each different sheet in order and then run them all through in fast repetition. Each complete set of sheets is stapled and stacked automatically.

- Copiers also can be linked to computers for direct electronic composition of graphic messages. The computer is programmed to produce a layout. The image is placed on the xerographic drum by a rapidly scanning laser beam.

- A growing use for copiers is to provide full color reproduction in some special applications. Both reflective and transparent artwork can be reproduced by these advanced copiers.

Review Questions

1. What is the name of the image carrier used in the spirit duplicating process?

2. What is the name of the image carrier used in the mimeograph process?

3. Which other printing process does mimeographing resemble?

4. Name the substance that performs the same function as ink in electrostatic copying.

5. What is another common term for electrostatic copying?

III

GRAPHIC ARTS

The first two parts of this book have shown how printing processes work. Concepts have been followed from the idea stage through the printed product. But the graphic arts process does not end there.

Good printing results when type, paper, ink, and technical skill are combined effectively. It is difficult to say which of the four parts is most important. The right kind of paper can add texture and visual quality. This is because paper is manufactured in many colors and finishes. Inks are also made in many colors for each of the major printing processes.

Color itself is an important aspect of graphic arts. Color offers visual appeal and excitement. Color can also provide much greater clarity of detail and contrast. Ask yourself whether you would prefer to watch a program on a black-and-white television or a color model. The answer sums up the importance of color printing.

MATERIALS

Finally, no job is complete until it is finished. Many printing products are not really finished when they come off the press. Magazines, for instance, must be stitched. Books must be bound. The outer edges of these products must be trimmed. They must be packaged for shipment to customers or distributors. Binding and finishing are vital aspects of graphic arts technology.

The units of this part cover:

12. *Ink and Paper.* This unit covers the variety of inks and how they are used in the major printing processes. It also deals with the various types of paper and how they are used. Topics include how ink and paper are manufactured for the graphic arts.

13. *Color.* This unit deals with color processing, including design, art preparation, film separations, and printing.

14. *Binding and Finishing.* This unit reviews the major binding methods for magazines, books, and other printed matter. Also discussed is finishing, a variety of operations that bring the printed product to its final form.

12 INK AND PAPER

INK FOR THE GRAPHIC ARTS: HOW IT IS MANUFACTURED

Printing inks are colored coating materials applied to the surface of paper or other image carriers, such as plastic, metal, glass, and wood. Ink manufacturing is complicated. Moreover, each printing process has its own special set of requirements. This requires many different types of ink made with different formulas. It would be easy to produce inks if all processes and printing surfaces were the same.

Ink manufacturers have their own formulas for the preparation of different inks. In general, the ingredients used in the manufacture of most printing inks include:

1. Vehicle   2. Pigment   3. Additives.

THE VEHICLE OF INK: THE BASIC INGREDIENT

The *vehicle* of the ink is the basic ingredient. The purpose of the vehicle is to act as a carrier for the *pigment* (color). It also provides a binder to adhere the pigment to the printed surface. There are several kinds of vehicles. They include petroleum oils, rosin oils, linseed oil, litho varnish, cottonseed oil, castor oil, and soybean oil. The kind of vehicle used determines what are known as the body, length, tack, and drying qualities of an ink.

Body. Another term for the body of a printing ink is *consistency*. There are thin inks and thick inks. A thin ink is a liquid that is absorbed easily into printing papers. A thick ink just coats the surface of the paper. It does not absorb easily. To illustrate, letterpress inks are thick when compared to the thinner gravure inks. This is because the bodies of the two inks are made to match the types of printing presses and processes they will be used for. Letterpress inks coat relief type and are transferred to the surface of paper. Gravure inks must collect in etched areas of plates and must be easily removable from non-printing surfaces.

Length. The ability of an ink to flow is known as its length. Inks are said to be either *short* or *long*. Short inks are thick like butter and do not flow easily. They are spread onto inking plates of presses with special, flexible-blade knives. Long inks are thin and flow easily. They can be poured into reservoirs of presses. For example, letterpress inks are generally short, and gravure inks are long.

Tack. The stickiness of an ink is called its tack. Tack is measured by the force required to separate or split an ink film between two surfaces. An example would be the force required to separate a film of ink between two rollers on a printing press. Tack is important in offset printing. This is because ink is transferred from ink roller to plate, from plate to rubber blanket, and from blanket to paper. Tack is also important in printing quality. A tacky ink will pick (lift) unwanted particles from the paper during printing. These paper particles can block the clean inking of the printed image.

Drying. The vehicle used helps determine the way an ink drys. Printing inks dry by several methods. Inks used on soft papers dry by soaking (absorption) into the fibers of the paper. Inks used on hard-surface papers generally dry by outside air (oxidation). In some cases, inks dry by a combination of the two methods.

INK PIGMENT: THE COLOR INGREDIENT

The ingredient that gives ink its color is the *pigment*. It is the pigment that is seen when you look at printed images.

Black pigments are generally prepared from furnace black and thermal black. Furnace black and thermal black are made from oil and natural gas. The various other ink pigments are made from mineral compounds such as zinc oxide, titanium oxide, and clays. Pigments are generally delivered as powders. These powders are mixed into the vehicle to produce colors. Varying the amounts of different pigments used in inks changes the shades of color. The ink manufacturer relies on a formula or recipe to mix inks. This insures the same color each time the ink is produced.

INK ADDITIVES: FOR SPECIAL PURPOSES

Ingredients known as *additives* are placed in ink for special purposes. Additives include driers, waxes, lubricants, reducing oils, and gums. Some of these additives are placed in the ink during manufacture. Additives are sometimes placed in the finished ink for special printing conditions. Some printers request the ink manufacturer to mix inks for certain paper and press conditions. For example, inks used on high speed web presses often have additives that help them dry quickly.

INK MANUFACTURE: METHODS MATCH USES

The end use of a printing ink determines the way in which it is manufactured. Most inks are made in large batches. Generally, ink making includes mixing, milling, and packaging.

Mixing. The mixing operation combines pigment with the vehicle in measured amounts. The mixing is done in containers or tubs fitted with large mixing blades. The speed of the blades is carefully regulated. Blade speed depends upon the kind of pigment and vehicle being mixed.

Figure 12-1. *Ink mills use rollers to completely blend the pigment into the vehicle of the ink.*

Milling. With some ingredients, a special operation is necessary to blend (mix completely) the pigment into the vehicle. A grinder, known as a mill, is used for the milling operation (Fig. 12-1). These machines include several steel rollers. The rollers revolve in opposite directions. The speed of the mill, temperature of the rollers, and pressure between the rollers are carefully controlled.

Packaging. The final step in the manufacture of ink is to place the product in containers for shipment to printers. Containers used for packaging include cans, drums, and cartridges. Each container is labeled to indicate stock number, name, and color of the ink.

In some instances, tanker trucks are used for large shipments to newspaper and magazine printing operations. Ink is often manufactured to fit individual customers' paper and press requirements. In these cases, the ink is packaged and labeled separately.

The manufacture of ink is a scientific and highly technical process. Quality control, ink color matching, and product research are all important in this industry. Chemists and other ink specialists work in this area of ink manufacturing (Fig. 12-2).

Figure 12-2. *Chemists and highly trained technicians are responsible for research, ink color matching, and quality control in this highly technical industry.*

Figure 12-3. *Papermaking begins with forests. This stand of trees is located on land owned by a major paper manufacturer. (Hammermill Papers Group)*

Figure 12-4. *Logs are sent to a chipping machine, where they are cut into small chips like these. (Hammermill Papers Group)*

Check Your Knowledge (True or False)

1. The vehicle of an ink carries its pigment.

2. Tack describes the ability of an ink to flow.

3. Pigment is the ingredient that gives an ink its color.

4. Steel rollers are used to mix ink.

PAPER FOR THE GRAPHIC ARTS: HOW IT IS MANUFACTURED

Most of the paper used today comes from trees (Fig. 12-3). Most trees used in papermaking are grown in areas where trees are planted especially for this purpose. These areas are known as *tree farms*. Since tree farms represent large investments of time and money, they are given expert care by professional growers. Most paper mills are located near tree farms and lakes and streams, where water is plentiful.

The manufacture of paper begins with the removal of bark from trees. Giant *debarkers* strip the bark from the trees. The trees are then cut into lengths of approximately four feet. The logs are sent to a *chipping machine*, which cuts them to chips about the size of a quarter (Fig. 12-4).

The wood chips are fed into a tall *digester*, where they are cooked in chemicals under pressure (Fig. 12-5). This process converts the chips to a *fiber*. The fiber is washed and passed through a chemical process that bleaches it into a white *pulp*.

The pulp is mixed in a *blender* with other papermaking chemicals. The materials are thoroughly mixed with water to the desired thickness. The pulp then flows onto an endless bronze screen belt at the front of the *papermaking machine.* The fine mesh screen moves and shakes to weave and mat the fibers together as the water drains off.

As the paper begins to form, the fibers align themselves parallel to the direction in which they are traveling. This forms a *grain* in the paper. The grain in paper is similar to the grain in lumber. The traveling pulp is passed over several suction boxes and rollers to remove more water. As grain is drawn through the papermaking machine, a continuous roll, or web, is formed.

About halfway through the papermaking process, the paper is given a coating to seal the surface. Toward the drying end of the papermaking machine, the web is carried through a set of steam-heated drying cylinders. This reduces the moisture content of the paper to about 5 percent. The web is then wound into huge rolls. Some rolls are shipped to printers as they come off the papermaking machines—in webs. However, most of the rolls are cut into sheets. These sheets are grouped in stacks (usually consisting of 500 sheets). The 500-sheet packages of paper are then wrapped and shipped to printers (Fig. 12-6). A package of 500 sheets of paper is called a *ream.* Other sheets of paper are packaged in cartons, ranging from about 1,000 sheets to 3,600 sheets, depending on size and thickness.

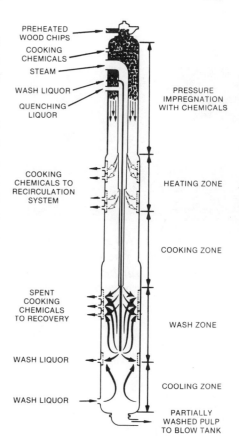

Figure 12-5. *A 200-foot-tall continuous digester can produce 700 tons of pulp per day.* (American Paper Institute)

Figure 12-6. *Paper is cut into sheets and stacked into 500-sheet reams for shipment from a papermaking plant.* (Hammermill Papers Group)

Figure 12-7. *After leaving the papermaking machine, paper is finished by further rolling and smoothing operations. (Hammermill Papers Group)*

PAPER FINISH: THE SMOOTHNESS FACTOR

The term *paper finish* refers to smoothness. Most papers are finished by additional rolling and smoothing operations. This is done by feeding the basic rolls from the papermaking machines into other machines equipped with steel rollers (Fig. 12-7). The common paper finishes include: antique, eggshell, machine finish (MF), and sized and super calendered (S&SC).

Antique. Paper with an antique finish has a velvety surface. Books and other such reading matter are often printed on antique paper. This kind of paper is also referred to as *text*. Antique paper is suited to book printing because its surface is dull and does not create glare or shine. The lack of reflection is easy on the eyes of the reader.

Eggshell. This paper gets its name from the fact that its texture is similar to that of an eggshell. The surface of eggshell paper has an irregular pattern of rounded hills and valleys. This kind of paper is used for programs and folders.

Machine finish. This finish is similar to that of antique paper. However, machine finish is smoother and less bulky. The smooth finish is applied to the paper in the papermaking machine. Typical uses for machine finish paper are magazines, booklets, and catalogs. Some books also use machine finish paper.

Sized and super calendered (S&SC). This paper has a very smooth, hard surface. Sizing, similar to clay, is added to the paper during the manufacturing process. The paper passes through an added number of metal rollers, which adds to its smoothness.

MORE FACTS ABOUT PAPER: WHAT THE TERMINOLOGY MEANS

Paper has a *wire side* and a *felt side*. This results from the basic manufacturing process. The side of the paper in direct contact with the bronze mesh screen

RECESSED DESIGN
GIVES DARK WORK

RAISED DESIGN
GIVES LIGHT WORK

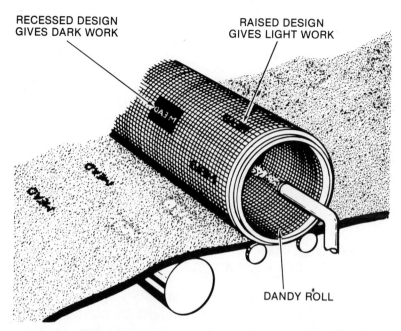

DANDY ROLL

Figure 12-8. *Watermarked papers have the watermark imprinted by a dandy roll. The design is pressed into the paper while it is still wet in the papermaking machine.*

of the papermaking machine is called the wire side. The other side of the paper is called the felt side. The felt side has a closer knit of fibers. The felt side has less grain and is the better printing side.

On watermarked papers, the printing should be done on the felt side. The *watermark* is placed in the paper while it is still wet in the papermaking machine. This is done with a *dandy roll* (Fig. 12-8). A dandy roll is made of fine wire on which the wording or design is raised. The design is pressed into the wet paper. The watermark is visible when a sheet of paper is held up to the light. If printing is done on the felt side, the printing will read the same way as the watermark.

The *grain* of paper is important in printing and binding. It refers to the direction of the paper fibers. During papermaking, most of the fibers flow with their length parallel to that of the papermaking machine. Paper folds smoothly with the grain but is stiffer across the grain. Books, magazines, catalogs, and programs usually have the grain running parallel to the binding edge. That is, the grain runs from top to bottom of the printed page, rather than from side to side.

Some papers, such as those with an antique finish, have deckled edges. A *deckled edge* is a feathery, ragged edge formed along the outer edges of the paper during manufacture. A deckled edge gives a pleasing look to certain kinds of printing. Examples would be a printed wedding invitation or concert program.

PAPER WEIGHT: AN IMPORTANT MEASURE

Most printing papers are identified by their basis weight. *Basis weight* is the weight in pounds for a *ream* (500 sheets) of paper in the *basic size* for that grade. For example, book paper has a basic size of 25 by 38 inches. A book paper with a basis weight of 60 means that 500 sheets of 25-by-38-inch book paper will weigh 60 pounds. The basic size is *not* the same for all grades of paper.

Paper is generally referred to in terms of its *ream weight*. Examples would be 20-pound bond and 70-pound book. However, most paper merchants list prices of paper by the thousand sheets. In graphic arts terminology, the letter "M" means 1,000. For example, 1M sheets of 25-by-38-inch 70-pound book paper weigh 140 pounds.

PAPER OPACITY: VITAL TO QUALITY

When an image printed on one side of a sheet of paper can be seen through on the other side, this is called *show-through*. The ability of a paper to resist show-through is called *opacity*. The thickness of the paper, ink coverage, and chemicals in the paper help to determine opacity. The amount of opacity in a paper is important in book, catalog, and magazine printing.

A special tool is used by the printer to measure a paper's opacity. If a paper has too much show-through, the quality of printed matter will be adversely affected.

As an example, a school textbook such as this one is usually printed on paper with an opacity rating of at least 90 percent. This means that less than 10 percent of the image printed on one side of the paper will be visible on the other side.

Check Your Knowledge (True or False)

1. A digester cooks wood fiber into pulp.

2. The grain of a paper is formed in the papermaking machine.

3. Paper with an antique finish is also referred to as text.

4. The wire side of a paper is the better printing side.

GRADES OF PAPER: IDENTIFYING NEEDS

There are many kinds, or *grades,* of paper. Each grade serves a certain printing need. You should learn to recognize some of the more common grades of paper. These include: business, book, cover, bristol, label, newsprint, and paperboard.

Business. Business-grade papers are used for financial and office purposes rather than for commercial printing. These uses include ledger sheets, money orders, bank checks, safety paper, stationery, and duplicating or copying papers. Paper used for these purposes must have long life and be able to retain images permanently. These printing papers are considered to be high in quality. This kind of paper is generally referred to as *bond*.

Most letterheads and business forms are a standard 8½-by-11-inch size. Four pieces of 8½-by-11-inch paper can be cut from the 17-by-22-inch basic size of business or bond papers. Weights of business papers generally range from 13 pound to 24 pound.

Book. Book grade is the most popular paper. Finishes include eggshell, antique, vellum, and super calendered. The basic size of book paper is 25 by 38 inches. Weights range from 30 pound to 100 pound.

Cover. Cover papers are available in a variety of grades, colors, and finishes. Cover papers serve the important task of covering and protecting other printed materials. These might include covers of programs, catalogs, schedules, or booklets. The basic size of cover paper is 20 by 26 inches. Weights range from 50 pound to 130 pound.

Bristol. This paper comes in three varieties: printing bristol, index bristol, and wedding bristol.

Printing bristol papers are used mainly for posters and point-of-purchase displays such as those found on grocery checkout counters. The basic size of printing bristol is 22½ by 28½ inches. Weights range from 90 pound to 200 pound.

Index bristol papers are used as file cards, postcards, booklet covers, business forms, menus, and advertising pieces. They are made to accept printing and writing and also to be erasable. The basic size of index bristol is 25½ by 30½ inches. Weights range from 90 pound to 170 pound.

Wedding bristol papers contain fancy vellum finishes. They are used for announcements, menus, and programs. The basic size of wedding bristol is 22½ by 28½ inches. Weights range from 120 pound to 240 pound.

Label. Label papers are not always used to make labels. They are used for such purposes as embossing, multicolor printing, die-cutting, and adhesive printed pieces. Label papers are used for book and record jackets, candy wrappers, and multipurpose seals and bands. The basic size of label paper is 25 by 38 inches. Weights range from 55 pound to 100 pound.

Newsprint. This is the standard paper on which newspapers and some magazines are printed. More than 90 percent of the newsprint manufactured today is supplied and used in rolls. The basic sheet size is 24 by 36 inches. Rolls of newsprint are made to fit the several standard sizes of rotary web-fed presses. Weights available are 30 and 32 pound.

Learning Activities

1. Obtain samples of several kinds of paper in your home. Examples would be a newspaper, a "slick" magazine (one whose pages are glossy), a piece of bond stationery, and a hardbound book. Feel the textures of the various kinds of paper. Observe the clarity of reproduction on those carrying printed matter. Hold a sample of each up to a light and note the relative opacity of each sample.

2. If possible, visit a printing firm that specializes in small printing jobs such as wedding invitations and social announcements. Ask to see samples of the paper kept in stock. Notice how packages of paper are labeled by the manufacturer as to grade, quantity, style, size, and so forth. Ask what kinds of ink are used on various grades of paper.

Paperboard. This is a heavy material generally used for packaging containers such as boxes and cartons. Paperboard has good printing qualities and is strong and durable. The thicker paperboards are printed on platen or screen process presses. Thinner paperboards are usually printed by offset lithography or gravure. The very thickest types of paperboard are referred to as *blanks*. These are used in package printing, outdoor advertising, and many commercial advertising pieces. The basic size of paperboard is 22 by 38 inches. Paperboard is manufactured in thicknesses up to 0.056 inch.

BUSINESS ENVELOPES: WIDE VARIETY IN SIZE AND STYLE

The world of business uses many different types of business envelopes. These envelopes are manufactured in many styles and sizes. Each style has a special use and is generally ordered by number. For example, a No. 10 envelope is for business use. It measures $4\frac{1}{8}$ by $9\frac{1}{2}$ inches.

Envelopes that contain a transparent window are used for statements and invoices. The address appears on the inserted material and shows through the window. This eliminates the necessity of typing addresses on envelopes. This is a major labor-saving device for many businesses.

Envelopes used for social invitations and wedding announcements are called *baronial*. A popular baronial size envelope for social occasions measures $4\frac{1}{8}$ by $5\frac{1}{8}$ inches. Blank paper for printing invitations is available for insertion in baronial envelopes.

Heavy kraft, or Manila, envelopes are manufactured for the mailing of magazines, pamphlets, reports, books, and a variety of similar materials. Kraft, or Manila, paper is a heavy material usually provided in a light brown color. Two common types of envelopes are made from this material. They are the *Manila clasp* envelopes that measure 8¾ by 11¼ inches and 9 by 12 inches. The description refers to a feature of the envelope. There are two metal leafs that form a clasp.

ESTIMATING PAPER: WHEN COSTS ARE VITAL

The *estimating* and cutting of paper is an important operation performed by the printer. Paper is a very expensive material, usually representing about 50 percent of the cost of the complete printing job. The printer must plan the cutting of the paper in advance to avoid waste.

The printer first determines the size of the sheets needed for the printing job. The size of the paper from which these sheets will be cut is then determined. The printer calculates, or estimates, how many pieces can be cut from one full sheet of basic size paper.

The dimensions of the sheet to be printed are written under the dimensions of a full sheet of basic size paper. By mathematical cancellation, the number of pieces that can be obtained from a full basic size sheet is determined. This shows how many pieces can be cut from each large sheet of the basic size paper (Fig. 12-9).

Figure 12-9. *Printers exercise great care in calculating how many pieces of a given size can be obtained from a standard size sheet of paper. As this diagram shows, incorrect calculations can be wasteful . . . and expensive.*

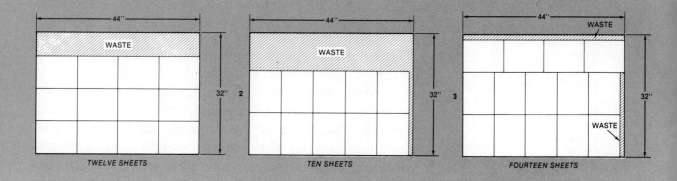

TWELVE SHEETS   TEN SHEETS   FOURTEEN SHEETS

Figure 12-10. *Computer-operated paper cutters can be programmed for a series of cuts, adjusting automatically for each dimension. Controls at the front of the machine require the operator to hold down buttons with the fingers of both hands in order to operate. (Challenge Machinery Co.)*

Vocabulary Checklist

1. vehicle
2. pigment
3. body
4. length
5. tack
6. milling
7. debarker
8. chipping machine
9. digester
10. fiber
11. pulp
12. blender
13. papermaking machine
14. grain
15. paper finish
16. text
17. wire side
18. felt side
19. watermark

In cutting paper for a printing job, it is necessary to add a few extra sheets as *spoilage allowance*. The extra sheets are used for press and bindery setups. Spoilage allowance also makes up for sheets damaged as the job is being printed.

There are two types of paper cutters used to cut paper to size. A simple hand lever model is used for limited cutting operations. An electrically powered model is used where large quantities of paper are cut. Some larger paper cutters include a computer (Fig. 12-10). This allows the cutter to be programmed for a series of paper cuts. This type of cutter automatically adjusts for each dimension in a series of cuts.

With any type of cutter, paper is placed on the cutting table and positioned for the desired size of cut. The paper is held firmly in position with a clamp as the blade makes the cut.

METRIC MEASUREMENTS FOR THE GRAPHIC ARTS

There are three measuring systems used in the graphic arts industry in the United States. One is the American standard, using inches and pounds. Another is the metric system, using millimeters and grams. The third is the printers' measurements of points and picas (there are no weight measurements in the printers' system). In graphic arts, as in other industries, the trend is toward conversion to the metric system. Eventually, metric measurements will be used exclusively in photo-offset lithography and photocomposition. The declining hot-metal and letterpress areas of the printing industry probably will not change over. Costs would be prohibitive, and not enough new equipment is being manufactured to warrant the expense.

Even in the United States, metric measurements have been used for many years in one area of graphic arts: photography. In fact, the familiar 8-, 16-, and 35-millimetre film sizes would seem strange expressed in inches (0.315, 0.63, and 1.38, respectively).

Paper measurement is an area in which the United States stands alone. The International Organization for Standardization (ISO) measures paper sizes on a unit of 1 square metre (1 m²) as the basic size. The slightly oblong basic sheet measures 1189 mm by 841 mm. The A series of paper measurement starts with the largest size being A1, measuring 841 by 594 mm. The short side of the sheet becomes the long side of the next smaller size. A2, therefore, measures 594 by 420 mm. A3 measures 420 by 297 mm, and A4 measures 297 by 210 mm. A4 is the closest equivalent to the standard American stationery size of 8½ by 11 inches. A4 is slightly narrower and somewhat longer, however, and does not fit well into American-made file drawers or copying machines. ISO, therefore, approved a sheet size of 280 by 210 mm. This size is exactly 11 inches long and slightly narrower than the customary American 8½-inch sheet (Fig. 12-11). The 210 mm width allows the sheet to fit into ISO standard C series envelopes.

ISO paper weight measurements are also given in metric terms, in grams per square metre (g/m²). For example, a ream (500 sheets) of 24-by-36-inch newsprint might weigh 12.29 pounds. In metric terms, this would be expressed as 20.0 g/m².

20. dandy roll

21. ream

22. "M"

23. opacity

24. business grade

25. book grade

26. cover grade

27. bristol grade

28. label grade

29. newsprint

30. ISO

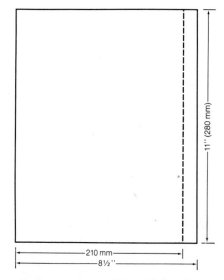

Figure 12-11. *The ISO sheet adopted to correspond to American measurement standards is shown here superimposed over a standard 8½ by 11 sheet.*

Unit Review

- Ink for the graphic arts industry includes three major ingredients: the vehicle, the pigment, and additives.

- The vehicle of the ink is its base. The pigment is its color. Additives are ingredients added for special purposes, either in manufacture or by the printer.

- Paper is generally made from trees. Paper mills are located close to the tree growing areas, usually in the midst of lakes and streams.

- Papers are identified by their basis weight. Basis weight is the weight in pounds for a ream (500 sheets) of a paper in its basic size. Paper is generally referred to in terms of its ream weight. Most paper merchants list prices by the thousand sheets. In graphic arts, the letter "M" means 1,000.

Review Questions

1. What is the basic ingredient of ink?

2. Which ingredient gives ink its color?

3. In which direction is the grain of the paper usually aligned in a book or magazine?

4. To which type of printing product is paper with an antique finish best suited?

5. What is the name of paper edges that are feathery and ragged?

6. How many sheets are contained in a ream of paper?

COLOR

13

THE IMPORTANCE OF COLOR IN MODERN GRAPHIC ARTS

Lengthy explanations are not needed to point out the value of color in our everyday lives. Color adds visual impact to the printed page as well as to the television or movie screen. Color lends lifelike quality to photographic reproductions (Fig. 13-1). Even printed pages with no illustrations are more attractive if one or two colors are added to the image.

Figure 13-1. *Photographic reproductions gain lifelike qualities when printed in color. (Photo by Andrew Mann)*

Color can be used on the printed page to set an overall mood. Sometimes, artists will use a second color for a single line of type—to draw attention to that headline. The uses of color are varied, depending on the kind of product being printed.

Living Color

Color is part of human life. It surrounds you. Color symbols tell you where you can go—and where you can't go. Color indicates safety—and danger. Color in your surroundings can add comfort to your life.

When you see a rainbow, this is a way nature has of displaying color. A rainbow is a good sign. It means clear weather ahead. Depending on your personal beliefs, a rainbow may mean a wish will come true.

One thing a rainbow does for sure is to display the full range of colors that exist. The full color range is called a spectrum (Fig. 13-2). A *spectrum* means a complete color display. Spectrum displays are used in design and printing.

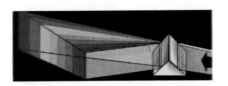

Figure 13-2. *When light is transmitted through a prism, the color spectrum becomes visible. All but the outermost two colors of the spectrum, infrared and ultraviolet, are visible to the human eye. (Reprinted from* Pocket Guide to Color Reproduction *by Miles Southworth, Graphic Arts Publishing Co., Livonia, NY 14487)*

USING COLOR IN DESIGN: MANY OPTIONS ARE AVAILABLE

Design and layout artists have a wide range of choices available to them in color printing. In earlier chapters, printing was discussed in one-color form. One-color printing is called *monochromatic,* or "mono." One-color printing does not have to consist of black type on white paper, although this is most common. A one-color printing job can have red type on yellow paper. The possible combinations are almost endless.

Multicolor printing means the use of more than one color of ink. When two or more inks are used on a printing job, the inks are transferred to the paper in sequence. On single-unit presses, a separate printing operation is required for each color. One press run is needed for each color. On larger presses, each printing unit can be used to apply a different color ink (Fig. 13-3). From two to four colors can be applied in a single run on a multi-unit press.

One obvious use of color is to reproduce four-color images. *Four color* generally means that an image is being reproduced in its full, natural colors. Four basic, or process, colors are used for such printing. Use of the four-color process is also known as process printing. These four colors—actually three colors and black as discussed below—can provide full-color reproduction of color images. The image can be a photograph of a person or scene. Four-color techniques are also used to reproduce works of art or printed items that benefit from color display. Sales catalogs or brochures are good examples of the value of full-color printing.

Consider, for example, the large, full-color publications of companies that sell from catalogs. A catalog published by organizations such as Sears, Roebuck or Montgomery Ward offers many items of merchandise for sale. Many of these items are expensive. Catalog merchandise can cost hundreds of dollars. Prospective buyers desire a visual "preview" or idea as to the appearance of the articles. Color printing is an important feature in buyer decisions on catalog purchases.

Full-color (known as four-color reproduction) illustrations are featured in this unit and in Unit 1 of this book. Merely glancing at pages with full-color illustrations will make clear the value of this method of reproduction.

One-color or two-color printing methods are used to add reader interest to printed items. Color can highlight the content of a printed product. In this book, for example, color is used for the type of the section headings. This helps the student identify topics to be studied. The headings printed in color stand out from the black type of the text itself. Also,

Figure 13-3. *Different color inks are applied to the paper in sequence in a multi-unit color press. (The Lehigh Press)*

color is used to highlight special review materials at the ends of chapters. The student gets accustomed to looking for uses of color in repeated patterns. With a textbook, therefore, the use of color helps guide a student using the text. Color type and design elements announce the purpose and content of the various parts of each unit.

Most publications, including newspapers and magazines, print black ink on white paper for basic text reproduction. Color is often added for design or emphasis of content. Advertisers often use color for added visual impact. Editors also specify color for special layouts.

Leading magazines and newspapers now use color photographs as part of their usual reading content. With large, modern web-offset presses, it has become possible to insert color illustrations anywhere within a publication. This ability to use color anywhere is known as *run-of-publication*—or *ROP*—color.

HOW COLOR PRINTING IS DONE: SEPARATING THE COLORS

Color printing is done with the use of inks containing different pigments. Colors must be *separated* so that each ink is applied from a different image carrier or plate. There are two kinds of color separations: mechanical and photographic.

Mechanical separations. Mechanical color separations are used for line copy and for black-and-white original copy. Art for multicolor reproduction is usually produced in black and white on a paste-up or mechanical. This is the first step toward achieving proper *registration* on the press. Registration is the alignment of the various color images on the printed sheet. There are two levels of registration: *hairline registration* and *commercial registration*. Hairline registration means that the alignment of color images must be

Figure 13-4. *Clear acetate overlays such as amberlith are used to separate copy designated for a second color on the press. The artwork on the paste-up board will be printed in the main color.*

precise. Commercial registration permits slight variations in color images.

In cases where hairline registration is not required, artwork for the key (main) color is prepared on the paste-up. Art for the other color or colors is prepared on clear acetate overlays. The overlays are hinged to the paste-up board in proper position (Fig. 13-4).

Separate film negatives are made for each color image. Each negative is used to expose a different plate for printing.

In cases where hairline registration is desired, all art appears on the same paste-up board. A tissue overlay is used to indicate color breaks. A *key line* is drawn where two colors meet or *butt*. Key lines are not reproduced in printing. They are keys, or guides, used in stripping film for offset platemaking.

Additional color values can be obtained by *overprinting* two or more inks, which may include black. Overprinting means that portions of the image are printed in more than one color of ink. The mixing of two or more color inks produces a third color that is different from the two ink pigments. For example, overprinting blue and yellow inks produces a green image.

Overprinting can be done in both solids and *tints*. A tint is obtained by using a *screen* to limit the amount of ink transferred to the paper (Fig. 13-5). Screens produce dot patterns when original copy is photographed with a process camera. The dot patterns vary in density. A 60 percent screen, for example, causes ink to be printed on 60 percent of the surface area. Such a screen will produce heavier ink coverage than a 20

Figure 13-5. *A screen is used to produce a tint. The screen limits the amount of ink that is transferred to the paper during printing.*

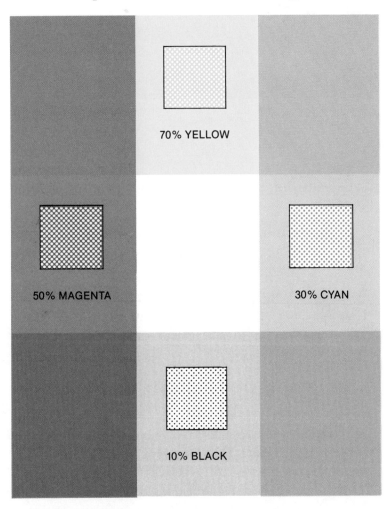

70% YELLOW

50% MAGENTA

30% CYAN

10% BLACK

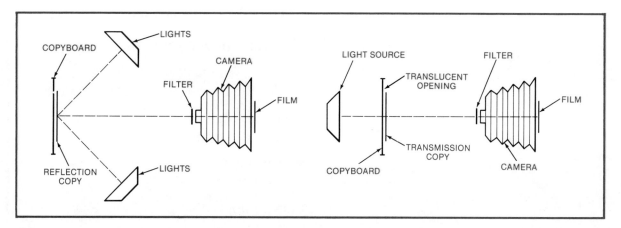

percent screen. Screens allow the layout artist to achieve a wide variety of color effects in multicolor printing.

Photographic separations. When a color photograph, painting, or color transparency is to be reproduced, the colors must be separated photographically. This is a more complicated method than mechanical separation.

Photographic separations are made for four-color, or process-color, printing. Process-color printing is described below. Two kinds of halftone copy are used in photographic separation: *reflection* and *transmission* (Fig. 13-6). Reflection copy consists of photographic prints or drawings. Light is directed *at* the copy and is *reflected* toward the camera lens and film. Transmission copy consists of a photographic transparency in which light is projected through it and toward the camera lens and film.

Figure 13-6. *Light is directed at reflection copy and is reflected toward the copy camera lens and film. Light is projected through transmission copy to the camera.*

PROCESS-COLOR PRINTING: AN OPTICAL ILLUSION

Process-color reproduction is based on a theory of three-color vision. The color white is composed of portions of three primary colors: blue, green, and red. The human eye has three different types of receptors.

Check Your Knowledge (True or False)

1. Printing done in black type on white paper comes under the heading of monochromatic.

2. Commercial registration is more exacting than hairline registration.

3. Overprinting of colors can be done in solids or tints.

4. A color photographic print is an example of transmission copy.

Each receptor is sensitive to one of the three primary colors.

When the eye views a color scene, the receptors react to the colors to which they are sensitive. Impulses are sent to the brain. The brain recreates the scene from the impulses that are transmitted by the eye's receptors.

The primary colors of blue, green, and red are called *additive primary colors* (Fig. 13-7). This is because three lights of these colors added together produce white.

Original copy is photographed three times, using different filters. Each filter corresponds in color and light transmission to one of the additive primary colors.

A *red* filter permits only red light to pass. Greens and blues are filtered out. Photography through a red filter produces a negative recording of all the reflected or transmitted red light. This is called the red separation negative. When a positive is made from this negative, the silver in the film will correspond to the other two colors. The negative has subtracted the red

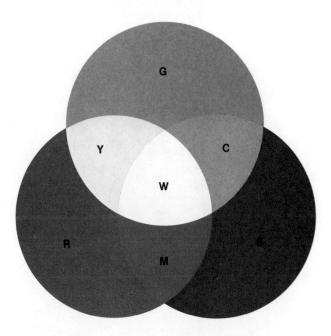

Figure 13-7. *The additive primary colors are blue, green, and red. These colors added together form white light. Subtracting any of these colors from white light (or mixing any two of them together) produces one of the subtractive primary colors. In graphic arts, these subtractive primaries are called the color printers. Red and green (white light minus blue) produce yellow. Blue and green (white light minus red) produce cyan. Blue and red (white light minus green) produce magenta.*

light. The positive is a recording of blue and green, which is called *cyan*. This is know as the *cyan printer*.

Photography through the *green* filter produces a negative recording of the green in the subject. The positive is a recording of the other additive primaries, red and blue, which is called *magenta*. The positive is called the *magenta printer*.

Learning Activities

1. Obtain several examples of multicolor printing. Good samples for comparison include a two-color page from a newspaper, a magazine advertisement, and a travel brochure. Look closely at the color areas. Observe how closely they are aligned with the black or other primary color on two-color pages.

2. Examine four-color reproduction of photographs. Using a magnifier, see if you can distinguish the separate colors on the page.

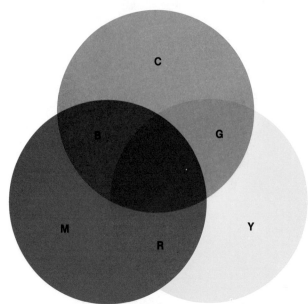

Figure 13-8. *Subtractive primary colors are called cyan, magenta, and yellow. Each is a mixture of two additive primary colors after one additive primary color has been subtracted from white light. The subtraction is accomplished by photographing original copy using filters for each additive primary.*

The *blue* filter produces a negative that records the blue in the original copy. The positive records the red and green, which when combined as additive colors produce *yellow*. This positive, therefore, is the *yellow printer*.

These colors—cyan, magenta, and yellow—are called *subtractive primaries* (Fig. 13-8). Each represents two additive primaries left after one primary has been subtracted from white light. Cyan, magenta, and yellow are the colors of the process inks used in process-color reproduction.

When these primary colors are overprinted, the viewer sees what appears to be a continuous-tone color print. This is the optical illusion created in process-color printing (Fig. 13-9).

Unfortunately, the use of the three process colors does not produce a faithful reproduction of the original copy. The inks used are not precise, and the gray and black areas appear *brownish*. To overcome this, a fourth, *black printer* is added. On high-speed presses,

Figure 13-9. *Color halftone plates are produced by photographing full-color original copy through filters. As the colors are printed from the yellow, cyan, and magenta plates, the inks blend to provide an optical illusion of full natural color. The black printer is used to fill in shadow areas and avoid muddiness that would be produced by the mixing of the three printers alone. (Photo by Andrew Mann)*

the other colors are reduced proportionately. This is so the inks will transfer or *trap* properly. The operation of reducing colors and printing a full black in shadow areas is called *undercolor removal*.

COLOR CORRECTION: ASSISTING THE INKS

Because of impurities in printing inks, it is almost always necessary to correct the separation negatives. This is called *color correction.* Color correction can be done photographically, manually, or electronically.

When done manually, corrections are made in halftone positives by reducing the size of the dots with chemical reducers. This is called *dot etching.* Dots in metal halftone plates for letterpress or gravure printing may be etched locally. This is called *fine etching* or *re-etching*.

When color corrections are done photographically, the operation is called *masking.* Numerous methods are used. *Positive masking* involves making a mask from each of the separation negatives. Each mask is placed over another separation negative to correct for color errors in different sets of full-color inks. The masks subtract color from the separation negatives in proportion to the strength of the masks. A simpler masking method uses color-masking materials made up of separate emulsion layers in a single film (Fig. 13-10). Only one mask is used. The mask is made

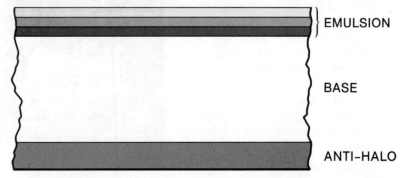

Figure 13-10. *Color film emulsion consists of several layers.*

EMULSION

BASE

ANTI-HALO

Figure 13-11. *Electronic scanners are used for most color separations in today's graphic arts industry. (Eastman Kodak Company)*

from the original and placed in contact with it in making the color separations.

The third correction method is *electronic scanning* (Fig. 13-11). Electronic scanning can be used to produce the equivalent of color correction by photographic masking. A light beam scanning the original is split into three beams. Each beam goes to a photocell covered with a filter corresponding to one of the additive primaries. This process separates each area of the original copy into its three color components.

Electrical currents from the photocell are fed into four computers—one for each color and one for black. The black is computed from the other three signals. The computers can be reset to modify currents according to printing conditions and inks being used.

The modified currents are fed to exposing lights. The lights vary in intensity according to the corrected value of each element in the area scanned. As the subject is scanned, light values are corrected for exposure of color separation films. Most scanners produce continuous-tone negative or positive color separation film. This film must be converted to halftones by conventional photographic methods.

SCREENS FOR PROCESS COLOR: EVERY ANGLE IS IMPORTANT

Each process color separation must be converted into a halftone negative or positive before printing. This conversion requires that the separations be screened.

The most popular screening technique for color separations, as for black-and-white work, is to use the contact screen. Gray contact screens are used. Magenta screens would act as filters.

The screen for each separation must be placed at a different angle (Fig. 13-12). This is necessary to avoid a condition in which the dot patterns of the four screens overprint each other. If two or more halftone patterns are printed on each other, a moiré results. A *moiré* is a pattern of wavy lines visible after halftone overprinting.

A moiré pattern can also be caused by improper transfer of ink, a condition called *poor trapping*. Proper trapping requires even transfer of ink to both the previously printed and unprinted areas of the paper.

SPECIAL COLOR TREATMENT: BEYOND FOUR-COLOR

High-speed web presses can print several combinations of ink colors in a single run. Pre-mixed inks are available in many dozens of colors. Ink manufacturers also have matching systems so that specific colors ordered by printing customers can be produced by the printer. This is done by mixing percentages of certain colors of ink (Fig. 13-13). The most popular system is known as the Pantone Matching System (PMS).

0°   15°   45°

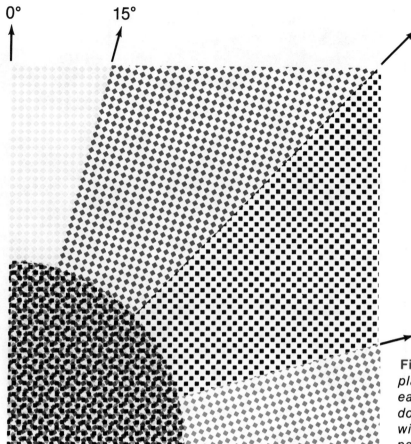

75°

Figure 13-12. *Screens must be placed at a different angle for each color separation so that dot patterns of the four screens will not create an objectionable pattern called moiré.*

Several pre-mixed or matched colors can be run on a single web of paper on modern web offset presses. In magazine printing, for instance, it is common to run two webs on a single press run. The amount of color depends on the number of printing units. One web may be run with four-color printing. On a six-unit press, the other web can be run as two-color. The unit printing the second color can print several colors, as long as space is allowed between colors. This separation on the press is called a *fountain split*. It prevents the inks in the fountain from mixing together. An eight-unit press can run two webs of four-color printing, delivering as many as 32 magazine-size pages.

Vocabulary Checklist

1. monochromatic
2. color separation
3. mechanical separation
4. photographic separation
5. hairline registration
6. commercial registration
7. masking
8. key line
9. butt
10. overprinting
11. tints
12. dot patterns
13. reflection copy
14. transmission copy
15. additive primary colors
16. cyan printer
17. magenta printer
18. yellow printer
19. subtractive primary colors
20. black printer
21. trap
22. undercolor removal

Figure 13-13. *Artists and printers can communicate about color through the use of ink matching charts such as the Pantone Matching System (PMS). (South-Western Publishing Co.)*

Some advertisers desire a special effect in their four-color advertising copy. Special metalsheen inks can be printed as fifth colors. Metalsheen inks give the finished product a metal-like appearance. Frequently used metalsheen colors are coppersheen and silversheen. For metalsheen printing, one web on a six-unit press would be run as a five-color job. Since only one unit would remain, the other web would be restricted to a single color. It is also possible to varnish a printed sheet on the press. This would be similar to a five-color job. However, varnishing simply supplies a fine glossy finish to the printed product.

23. color correction
24. dot etching
25. fine etching
26. re-etching
27. positive masking
28. electronic scanning
29. moiré
30. fountain split

Unit Review

- Color is a highly desirable part of graphic arts. Color provides visual stimulation and lifelike quality to photographic reproductions.

- Artists have a wide range of choices available in color printing. Multicolor printing means the use of two or more colors of ink on a single job. Different color inks are transferred to the printing surface in sequence. Single-unit presses require a separate printing operation for each color. Large, multi-unit presses can print separate colors on each unit.

- Colors must be separated. Each ink color requires its own image carrier.

- There are two kinds of color separations: mechanical and photographic. Mechanical separations are used for line copy. Halftone copy requires photographic separations, usually made for four-color, or process-color, printing.

- Registration is the alignment of two or more color printing images on a press. Hairline registration calls for precise alignment of color images. Commercial registration allows slightly greater variations.

- In mechanical separations, secondary color printing areas are masked so they do not photograph with the primary copy. Separate film negatives are made for each color image. Each negative is used to prepare a separate printing plate.

- Additional color values can be obtained by overprinting two or more inks, thus mixing ink colors on the press.

- Tints are obtained by the use of screens to limit the amount of ink transferred to an image area. Screens produce dot patterns of varying intensity. The use of tints allows great variety in color printing.

- There are two kinds of color halftone copy: reflection and transmission. Reflection copy reflects light through the camera lens. Light is projected through transmission copy to the lens.

- The primary colors of blue, green, and red are called additive primary colors. Filters of these colors are used to photograph original copy. The resulting negatives record one of the three primary colors. Positives made from these negatives contain the other two colors. The red filter produces a mixture of blue and green, called cyan. The green filter produces red and blue, or magenta. The blue filter produces red and green, or yellow. The three positives are called the cyan printer, the magenta printer, and the yellow printer.

- Cyan, magenta, and yellow are called subtractive primaries. This is because each color represents the two colors remaining after one primary has been subtracted from white light.

- Ink colors are not precise. Therefore, a fourth, black printer is used to produce a full black in shadow areas.

- Inks contain impurities. Therefore, it is almost always necessary to correct the color separation negatives. Color correction can be done mechanically, photographically, or by electronic scanning.

- Process color separations are converted into halftone negatives or positives before printing. This conversion requires screening of the separations, using gray contact screens. Screens have different angles for each color. The varying angles help avoid a wavy pattern called moiré.

- Printers have a wide variety of pre-mixed inks to choose from in matching colors. Multi-unit web presses can run extra colors in addition to four-color reproduction. More than one color can be run per unit, provided fountain splits are maintained to separate the inks.

Review Questions

1. What is single-color printing called?

2. Which kind of separations are made on line copy?

3. What kind of copy is separated through a photographic process?

4. Which kind of registration is used for precise image alignment in multicolor printing?

5. What is the name for copy that consists of photographic film transparencies?

6. What are the colors blue, green, and red called?

7. What kind of colors are cyan, magenta, and yellow?

8. Two methods of correcting color separation negatives are the mechanical and photographic processes. What is the third process called?

9. Color separation screens have different angles. What undesirable printing effect does this variation in angles help avoid?

10. What term do printers use to describe improper placement of ink transfer on a printing press when running multicolor work?

BINDING AND FINISHING

14

BINDING AND FINISHING: THE FINAL PRODUCTION STEP

Every process has an end. Graphic arts work is no exception. The final step in the production of a printed job usually includes some form of binding or finishing.

An example of a binding operation would be the cover of this textbook. Placing books in cardboard boxes for shipment is a finishing operation.

Some large printing presses are equipped to handle folding, gluing, and cutting operations. Most printed jobs, however, require some special handling in the binding and finishing department. This unit covers the basic operations and terminology included in these two areas of the graphic arts.

BINDING: HOLDING EVERYTHING TOGETHER

Binding is any method used to hold printed sheets together. Sheets of paper, folded or unfolded, are bound together. Several different methods are available.

Some binding methods are designed for low cost and short life. An example is the popular books sold

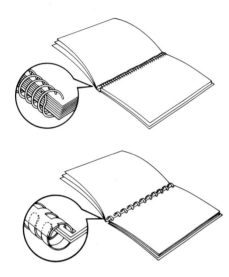

Figure 14-1. *Spiral (top) and plastic fastening are two common methods of mechanical binding, requiring that holes be punched in the paper. (A.B. Dick Co.)*

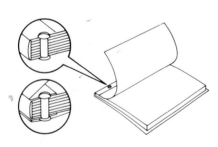

Figure 14-2. *Loose-leaf fastening may be done with posts (shown here) or movable rings. (A.B. Dick Co.)*

in racks at supermarkets. A hardcover textbook like the one you are reading is bound so that it can withstand hard use for a long life.

The most common binding methods include:

- Mechanical
- Loose-leaf
- Wire stitching
- Sewn soft cover
- Sewn case bound
- Perfect
- Padding.

Mechanical. Mechanical binding requires the punching of holes in the paper. Metal or plastic wire or strips are threaded through the holes. Two common methods include *spiral* and *plastic* (Fig. 14-1). An advantage of mechanical bindings is that pages can lie perfectly flat when a book is opened. Mechanical binding is very popular for fastening books, catalogs, manuals, and similar volumes.

Loose-leaf. This method gets its name from the fact that pages remain loose within their binders. Pages are held together by movable rings or posts (Fig. 14-2). This allows for the removal and addition of pages. With *ring binding,* pages may be opened flat. Since holes must be punched for this type of binding, a relatively wide clearance is necessary along the binding edges of the paper.

Wire stitching. There are two methods of wire-stitching binding: saddle-wire and side-wire. *Saddle-wire* binding consists of wires or staples inserted on the fold lines of the pages. This method is also called *saddle stitching* (Fig. 14-3). With the *side-wire* method, staples are inserted close to the fold and clinched at the back. This method is also called *side-stitching* (Fig. 14-4). Pages of a side-wire stitched book cannot be opened flat. This type of fastening also requires extra allowance on the margins to accommodate the staples.

Sewn soft cover. For sewn bindings, sets of printed pages are actually sewn together at their folded seams (Fig. 14-5). Sewn bindings are the most permanent way to fasten pages. For permanence, however, the sewn seams should be protected by a sturdy cover. This is not the case with sewn soft cover publications. Thus, publications with this type of binding do not withstand hard use. However, information bulletins are often bound this way. This is because such items are used for only a short time.

Sewn case bound. *Case binding* is a term that describes books with hard covers. Such books are designed for hard use and long wear (Fig. 14-6). Books bound in this manner are assembled in units called *signatures*. Signatures are printed pages usually printed and folded in multiples of 4, 8, 16, or 32 pages. The signatures are assembled and sewn together with strong thread. The thickness of the signatures forms a wide *spine*, or end, to which the cover is glued. Sewn case-bound binding is the most expensive method. But this method also produces the longest-lasting books.

Perfect. In perfect binding, the pages are held together with a flexible cement (Fig. 14-7). Books bound in this manner lie flat when open and are less expensive to bind than sewn books. Perfect binding is fast, relatively economical, and results in an attractive printed product. Perfect binding is used for products such as telephone books, some magazines, pocketbooks, and mail order catalogs.

Padding. This method uses a flexible coating of adhesive cement applied to one edge of a pile of printed or blank sheets. When dry, the booklets are individually separated and trimmed to final size on a

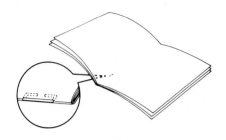

Figure 14-3. *In saddle stitching, the wires (staples) go through the fold lines of the pages. (A.B. Dick Co.)*

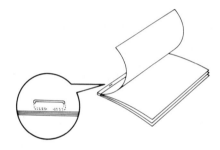

Figure 14-4. *Side stitching, or side-wire binding, involves the insertion of staples close to the fold. The staples are clinched at the back. (A.B. Dick Co.)*

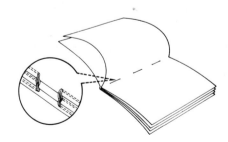

Figure 14-5. *Soft sewn bindings are best for publications that will not be subjected to heavy use. (A.B. Dick Co.)*

Figure 14-6. *Case binding usually refers to books with hard covers. Signatures are sewn together with strong thread, and the cover is glued to the spine. (A.B. Dick Co.)*

paper cutter. Familiar items bound with adhesive cement are tablets, notebooks, and memo pads.

Check Your Knowledge (True or False)

1. Wire stitching is an example of mechanical binding.

2. Pages of a saddle stitched book cannot be opened flat.

3. Case binding is used for books with hard covers.

4. Memo pads and notebooks are assembled by a binding process called padding.

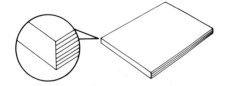

Figure 14-7. *Pages are held together with a flexible cement in perfect binding. (A.B. Dick Co.)*

FINISHING OPERATIONS: WHATEVER THE JOB REQUIRES

Not all printed sheets are bound into books or other units. Some need only to be cut to size. Other sheets are folded, drilled, or simply wrapped for shipment. These methods are known as finishing operations. The finishing department of a printing plant is generally a part of the binding area.

Most printed jobs have some form of finishing as the final step in their production. Some of the more common finishing operations include:

- Cutting and trimming
- Folding
- Punching
- Drilling
- Gathering

- Collating
- Scoring
- Perforating
- Die Cutting
- Hot stamping.

Figure 14-8. *Paper cutters come in a variety of sizes and capacities. (Challenge Machinery Co.)*

Cutting and trimming. After pages for magazines, books, pamphlets, and booklets are printed, they are cut and trimmed. This is usually done after the pages have been printed, folded, and bound. The printed sheets are cut so that they can be folded. Paper cutters come in many sizes and models (Fig. 14-8). These include models that make one cut at a time and are hand operated. There are also models that make one cut at a time but are power operated. For mass production, there are models that trim all three sides of a job automatically. These are called three-knife trimmers and are generally used to trim the top, right, and bottom sides of a book, magazine, or booklet.

It is a common printing practice to place a job in several positions on a large sheet of paper. This method saves valuable time on the press. Sheets that are printed in this way generally end up being cut apart and trimmed to final size. This is done on a single-knife paper cutter.

Figure 14-9. *Automatic folders handle booklets, programs, and flyers. (Challenge Machinery Co.)*

Figure 14-10. *In addition to its function as a punch, this manually operated machine is a binder. (General Binding Corp.)*

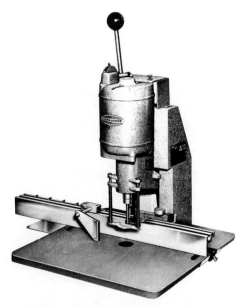

Figure 14-11. *This is a single-head drill. The bit is hollow to permit paper chips to escape. (Challenge Machinery Co.)*

Folding. Booklets, flyers, and programs require folding. This operation is done on automatic folding machines (Fig. 14-9). Folders come in many sizes and have many capacities. All folders, however, operate by forcing the paper between metal rollers.

In designing a printed job, the different types of folds and the limitations of folding equipment must be considered.

Punching. Machines for punching are used to cut rectangular or specially shaped holes in paper for plastic and spiral binding (Fig. 14-10).

Drilling. Some printed materials require holes for use in ring binders. This process is called drilling. Drilling machines vary in size and capacity. These include single-drill (Fig. 14-11) and multiple-drill types. For drilling holes in paper, a bit, or drill, must be hollow. This allows the paper chips to escape to a compartment at the rear of the machine.

Gathering. Placing signatures or individual sheets in correct sequence is called gathering. This operation involves placing piles of signatures or pages in order along the edge of a table. One sheet at a time is picked up from each pile and assembled in proper sequence.

Automatic gathering machines are used by high-volume printing firms. Desk-top, semiautomatic machines are used where small volumes of work are handled.

Collating. Collating and gathering are often confused. Collating is an operation performed to see that the correct number of pages or signatures are gathered (Fig. 14-12). Collating marks are printed in different positions on the binding fold of signatures. After the book or magazine has been folded and gathered, a pattern is visible on the spine. Errors are quickly seen and easily corrected.

Safety Tip

- **Binding and finishing machines are dangerous and should be operated with great care at all times. This machinery contains a variety of hazardous components, such as sharp blades, drill bits, and other pieces that can cause serious injury. Always be alert when operating these machines. Particular care should be practiced when operating automatic machinery. There will always be safety-protection devices on these machines. Make sure these safety units are used.**

Figure 14-12. *Collating machines ensure that the correct number of pages or signatures of a job are gathered. (Challenge Machinery Co.)*

Scoring. Placing a crease in a sheet of thick paper or cardboard to aid in folding is known as scoring. The crease produces a raised ridge on the sheet. The fold is made with the ridge on the inside of the sheet to avoid stretch. The width of the crease varies according to the thickness of the paper. Thin paper requires a narrow crease. Thick paper requires a wide crease. The object of scoring is to aid in the folding of certain kinds of paper. A special roller similar to a die is used to provide a crease in the paper. Scoring is generally performed on automatic machines (Fig. 14-13).

Perforating. Some printed jobs require that a portion be removable. A ticket stub or a magazine tear-out insert are examples of perforated items. A series of narrow holes is cut in the paper, allowing the pieces to be separated. Perforating is usually done on the press as a job is printed. It can also be done on folding equipment.

Die cutting. In die cutting, irregular shapes or designs are cut in paper and cardboard. Familiar examples are counter displays, record album jackets,

Figure 14-13. *This versatile machine performs a number of tasks. It is a combination scorer/perforator/creaser/slitter. (F.P. Rosback Co.)*

Vocabulary Checklist

1. binding
2. finishing
3. mechanical binding
4. loose-leaf binding
5. wire stitching
6. saddle-wire binding
7. side-wire binding
8. sewn soft-cover binding
9. sewn case-bound binding
10. perfect binding
11. padding
12. signature
13. spine
14. ring binding
15. cutting and trimming
16. folding
17. punching
18. drilling
19. gathering
20. collating
21. scoring
22. perforating
23. die cutting
24. hot stamping
25. foil

and cardboard containers. A metal die is prepared in the shape of the required design. A die is a cutting edge that matches the outline shape of the design. The die is mounted on a wooden board with the cutting edge up. A die is similar to a cookie cutter. Die cutting presses are similar in construction to letterpress printing presses.

Hot stamping. Gold, silver, and colored images of type or drawings are frequently placed on the covers of books, business letterheads, and certificates. Hot stamping is used for this purpose. Hot stamping is a letterpress process that uses relief images and heat. Gold, silver, or colored foil is positioned between the type or drawing and the surface to be stamped. Foil consists of a thin strip of cellophane coated on one side with a colored metallic material. Using pressure and heat, a permanent image is formed.

Hand-operated machines are used for small amounts of hot stamping. Heavy-duty automatic equipment is used where a large volume of work is required, such as the covers of pocketbooks.

Learning Activities

1. Gather samples of various binding operations from your home and in your school library. You should be able to find at least one example of each of the major types of binding. Compare how the different books, magazines, and other printed products appear and how they are suited for their uses.

2. If possible, visit a printing firm. Ask to see the various pieces of equipment used for finishing operations. If possible, watch some of this equipment in operation.

- Most printing jobs involve some form of binding or finishing operation as the final step in production. Equipment used for these functions is often automatic.

- Binding is any of several methods used to hold printed sheets together. The most common binding methods are: mechanical, loose-leaf, wire, sewn soft cover, sewn case bound, perfect, and padding.

- Not all printing jobs involve binding. Some need only to be cut to size. Some are folded, drilled, or just wrapped for shipment. These are finishing operations.

- Common finishing operations include: cutting and trimming, folding, punching, drilling, gathering, collating, scoring, perforating, die cutting, and hot stamping.

1. Which form of binding includes the spiral and plastic methods?

2. Which type of binding is the most permanent method of fastening pages?

3. Wire stitching is divided into two methods. Saddle-wire is one. Name the other.

4. What are the printed units called that are assembled in book binding?

5. Which type of binding is generally used for telephone books?

6. Which process is used to cut irregular designs or shapes in paper and cardboard?

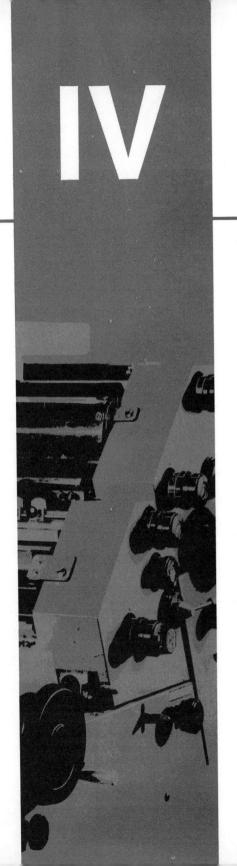

IV

GRAPHIC ARTS

The graphic arts industry, like other fields that use modern technology, is growing rapidly. In graphic arts, the introduction of electronics and other modern methods has taken place only recently.

As you have learned, advancement in graphic arts methods has been relatively slow until recent years. The first major development leading toward modern printing came when the Chinese developed wood-block methods in the ninth century.

Almost 600 years passed before the second major step in graphic arts growth was taken. This came when Gutenberg invented movable type and the first printing press in 1452.

More than 300 years later, a third major invention came about. Alois Senefelder invented the lithographic process in 1798. This planographic (flat) printing process led to the development of today's photo-offset printing.

Almost another full century passed before the next major step in printing technology. This was the invention of the Linotype by Ottmar Merganthaler in the late nineteenth century. The development of typesetting machines greatly increased the amount of work printers could complete. Machine-set type and high-speed presses made possible the

PROGRESS

modern newspaper and other printed forms of mass communication.

The rate of graphic arts progress has increased dramatically since the beginning of the twentieth century. In particular, the development of computers and other electronic equipment has been important in graphic arts progress.

The final part of this book tells you about some of the newest developments in graphic arts. Some of these developments are already here. Others are just beginning—or are expected in the near future. Certainly, all of the methods described will be part of the graphic arts field during your working lifetime. Graphic arts has become—and will continue to be—a fast-moving industry. Opportunities in graphic arts exist now and will continue to be available.

The content of this part is for your information and guidance only. Don't try to memorize the content. Do use this information to help you think about career decisions and future studies.

Because of this special purpose, there are no review questions in this part. Instead of answering questions, use this information to ask questions of your own. Then follow these questions into an exploration of your own future.

15

NEW AND FUTURE TRENDS

TELETEXT

Teletext is an electronic system that delivers news text to television screens. In effect, Teletext is a video newspaper (Fig. 15-1). In the future, it is expected that news and information text programming will play a major role in the communications industry. In particular, Teletext is expected to be an important part of cable television.

Teletext programming is already being offered in selected cities. The programs typically include news summaries. In some areas, the brief news stories are accompanied by page references to local newspapers. These references guide viewers to stories with more complete information.

In effect, a Teletext program is a short news bulletin or newsletter. Viewers can read the items for clear understanding. People who are promoting Teletext feel that this method offers a way to present real, pure news on TV. These people claim that personalities of broadcasters influence or distort the delivery of TV news. In some areas, advertisements are also being presented on Teletext programs. Drawings and photos are also being added on some programs.

Figure 15-1. *Teletext delivers news text to television screens. This technology will produce, in effect, a video newspaper.*

One clear advantage of Teletext is that the news can be presented immediately. It is possible, for example, to display news copy as it comes from news service teletypewriters. Thus, Teletext news presented on special channels is available to the public even before routine news shows. Obviously, text can be delivered on TV systems much faster than through the printing and distribution of newspapers.

Supporters feel that this growth will continue as the public learns about and accepts the Teletext format. The greatly increased number of channels available on cable TV could serve both to make room for and to support Teletext programming.

TELEVISION FACSIMILE PRINTERS

Another trend for delivery of news and information on home TV sets is the introduction of facsimile printers. These will be devices that, in effect, print the images from your TV screen onto paper—right in

Figure 15-2. *Television facsimile printers may make newspaper delivery unnecessary in the future. Images from your television screen will be printed on paper—right in your home.*

your home (Fig. 15-2). Newspapers and other printed documents may be delivered through this method in the future. An advantage would lie in the speed of getting newspapers into the home. Costs of delivery would also be reduced—as compared with printing newspapers and having them carried to your door.

ELECTRONIC PLATEMAKING AND PRINTING

Electronic (TV-like) methods of forming messages and images will also be used for printing on presses. Imagine a television picture hooked up directly to a printing press or a platemaker. Scientists and engineers have already imagined this possibility. They have begun to do something about building video (TV) systems into graphic arts processes.

You have already learned about xerography. Xerographic printing is a step in this direction. In xerography, a metal or other special surface, is sensitized to form images from ink-like materials. In newer methods, the paper itself is sensitized in much the same way. A smoke-like ink is then sprayed in front of the sensitized paper. Ink is attracted to form the image. This method is already being used on some high-speed computer printers. In the future, smoke printing may well be used for publications or for general printing. Under this method, platemaking and press setup functions are eliminated or reduced greatly. Images are transfered to paper through use of electronics.

At present, smoke printing is not a high-quality process. For improved speed, lower costs, and acceptable quality in press-type printing, plates are being made electronically. TV-like images are transferred directly from original artwork to printing plates. The plates are produced without photographic chemicals or processing. Thus, this is known as a dry platemaking process.

Electronic platemaking methods are being developed for both black-and-white and color. As you learned in earlier units, electronic scanning is already widely used. Scanners prepare metal and plastic engravings as well as platemaking film. Dry platemaking will be a future improvement. With these methods, it should become possible to improve service while reducing costs.

TYPESETTING FROM WORD PROCESSING SYSTEMS

This technology is already receiving rapid acceptance. *Word processing* describes techniques for storing, using, and delivering information electronically. Word processing systems use computers or special electronic equipment.

The basic idea of word processing is to save time (eliminating extra keyboarding) and cut costs in office operations. Word processors can be used much the same as typewriters. Letters and other documents are typed on these machines. Instead of creating images

Figure 15-3. *Word processing enables the operator to "store" text that has been entered into a terminal. Storage is accomplished through some form of magnetic recording. Copy can be recalled and reformatted without having to be rekeyboarded. (Addressograph-Multigraph Corp.)*

directly on paper, many word processors display text on video screens. The devices that include keyboards and video screens are called *terminals*. Typing and the composition of texts is done on these terminals.

After text has been entered into a terminal, it is stored electronically. This is done through some form of magnetic recording (Fig. 15-3). The recorded text can then be reviewed, corrected, or changed as necessary. This ability to change text without retyping is the key to word processing. Using stored text, new documents are created in a fraction of the time that would be required for complete retyping.

Many organizations, large and small, are already using these basic methods. Word processing has become one of the country's fastest-growing industries. Graphic arts processes are already being affected. Text materials can be sent directly from word processors to electronic typesetters. Text can be converted into type at electronic speeds. Virtually all newspapers use some version of this method. So do many magazines. In the future, books and other printed media will also use these methods. This book was prepared through such advanced techniques. The text was entered initially into a word processing

Check Your Knowledge (True or False)

1. Teletext programming permits rapid presentation of news.

2. Facsimile printers deliver the ''newspapers'' of the future.

3. Smoke printing is a high-quality process.

4. Word processing is not adaptable to newspaper production.

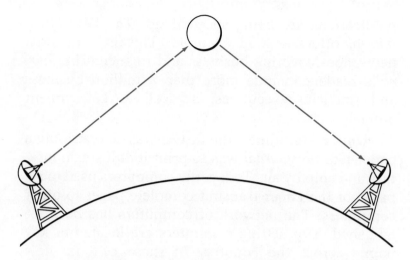

Figure 15-4. *Satellite transmission between computers provides great flexibility for publications that produce regional editions.*

system. Initial editing took place on the computer. The edited text was then transmitted directly to typesetting equipment. The words you are reading are an end product of this electronic processing.

SATELLITE COMMUNICATIONS

Space-age communication methods are adding to such advances as computers, word processing, and Teletext. Satellites are adding still greater capabilities for people to communicate. With satellites, it has become possible to communicate directly and immediately— all over the earth. It is no longer necessary to string long-distance wires or to erect radio relay stations. Ground stations direct their signals to satellites. The satellites relay the signals directly to other ground stations (Fig. 15-4).

Many of the TV programs you watch are already being delivered with the aid of satellites. The same is true for long-distance telephone calls. The graphic arts industry has also become a major user of satellite communication services.

Already, major news services, newspapers, and magazines are using satellite transmission. Both distribution of information and production of finished publications are being speeded up. *The Wall Street Journal* offers a good example. This is a national newspaper covering business and finance. The *Journal's* readers include more than a million business and financial executives, as well as government officials.

Until recent times, the fastest way to distribute a paper like the *Journal* was to print it at a single location and ship by air. Today, the computers used to set pages of the paper transmit complete pages to other computers. The network of computers has been established. Typesetting computers are located at key points across the country. At these centers, new sheets of platemaking film are created on computers. Plates are made and copies are run at plants located thousands of miles apart. These techniques make it possible to print and distribute newspapers at many points at the same time. Printed media are delivered to the whole country at the same time. Satellite communications have made such widespread graphic arts operations possible.

Similar methods are used by the nation's major weekly newsmagazines, including *Time, Newsweek,* and *U. S. News and World Report.* The combination of satellite transmission and advanced photocomposition has greatly improved production methods at these publications. An example can be seen in the service of these publications to the automotive industry.

In recent years, the major auto makers have tried to gear their advertising to the results of 10-day sales reports. These reports show how many new cars were bought and licensed in each 10-day period. The reports help auto makers plan their production, sales, and advertising programs. Last-minute decisions are made on the basis of how various models are selling.

Formerly, news magazines could not qualify for this type of advertising. It took too long to get ads into print. By the time a news magazine carried an ad, new reports—and new market trends—would exist. Income was lost in this specific area. Now, however, the combination of computerized composition and satellite transmission has changed that picture. All three of the major news magazines can accept full-color ads on Friday for issues to be distributed the following Monday. Within the graphic arts area, this is a major triumph for technology.

REGIONAL COMMUNICATION

Satellites make possible wide, general communication. With a satellite network, service to the entire nation is possible. The same methods also make it possible to develop printed communications media for local or regional areas.

For example, a manufacturer may sell products only in the East or Midwest. National manufacturers may want to conduct marketing tests for products in one part of the country. It is now possible to place such special, directed advertisements in major publications (Figure 15-5). All of the major news magazines, for example, now publish special, local, *demographic* editions.

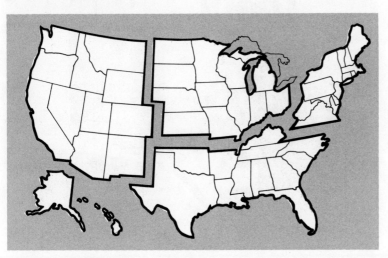

Figure 15-5. *Demographic publishing allows advertisers to choose selected audiences for their messages.*

This means that the magazine is slightly different in different areas or regions. Special news stories or advertising pages may be added in copies of the magazine that are sold in one city or a single region. These materials do not go to the entire country. The advertisers pay only for the markets they reach. Demographic publishing has become an important segment of advertising in recent years. Advertisers gain the prestige and efficiency of major publications while limiting their costs.

OPTICAL CHARACTER RECOGNITION

The billions of purchases made around the world with credit cards are possible because of optical character recognition (OCR) technology. *Optical character recognition* is the reading of printed or handwritten documents by machines. The key device in an OCR system is a scanner (Fig. 15-6). The scanner, in effect, looks at and recognizes letters and

Figure 15-6. *The scanner is the key device in optical character recognition (OCR) technology.*

numbers. When credit card sales slips are put through a scanner, the machine reads the customer's account number. The amount to be charged is also read by the scanner. The information is recorded for computer processing.

OCR techniques are finding increasing use in the graphic arts field. With OCR methods, virtually any typewriter can become a typesetting machine. Under most systems in use today, the typewriter has to be equipped with specific type fonts. These are known as OCR fonts. The typewritten pages can then be fed directly into OCR readers. The text is usually recorded for computer processing.

Many newspapers converted to phototypesetting through OCR techniques. Reporters wrote their stories on OCR-equipped typewriters. Also, classified ads were typed in OCR fonts by persons accepting the orders over the phone. Page readers were used to enter the text into computers for typesetting. More recently, most newspapers have converted to systems using video terminals. Reporters and classified ad personnel create text on terminals. Copy is fed directly to computers.

However, OCR still has many uses and great potential for growth in graphic arts. This potential stems partly from two new developments that are taking place. One of these developments is the *optical wand*. Large machines that read whole pages of copy are being replaced by pencil-like wands. These wands use a technology known as *fiber optics*. Fiber optics involves the use of long threads made from a glass-like material. Light is transmitted through these optical fibers. Images sensed at one end of the optical fibers are delivered at the other end.

Fiber optic wands are already being used for some business jobs. For example, salespeople in stores read tags on packages or labels on clothing or other merchandise. Information on the tags is delivered to a computer system. In the near future, editors should be able to read typewritten copy with OCR wands. The text will be entered directly in a computer terminal. The editor will be able to make changes in the text on a keyboard that is part of the same terminal system. Entry of text for typesetting will become easier and faster.

The other major OCR development is an *intelligent reader*. Instead of requiring that copy be composed in special OCR fonts, these machines can read any typewritten or printed text. If the machine finds a character it cannot read, the character is displayed on the screen. The operator then uses a keyboard to identify that character. From then on, the system will remember the character and read it automatically. In this way, the system can be instructed in a short time to read any type font.

Intelligent OCR systems are already being used for book reprints. When old, classic books are to be reprinted in modern editions, copies of the original text are entered. Following operator instructions, the OCR device enters the complete text into a computer. Entire book texts are processed in this way.

Check Your Knowledge (True or False)

1. Satellite communication works well for the electronic media, but it is not of much use to the printing industry.

2. Demographics is the art of political advertising.

3. The key device in optical character recognition is a scanner.

AUDIO-RECOGNITION SYSTEMS

Straight out of the pages of science fiction comes a new concept: Talk to a machine and it will display the text of what you say, right in front of your eyes on a video screen.

The new technology still doesn't have a formal name. It has been called *audio-recognition* and *voice-activated transcription*. By any name, the principle is exciting: A human voice is processed through a computer-controlled system. The sounds are converted to words through the use of a dictionary and special commands stored in the computer. The words are then fed into a standard word processing system.

In limited forms, audio-recognition systems are already at work. Some dictation machines are voice-activated. These systems are usually connected to telephones. Executives dial a specific number and dictate letters or other documents. The recording machine stops and starts at the sound of the speaker's voice. The process conserves recording tape. Because the dictation is tied together in compact messages, typing transcription is easier to handle.

A few audio-recognition systems with limited vocabularies have already developed. They respond to a few specific, spoken commands. For example, a few systems have been used in warehouses that store materials (Fig. 15-7). These warehouses have automatic systems to move materials and to place boxes in storage locations. Persons in charge of the warehouses are busy handling many details.

Instead of requiring them to enter instructions into keyboards, the new systems make it possible to give instructions by voice. The audio-response equipment can recognize a limited number of sounds. These include spoken numerals and a few commands covering specific operations. Examples of commands

Figure 15-7. *Audio-recognition, also called voice-activated transmission, enables an operator to direct a computer through vocal commands.*

might be "put" and "get." With this specific vocabulary, an operator can complete many warehousing operations by talking to a machine.

In the future, the vocabulary of audio-response systems will expand greatly. Equipment now under development is expected to allow a dictionary of 30,000 words or more. When these systems are introduced, computers should gain the ability to transcribe spoken text automatically. Once the texts are in word processing equipment, they can be used for many purposes. These include the writing of business letters, typesetting, Teletext, or other graphic arts jobs.

It is expected that audio-response transcription for full texts will be a reality some time before the end of the 1980s. Certainly, these methods should be standard communication and graphic arts tools by the year 2000.

LANGUAGE TRANSLATION

A major stumbling block to worldwide mass communication lies in languages. People who can't read, write, and speak each other's languages can't communicate effectively. Even if texts are translated from one language to another, it is difficult to be accurate. You may have heard the expression about a play or story: 'Something was lost in the translation.'' This means that the exactness of the meaning has suffered in converting text from one language to another.

In technical and business areas, it is important for people in different countries to be able to communicate. Translations are necessary. Computers have already been put to work in this area. Routine technical or business language can be translated by computer systems. OCR techniques can be helpful in this work. For example, it is possible to read a page of a book in English and have the computer display a text in Russian or Spanish.

However, people who are expert in two or more languages still have to look at and edit the translations. The problem is that words have different meanings within any language. When words are given special or unusual meanings, they are referred to as *idioms.*

Idioms are so basic to everyday speech that most people don't even think about the difficulties they can create. For example, young people might use the words ''right on'' to indicate they approve of something. You could also say that someone's house is ''right on my way home from school.'' In addition, you could say a book is ''right on my desk.'' The words ''right on'' have three different meanings in these statements. These meanings, however, might not be exactly the same in another language.

Even with such problems, computerized translation is already an important tool for worldwide communication. Methods are improving all the time. In the future, these techniques should greatly improve the exchange of information and expand the graphic arts industry.

ADVANCES IN PRESSES AND INKS

In the future, the printing press may well become a completely automated manufacturing plant. Massive groups of equipment will print, bind, and trim printed products. Then the printed products will be counted and packaged. All of this will take place in one continuous operation.

This type of automation has already moved well along in the printing industry. Such operations are necessary to keep costs in line. Reducing the labor needed in printing is a primary factor in controlling costs. Lowering labor costs balances increases in the costs of materials.

To illustrate, many types of paper had cost increases of 20 times (2,000 percent) between 1947 and 1982. By comparison, automobile prices increased approximately five times (500 percent) in the same period. Thus, in the printing field, increased automation is one of the primary ways of controlling prices. Without such controls, people would find it hard to afford to buy printed products.

One trend that has helped automate printing is the continuous-belt press. Instead of being mounted on printing cylinders, the printing plates used on these presses are attached to a long, endless belt. Thus, rather than printing a limited number of pages at a time, complete books can be produced in single press runs. Folding, cutting, and binding take place as the printed products are moved to other units of equipment—all automatically.

Along with these developments in printing equipment, it will be necessary to develop improved inks. Printing inks of the future will have to spread more evenly and dry faster than those that have been used in the past. Ink development will have to match the needs of equipment. As more and more presses are equipped with high-speed dryers, inks will have to match these needs. Inks of the future will have to be able to handle the high temperatures of the dryers. These inks will have to form permanent images quickly and surely.

FUTURE CAREERS IN GRAPHIC ARTS

Change brings opportunities for people who are prepared for new developments. Certainly, as you have learned, the graphic arts industry is changing rapidly. This pace of change is likely to increase even further in the years ahead. The reason is that new technologies will keep contributing to graphic arts methods.

New technologies will bring many new career opportunities in graphic arts. However, taking advantage of these opportunities will require new training and career changes. The artist who pastes up type today may be working at a computer terminal in the future. The operator of a process camera may be retrained to work on an electronic scanner. But, no matter how graphic arts products are produced, people will need more and more information.

Meeting the needs for this growing supply of information will continue to produce challenges and opportunities. All you will need to begin with will be a solid foundation of understanding about the processes of graphic arts. After that, a willingness to learn should carry you a long way on an interesting career path in this field.

Vocabulary Checklist

1. Teletext
2. facsimile printer
3. smoke printing
4. dry platemaking
5. word processing
6. terminal
7. magnetic recording
8. stored text
9. satellite
10. demographic publishing
11. optical character recognition (OCR)
12. scanner
13. optical wand
14. fiber optics
15. audio-recognition
16. voice-activated transcription
17. idiom

Unit Review

- Teletext is bringing "instant news" to home television screens. Words on the TV screen provide an electronic newspaper. It is expected that facsimile printers soon will be available for home use. Facsimile printers will print video images onto paper. This is how your daily newspaper may be delivered in the future.

- Electronic platemaking and printing processes are being developed that will improve services and reduce costs. Electronic typesetting methods are in wide use today.

- Satellite transmission is greatly increasing the speed and flexibility of producing and distributing national publications.

- Regional and demographic editions of national publications are made available by satellite networks. This is particularly important in providing audiences and markets for advertisers.

- Optical character recognition (OCR) is the reading of printed or handwritten documents by machines. Product labels and credit card slips are read by OCR scanners, that transmit information to computers. A newer OCR development is the intelligent reader that can read almost any typewritten or printed text.

- Computer-based automation is bringing rapid advances in the more traditional areas of printing presses. Increased speed and quality of printing will result from these improvements.

GLOSSARY

additive primary colors In photographic color separation, the primary colors of blue, green, and red are called additive primary colors. This is because three lights of these colors added together produce white.

aniline dye carbon paper A special carbon paper used in the spirit duplicator process.

antique finish Describing the surface of paper that has a natural rough finish. Antique paper is suited to printing books and other reading matter because its surface is dull and does not create glare or shine.

aqua film One of two kinds (the other is lacquer film) of hand-cut film for screen process printing. Aqua film is adhered to the screen mesh with water. It requires the use of a lacquer-base ink.

basis weight The weight in pounds for a ream (500 sheets) of paper in the basic size for that grade.

binding Any method used to hold printed sheets of paper, folded or unfolded, together.

black printer A term used in four-color printing. When cyan, magenta, and yellow are overprinted, the viewer sees what appears to be a continuous-tone color print. The inks used are not precise, however, and the gray and black areas appear brownish. To overcome this, a fourth, black printer is added.

blanket In photo-offset lithography, a rubber sheet clamped around the blanket cylinder. It transfers the image from the plate to the paper.

blockout A mask, made of paper or liquid, used to cover the non-printing areas in screen printing.

book-grade paper The most popular paper for book and magazine printing. Finishes include eggshell, antique, vellum, and super calendered.

bristol paper Paper that comes in three varieties: *Printing bristol* is used mainly for posters and point-of-purchase displays such as those found on grocery checkout counters. *Index bristol* is used for file cards, postcards, booklet covers, business forms, menus, and advertising pieces. *Wedding bristol* is used for announcements, menus, and programs.

business-grade paper (bond) High quality paper that has long life and is able to retain images permanently. Uses include ledger sheets, money orders, bank checks, safety paper, stationery, and duplicating or copying papers.

California job case In hot-metal typesetting, the case in which all upper case and lower case letters and special characters are stored.

carrier A surface that carries ink to paper or other material.

center line A vertical line drawn to indicate the center of a page or sheet.

chase In letterpress printing, a rectangular metal frame in which the type form is locked up (held firmly in place) ready for printing.

clip art Preprinted artwork covering almost any subject. Can be cut from sheet and inserted on mechanical by paste-up artists.

cold type Any typesetting process, such as phototypesetting, that does not use molten metal. The two basic cold-type composition methods are mechanical and photographic.

color correction In four-color printing, any method, such as dot etching, re-etching, or masking, used to improve color rendition. It can be done photographically, manually, or electronically.

color separation The division of colors of a continuous-tone full color original, each of which is printed with a separate printing plate.

composing stick In letterpress printing, a hand tool in which type is assembled and justified by a compositor. Characters are selected from a type case and assembled in the composing stick until they make up a full line.

compositor One who puts together pages of materials (type and illustrations) to be printed; sometimes used to mean a typesetter.

comprehensive layout ("comp") A detailed drawing of the final printed product-to-be. It shows styles and sizes of type and illustrations in great detail.

contact print A same-size photographic print made from either a negative or a positive. It is made by placing a film negative or positive in direct vacuum contact over a sheet of film or photoprint paper.

contact screen A photographically prepared halftone screen having a dot structure of graded density. Used in vacuum contact with the photographic film to make a halftone.

continuous tone copy Photographs or other artwork that contain various shades of gray.

copyboard The part of a process camera that holds the copy to be photographed. It has a large flat surface on which the copy is positioned, and a hinged glass cover that keeps the copy in place in front of the camera.

cover paper Paper that covers and protects other printed materials, such as magazines, programs, catalogs, schedules, or booklets.

crop To selectively reduce the size of an illustration by cutting off, trimming, masking, or opaquing part of it.

Cursive type style A typeface similar to Script. The letters resemble handwriting but do not necessarily connect.

cyan printer A term used in four-color printing. A red filter permits only red light to pass. Greens and blues are filtered out. Photography through a red filter produces a negative recording of all the reflected or transmitted red light. The positive, called the cyan printer, is a recording of the other additive primaries (blue and green).

dampening unit A part of an offset press similar to the inking unit. The fountain roller rotates in a container of water mixed with etch (a mild acid). The mixture is called fountain solution. It keeps the nonimage areas of the printing plate from inking up.

dandy roll In papermaking, a fine wire cylinder on a papermaking machine that presses a watermark into the paper.

dead form A form which has been printed and is ready to be disassembled, with the type being sorted and returned to its proper compartments in the type case.

delivery unit The end of the offset press on which the printed sheets are delivered and stacked.

diaphragm On a process camera, a device that controls the size of the opening in the lens.

direct entry A phototypesetting machine on which the typed line is immediately sent to a computer and then produced on film or film paper. The text is not stored on paper tape or magnetic disc.

display type Type used for headings or titles, usually 14 point or larger.

doctor blade In gravure printing, a flexible rubber knife-edged blade pressed against the engraved printing cylinder. It removes excess ink from the nonprinting surface area of the cylinder.

dot etching In four-color printing, a manual method of improving or correcting the colors in halftone positives by reducing the size of the dots with chemical reducers.

dot values The dot values of a halftone are usually expressed in terms of a percentage comparing black areas to white areas. See also **screen ruling.**

drypoint engraving The least expensive and simplest form of gravure printing. Prints consist of lines only.

duplicator A small offset press, up to a sheet size of about 11 by 14 inches.

eggshell finish A paper finish similar in texture to an eggshell.

electronic scanning In color printing, a method of color correction. A light beam scanning the original is split into three beams. Each beam goes to a photo-cell covered with a filter corresponding to one of the additive primary colors. This process separates each area of the original copy into its three color components.

electrostatic copier An office duplicating machine that prints one or more copies directly from typed, handwritten, or printed originals.

electrotype A letterpress metal printing plate. The surface is usually treated with a coating of chromium or nickel. This hardens the surface so that the electrotype lasts longer when used on a press than a stereotype.

emulsion A light-sensitive coating, containing gelatin and silver salts, on a photographic film's transparent plastic base.

engraving A metal plate that is prepared by cutting or etching an image into its surface.

engraving and etching press A small hand-operated gravure press that is suitable for small quantities of printing from a plate that is usually cut by hand methods.

etching A printing plate that is prepared by applying chemicals to a metal plate to remove, or dissolve, areas. Cavities are formed on the surfaces of the plate.

feeder unit The part of an offset press that separates the sheets of paper and feeds them into the press.

felt side The smoother side of paper that has less grain and is the better printing side. It is opposite from the wire side of the paper.

film negative A photographic film on which the image area is transparent and the nonimage areas are opaque. Photographing the original art (positive) on a process camera produces a negative.

film positive A photographic film on which the image areas are opaque and the nonprinting areas are transparent.

finishing The final step(s) of most printed jobs. It includes (1) cutting and trimming of printed sheets, booklets, magazines, or books, (2) automatic folding of booklets, flyers, and programs, (3) machine punching of rectangular or specially shaped holes in paper for plastic and spiral binding, (4) drilling of hole in paper for use in ring binders, (5) gathering of signatures or individual sheets of paper in correct sequence for binding, (6) collating, (7) scoring, (8) perforating, (9) die cutting, (10) hot stamping.

flash exposure The second exposure made in halftone photography. It is made in the darkroom with an amber light. It forms dots in the negative where there are shadow areas in the original copy.

flat In offset lithography, the assembled sheet of negatives. The flat is used to prepare an offset printing plate.

flat-bed cylinder press A letterpress printing press that operates with the type form held in a large flat bed of the press. The bed moves backward and forward on a track beneath an impression cylinder. Sheets of paper are fed in at the top and are carried around the cylinder. Each sheet receives its impression by a rolling contact with the type. Only a small area of the cylinder actually touches the type at one time.

flexography A form of letterpress printing in which a flexible rubber plate is used as the image carrier. The rubber plate is attached to a cylinder on the press. Products such as cellophane, foil, and plastic bags are printed by flexography.

flywheel A part of a platen press that, on most presses, revolves counterclockwise toward the rear of the press. It balances the press and gives it a steady, even motion.

folio A page number.

font A complete set of letters for a given size and style of type, including figures, punctuation marks, and other signs and accents needed for typesetting.

form All the pages being printed on a press at one time. Also, when type and related printing elements in a galley are tied up and ready to be proofed or printed, they are called a form.

formal balance In design, the images on the page are centered horizontally. An equal amount of each unit is positioned on either side of an imaginary center line.

fountain solution A mixture of water and etch (a mild acid) used in the dampening unit of an offset press. It keeps the nonimage areas of the printing plate from inking up.

fountain split In color printing, an ink color separation on the press.

f-stop In a process camera, the size of the lens opening produced by the diaphragm. A series of f-stop numbers (as f/8, f/11, f/16, f/22, f/32, and f/45) is stamped on the lens collar. Each number represents a different, measured value of light that will be passed through the lens. The larger the f-number, the smaller the opening in the lens, and the smaller the amount of light that will be passed through the lens.

galley Typeset material from the typesetter, usually in sections 12 to 14 inches long. In hot-metal composition, a shallow three-sided tray into which type is transferred from the composing stick. The printer arranges or makes up a job in the galley according to the layout specifications.

galley proof   A proof of typeset material, such as a photocopy or ozalid reproduction, to be used for proofreading.

gauge pins   Small pin-like metal guides used to hold the paper in position on the tympan of a platen press during printing.

gothic   A Sans Serif typeface with plain block letters.

grain (paper)   The direction in which most of the fibers of the paper run.

gravure   An intaglio process of printing; the exact opposite of letterpress. The images are etched into the metal plate image carrier. Plates are generally made of copper and are either flat or curved, depending on the type of press to be used. The image is filled with ink, which is then transferred to paper by pressure of the plate against the paper.

gravure cylinder   The part of a gravure rotary web-fed press on which the images to be printed are etched.

gray scale   A strip of 12 standard gray tones (called steps), ranging from white to black, placed next to the original copy during halftone photography. It is used as an aid (or aim point) in film processing. Another type of gray scale, with 21 steps, is placed beside the negative or positive during plate exposure to determine the correct exposure time.

gray screen   A halftone contact screen. It is light gray and can be used to photograph colored copy.

gripper margin   In printing, the distance between the top edge of the sheet of paper and where the printed image begins.

grippers   Metal fingers on a sheet-fed press that hold the paper during its printing cycle.

ground glass   A piece of glass, etched on one side, that forms a viewing image for the process camera operator to check before taking the picture. It acts as a screen, displaying the image that comes through the lens. It is positioned on the same plane as the film. It is removed or swung out of the way during film exposure.

halation   In photography, an undesirable spreading or reflection of light on a photographic negative. Halation appears as a halo around bright objects or areas.

halftone (continuous tone) copy   Photographs and other artwork that contain a complete range of tones from white to black.

halftone engraving   A letterpress printing plate which, when used to print with one color of ink, produces an image that appears to have been printed in various tones of that color. The tones may vary from black to white.

halftone photography   The reproduction of a photograph or other continuous tone artwork that contains various shades of gray. It is made by placing a halftone screen in front of the negative during photographing. The detail and tone values of the image are represented by dots of varying size and shape.

halftone screen   A screen placed against photographic film to form a dot pattern on the film. During exposure, light passes through the camera lens and then through the screen before striking the film.

hand-set type   Hot-metal type that has been assembled by hand by a compositor in a composing stick.

highlights   The whitest areas of the original halftone copy.

hot-metal composition (typesetting)   Includes all methods of setting metal type into lines and pages by hand or by machine.

hot type   Type set from molten metal. Three-dimensional types.

image carrier   The plate containing images in the printing process.

impression cylinder   One of three cylinders on the main printing unit of an offset press. It transports the paper in contact and under pressure with the blanket cylinder. On gravure and letterpress rotary web-fed presses, the impression cylinder brings the web of paper into contact with the plate cylinder.

indirect entry   A phototypesetting process in which typed lines are stored on punched paper tape or magnetic media such as a disc, tape, drum, or cassette.

informal balance   In design, allows images to be placed at different locations on the page. It is considered more modern than formal balance.

ink fountain   The container, or pan, into which the press operator puts the printing ink before running the job.

inking unit A part of an offset press that generally consists of three to four metal vibrating rollers, four or more rubber rollers, and two to four rubber form rollers. They pick up ink from the ink fountain and spread it evenly on the image of the plate.

intaglio printing A method of printing, also called gravure printing. See **gravure.**

italics Letters that slant to the right, as different from upright Roman letters.

justify To set type so that all lines align at the left and right sides. This is done by varying the amount of space between words, and sometimes between the letters of the words in a line.

lacquer film One of two kinds (the other being aqua film) of hand-cut film for screen process printing. It is adhered to the screen mesh with lacquer thinner.

latent image An invisible image caused in the emulsion of photographic film.

layout The drawing or sketch of a proposed printed product (such as a page, advertisement, or calendar). It is a working diagram for a typesetter, compositor, or printer to follow.

layout dummy A series of design layouts. It is drawn to show all areas of type and illustrations.

lead edge The edge of the paper that enters the printing press first.

leading In hot-metal composition, the distance, expressed in points, from the bottom of one line of type to the top of the next line of type. Strips of metal called leads (usually 2 points thick) and slugs (usually 6 points thick) are inserted. These strips of metal are referred to as leading. In cold-type composition, the computer of the typesetting machine is programmed to move down a certain number of points from one line to the next line. Thus, leading is the distance from the baseline of one line to the baseline of the next line of type.

leads In hot-metal typesetting, strips of metal (usually two points thick) placed between lines of type to create space.

lensboard On a process camera, a board to which the lens assembly is fastened.

letterpress printing A relief method of printing. Printing is done from metal type, wood type, or metal plates on which the image area is raised. Ink is applied by rollers only to the raised image. The inked image is transferred directly to paper.

letterspace To insert space between the letters of words in type.

line copy Pasted up copy or artwork which is black and white only. It does not contain shades of gray.

line engraving A letterpress printing plate made from an illustration having solid blacks and pure whites. There are no gray tones.

line gauge A measuring ruler used by printers and layout artists.

line negative A photographic negative made from line copy.

linoleum block A letterpress plate prepared by cutting into a flat surface of a special type of linoleum used for decorative or printing purposes. The image area is left raised on the block. Nonimage areas are cut away.

Linotype A machine that casts a single, complete line of type called a "slug." The type line consists of characters and spaces on a single body rather than characters on individual bodies.

lithographic plate The image carrier in offset printing. Litho plates are made from many kinds of materials such as aluminum, zinc, and stainless steel. For short press runs, direct-image paper masters can be used on small presses.

lithography See **planographic printing.**

loose-leaf binding Pages are held together by movable rings or posts, but remain loose within their binders.

lower case letters The small letters of a typeface; not capitals or small capitals.

Ludlow A machine that casts lines of type from matrices that are set by hand in a special composing stick.

machine finish A paper finish similar to that of antique paper, but smoother and less bulky. Machine-finish paper is often used for magazines, booklets, and catalogs, and sometimes for books.

magazine A storage compartment where matrices are held in a Linotype machine.

magenta printer A term used in four-color printing. Photography through a green filter produces a negative recording of the green in the subject. The positive is a recording of the other additive primaries, red and blue, which is called magenta. The positive is called the magenta printer.

magenta screen A halftone screen that is colored magenta (purplish red). It is used for black-and-white original copy only.

main exposure In halftone photography, the first exposure. During this exposure the contact screen converts into dots the highlights and middletones within its screen range.

main printing unit The main printing unit of an offset press generally includes three cylinders. These are: plate cylinder, blanket cylinder, and impression cylinder.

mark-up The process of writing the typesetting instructions on a manuscript or a piece of copy. It includes typefaces to be used, sizes of type spaces between and arrangement of sections of copy.

mask In screen printing, something that covers an unwanted or nonimage area of the screen mesh. It prevents the ink from flowing into that area. Masks are generally made of paper or liquid (water or lacquer).

masking In four-color printing, color correction done photographically. Numerous methods are used. One is called *positive masking* (see below). A simpler masking method uses color-masking materials made up of separate emulsion layers in a single film. Only one mask is used. The mask is made from the original and placed in contact with it in making the color separations.

masking paper In preparing offset lithographic plates, the goldenrod layout sheet on which negatives must be assembled and taped into position. The masking paper holds back light rays so that certain areas of the printing plate will not be exposed. This process is referred to as stripping.

mechanical A pasted-up page (text and illustrations) ready to be photographed. Also called *camera-ready copy.*

mechanical binding Holes are punched in the paper, and metal or plastic wire or strips are threaded through the holes. The common methods include spiral and plastic binding.

mechanical cold type The four popular methods of preparing cold type by mechanical means are hand lettering, transfer type, clip art, and strike-on.

mechanical separation Color separation that is used for line copy and black-and-white original copy. Art for multicolor reproduction is usually produced in black and white on a paste-up or mechanical. If hairline registration is not required, artwork for the key (main) color is prepared on the paste-up. Art for the other color(s) is prepared on clear acetate overlays.

mesh count In screen printing, the number of openings per square inch of the fabric used to make the screen. A coarse mesh fabric would be 6XX. A closely woven fabric for fine detail printing would be 18XX. For general printing purposes, 12XX mesh is used.

middletones The areas of gray on the original halftone copy (usually 50 percent tones). On the printed page, they are viewed as equal-size (checkerboard) black-and-white dots. These areas are between the shadows and the highlights.

mimeograph An office duplicating machine that uses a stencil. The images are formed on the stencil by typing or drawing. The stencil is placed over an inked drum. Each time the drum turns ink is forced through the holes in the stencil to create an image on a piece of paper.

In four-color printing, an undesirable pattern of wavy lines visible after halftone overprinting.

monochromatic Having only one color. In printing, means only one color of ink is used.

Monotype A hot-metal typesetting system that uses two machines: a keyboard and a caster. The keyboard machine punches or perforates a roll of paper tape as the operator presses the keys. The tape is then run through the caster, which casts single characters properly spaced in lines of preset width.

multicolor press A press capable of printing more than one color in a single pass of the paper through the press. It consists of several printing units connected in a row to form one press. Each unit can run a different plate and a different color of ink.

negative In photography, a negative picture has white (or clear) images on a black background. It is reverse reading.

newsprint Paper made mostly from ground wood pulp and small amounts of chemical pulp. Mostly supplied and used in rolls. It is the standard paper on which newspapers and some magazines are printed.

opaquing The painting out of pinholes or scratches or other areas on a negative which are not to print.

optical center The optical center of a page is about two units from the top and three units from the bottom of a page. If a single line of type on a page is placed in the optical center, it will appear balanced on the page.

optical character recognition (OCR) The reading of printed or handwritten documents by a machine called a scanner.

orthochromatic (ortho) film Photographic film that is sensitive to blue, green, and yellow light. Because of this, light blue guidelines left on paste-up copy will not show on the film. Since ortho film is not sensitive to red light, red safelights can be used to light the darkroom, and it "sees" red as black. This kind of film is used for most line and halftone work.

overprinting Double printing; printing over an area that has already been printed. Additional color values can be obtained by overprinting two or more inks, which may include black. For instance, overprinting blue and yellow inks produces a green image.

padding This method uses a flexible coating of adhesive cement applied to one edge of a pile of printed or blank sheets. When dry, the booklets are individually separated and trimmed to final size on a paper cutter. Used for tablets, notebooks, and memo pads.

panchromatic film Photographic film that is sensitive to all colors (blue, green, and red). It must be processed and handled in complete darkness. Its major use is in color separation work for color printing.

paperboard A heavy material generally used for packaging containers such as boxes and cartons.

paste-up The process of putting together typeset copy and illustrations on a piece of white illustration board. Hot wax is usually applied to the back of the elements so they will adhere to the board. The completed board is called a *mechanical*, or camera-ready copy.

perfect binding The pages are held together with a flexible cement. Perfect binding is used for telephone books, some magazines, pocketbooks, and mail order catalogs.

perfector A press that prints on both sides of the sheet at the same time. It may be sheet-fed or web-fed; it may be single-color or multi-color.

photodisplay machine A photographic machine that sets display type.

photoengraving A metal relief plate made by acid etching a photographically produced image, which can have words and pictures, on it. Also the process by which original relief image carriers are produced by photographic, chemical, and mechanical means.

photographic separation The division of colors of a continuous-tone full color original such as a color photograph, painting, or color transparency. Each color will be reproduced by a different printing plate. Photographic separations are made for four-color, or process-color, printing. See **reflection copy** and **transmission copy**.

photo-offset lithography See **planographic printing (lithography)**.

phototypesetting Also called photocomposition. The setting of type by a photographic process directly onto paper or film. Used to prepare material for photo-offset printing.

pica A printer's unit of measure equal to 12 points, or 1/6 inch. It is used to measure the width of lines and the depth of typeset pages.

pigment (ink) The ingredient that gives ink its color. It is the pigment that is seen when you look at printed images.

planer In locking up a form for letterpress printing, a device used to level the form.

planographic printing (lithography) Printing done from a flat (plane) surface plate. The image to be printed is level with the rest of the plate, but it is treated to accept a greasy ink, which the nonprinting parts of the plate (dampened with water) reject. This process is based on the principle that grease (or oil) and water do not mix easily. Also called *photo-offset lithography, offset lithography, offset,* and *lithography.*

plate cylinder The cylinder in the main printing unit of a press, which contains the image carrier.

platemaker One who produces the plates from which printing is done, using the film put together by a stripper. Also, a machine used to expose a flat to a plate.

platen press A letterpress printing press that operates on the same principle as a clam shell opening and closing. The type form is held vertically. The form is inked by rollers which pass over it. The paper is fed onto a flat metal surface (the platen) that is hinged below the form and swings against it to transfer the impression from the plate to the paper.

point The basic unit for measuring type. Twelve points equal one pica. Six picas equal one inch.

positive In photography, a positive picture has black images on a white background. It is right reading.

positive masking In four-color printing, a method of photographic color correction. A mask is made from each of the separation negatives. Each mask is placed over another separation negative to correct for color errors in different sets of full-color inks.

presensitized plate A metal or paper plate that has been precoated with a light-sensitive chemical.

press form A section or sections of a magazine printed as a single press run.

press operator One who runs a printing press.

process camera A camera that produces film for use in making plates, screens, or other image carriers in printing.

process-color (four-color) printing Printing of color originals using cyan, magenta, yellow and black inks, each color requiring a separate plate. Plates are made from photographic color separation negatives.

production schematic A master dummy. It contains simplified instructions for individual pages. It shows the position of all elements, as well as where color printing is to be used.

quoins In letterpress printing, metal devices that act as wedges to hold a form firmly inside a chase. A quoin key is used to tighten the quoins.

ream Five hundred sheets of paper.

reflection copy In photographic color separation, one kind of halftone copy is used. Light is directed at the copy and is reflected toward the camera lens and film. See also **transmission copy**.

registration In photo-reproduction and color printing, the alignment of the various color images on the printed sheet so that each color is in its proper place. There are two levels of registration: *Hairline registration* means that the alignment of color images must be precise. *Commercial registration* permits slight variations in color images.

relief printing Printing in which the image area is raised on the plate and is inked. The ink is transferred to the paper by pressure.

reverse reading Said of a carrier that has a mirror image of the final printed item. To deliver right-reading products, a printing process must be done from a reverse-reading carrier.

rhythm In design, rhythm involves use of the same image or design over and over to create a visual pattern.

right reading Said of a document that reads correctly when you look at it.

Roman Oldstyle Typefaces designed after the lines of the first Roman lettering to appear in printing. They have full, round serifs, and are soft, rich, and warm. Examples: Garamond, Caslon.

Roman type The normal form, not italic or bold, of a typeface.

rotary press A printing press that uses an impression cylinder to press the paper against a printing plate cylinder. The plates are curved to fit the shape of the printing cylinder. Most rotary presses print on both sides of the paper in a single pass through the press. This type of press is called a perfector. A rotary press may be sheet-fed or web-fed.

rotogravure press A gravure press that uses a rounded plate cylinder rather than a flat plate. Rotogravure presses are usually web type (print from a roll of paper), are extremely fast, and produce good quality color printing.

rough layout A drawing that is the same size as the intended printing job.

routing The process of cutting away large non-image areas of a letterpress plate.

safelight The special darkroom lamp that can be used for illumination without fogging the sensitized films and photographic papers.

Sans Serif typeface Typefaces of the simplest designs that are straight up and down and rectangular, with no serifs. They have little or no variation in the strokes of letters. Included are the plain block letters graphic artists call *gothic*. Examples: Futura, Optima, Helvetica.

screen printing A process that uses a porous (open) stencil as the image carrier.

screen ruling In halftone photography, it describes the number of openings in one linear inch of the screen.

Script A typeface in which the letters slant and connect. This design imitates handwriting.

serif A short cross-line at the end of a stroke of a letter.

sewn case bound Describing sets of printed pages called signatures that are sewn together at their folded seams and covered with a hard cover. Also called *case bound*.

sewn soft cover bound Describing sets of printed pages that are sewn together at their seams and protected by a heavy paper cover.

shadows In halftone photography, the darkest areas of the original copy. They determine the second (flash) exposure given a halftone.

sheet-fed press A printing press that accepts paper cut into individual sheets.

shutter A device that controls passage of light through a camera lens.

signature A folded printed section of a magazine, book, or booklet; usually 4, 8, 16, 24, 32, or more pages.

sized and super calendered (S&SC) finish The finish of paper that has a very smooth, hard surface. Sizing, similar to clay, is added to the paper during the manufacturing process. The paper is passed through a number of metal rollers, which adds to its smoothness.

sizing The treatment of paper that gives it resistance to penetration of liquids (particularly water).

slug A strip of metal, usually six points thick, inserted to create space between lines of type in hot-metal typesetting.

small caps (sc) Small capital letters approximately the height of the lower case x of a typeface.

spine The back of a bound book connecting the front and back covers.

spirit duplicator An office printing machine that uses a paper image carrier.

Square Serif type style A typeface that contains strokes of approximately uniform weight and straight serifs of the same weight. There is little or no contrast within individual letters. Square Serif is frequently used in headlines or for areas of smaller type copy. Examples: Beton, Memphis.

squeegee In screen printing, a rubber blade attached to a handle that is used to force ink through the open areas of the stencil and mesh.

stock Paper to be printed on.

strike-on A cold-type method of mechanical typesetting done on typewriters or machines similar to typewriters. The operator types the copy directly onto specially coated paper with an extra-bright white surface.

stripping The positioning of negatives containing images of type and illustrations on a layout sheet of masking paper to make a complete flat, ready for the platemaker.

Strip Printer A machine used to set display type manually. It uses a film strip font that contains a single size and style of type. The operator inserts the film strip between the lamp and the photographic paper.

stylus A sharp-pointed metal writing instrument with a hard edge. It is used for writing, marking, or engraving.

subtractive primaries In four-color printing, the colors cyan, magenta, and yellow. Each represents two additive primary colors left after one primary color has been subtracted from white light. They are the colors of the process inks used in process-color reproduction.

Teletext An electronic system that delivers news text to television screens.

television facsimile printer These are devices that print the images from your TV screen onto paper, in your home. Newspapers and other printed documents may be delivered through this method in the future.

template A solid plastic or metal sheet with letters and other symbols cut out. It is used to trace the cutout images onto artwork.

text type Type used for the body of a book or brochure, usually no larger than 14 point.

thumbnail sketch A small drawing in the same shape and proportion as the job being designed. Often drawn with pencil. Usually about 2 by 3 inches in size.

transfer type   Alphabets of letters preprinted on transparent acetate transfer sheets. They are applied directly to the paste-up by rubbing. Some transfer lettering has an adhesive backing mounted on an acetate sheet.

Transitional type style   Similar to Roman Oldstyle, but with a gradual flattening and refinement of the serifs; has more contrast between thick and thin strokes of letters. Examples: Baskerville, Bulmer.

transmission copy   In photographic color separation, one kind of halftone copy. Transmission copy consists of a photographic transparency in which light is projected through it and toward the camera lens and film.

trapping of inks   In color printing, the ability of an already printed ink to accept the transfer through overprinting of another color of ink to produce a desired third color.

trim size   The final size of pages or other printed matter after trimming.

tympan   On a platen press, a cushion against the paper being printed. A complete tympan generally consists of one or two sheets of pressboard and three or four sheets of book paper, which are held under the drawsheet on the platen.

type   A small, rectangular piece of wood or metal having on its surface a letter, figure, or other character; a printed letter or other character.

type element   A ball-shaped metal type font that fits onto the moving striking mechanism of certain typewriters and typesetting machines.

typeface   A particular design of type, usually named for its designer. Six groups of typefaces are Roman Oldstyle, Sans Serif, Square Serif, Script and Cursive, Textletter (or Blackletter), and Decorative.

type family   All the different series of one typeface. It may include Roman, italic, bold, and other weights, as well as all sizes.

type high   In letterpress printing, the height from the bottom of a piece of type or type slug to its face (.918 inch). This is standard for all letterpress type.

type series   All the sizes of one style of a typeface.

typographer   One who sets type for materials to be printed.

undercolor removal   In four-color printing, the operation of reducing colors and printing a full black in shadow areas.

upper case   The capital letters in any typeface.

vacuum back   The back, usually metal, of a process camera that holds the film. In the metal surface are many small holes. A motor and vacuum pump draw air out of the vacuum back through the holes. This holds the film flat against the back.

vehicle (of ink)   The basic ingredient. It acts as a carrier for the pigment (color) and provides a binder to adhere the pigment to the printed surface. Kinds of vehicles include petroleum oils, rosin oils, linseed oil, litho varnish, cottonseed oil, castor oil, and soybean oil.

watermark   In papermaking, a design or name pressed into the wet paper by a dandy roll. The watermark is visible when a sheet of paper is held up to the light.

web   A continuous roll of paper fed into a rotary web press.

web press   A high-speed press that prints from a continuous roll (web) of paper.

wire side   The side of paper in direct contact with the bronze mesh of the papermaking machine; opposite from the felt side. The wire side has a looser knit of fibers, fewer short fibers, and more grain. It is not as good to print on as the felt side.

wire-stitching binding   There are two methods of wire-stitching binding: Saddle-wire binding, or saddle stitching, consists of wires or staples inserted on the fold lines of the pages. Side-wire binding, or side stitching, consists of inserting staples close to the paper fold lines and clinching the staples at the back.

xerography   A method of printing in which a metal or other special surface is sensitized to form images from ink-like materials.

yellow printer   Used in four-color printing. Photography through a blue filter produces a negative that records the blue in the original copy. The positive records the red and green, which when combined as additive colors produce yellow. This positive, therefore, is the yellow printer.

INDEX